Exoteric Modernisms

Modern American Literature and the New Twentieth Century
Series Editors: Martin Halliwell and Mark Whalan

Published Titles

Writing Nature in Cold War American Literature
Sarah Daw

F. Scott Fitzgerald's Short Fiction: From Ragtime to Swing Time
Jade Broughton Adams

The Labour of Laziness in Twentieth-Century American Literature
Zuzanna Ladyga

The Literature of Suburban Change: Narrating Spatial Complexity in Metropolitan America
Martin Dines

The Literary Afterlife of Raymond Carver: Influence and Craftsmanship in the Neoliberal Era
Jonathan Pountney

Living Jim Crow: The Segregated Town in Mid-Century Southern Fiction
Gavan Lennon

The Little Art Colony and US Modernism: Carmel, Provincetown, Taos
Geneva M. Gano

Sensing Willa Cather: The Writer and the Body in Transition
Guy J. Reynolds

Gertrude Stein and the Politics of Participation: Democracy, Rights and Modernist Authorship 1909–1933
Isabelle Parkinson

The Regional Development of the American Bildungsroman, 1900–1960
Tamlyn Avery

Exoteric Modernisms: Progressive Era Realism and the Aesthetics of Everyday Life
Michael J. Collins

Forthcoming Titles

The Big Red Little Magazine: New Masses, 1926–1948
Susan Currell

The Reproductive Politics of American Literature and Film, 1959–1973
Sophie Jones

Ordinary Pursuits in American Writing after Modernism
Rachel Malkin

The Plastic Theatre of Tennessee Williams: Expressionist Drama and the Visual Arts
Henry I. Schvey

Black Childhood in Modern African American Fiction
Nicole King

The Artifice of Affect: American Realist Literature and the Critique of Emotional Truth
Nicholas Manning

Visit our website at www.edinburghuniversitypress.com/series/MALTNTC

Exoteric Modernisms

Progressive Era Realism and the Aesthetics of Everyday Life

MICHAEL J. COLLINS

EDINBURGH
University Press

Edinburgh University Press is one of the leading university presses in the UK. We publish acadademic books and journals in our selected subject areas across the humanities and social sciences, combining cutting-edge scholarship with high editorial and production values to produce academic works of lasting importance. For more information visit our website: edinburghuniversitypress.com

© Michael J Collins 2023, 2025

Edinburgh University Press Ltd
13 Infirmary Street
Edinburgh EH1 1LT

First published in hardback by Edinburgh University Press 2023

Typeset in 10/13 ITC Giovanni Std Book by
Cheshire Typesetting Ltd, Cuddington, Cheshire

A CIP record for this book is available from the British Library

ISBN 978 1 4744 5672 2 (hardback)
ISBN 978 1 4744 5673 9 (paperback)
ISBN 978 1 4744 5674 6 (webready PDF)
ISBN 978 1 4744 5675 3 (epub)

The right of Michael J Collins to be identified as the author of this work has been asserted in accordance with the Copyright, Designs and Patents Act 1988, and the Copyright and Related Rights Regulations 2003 (SI No. 2498).

CONTENTS

List of Figures vi
Acknowledgements vii

Introduction: Modern Times; Or, Re-Reading the Progressive Era 1
1. Culture and Anarchy: Time, Narrative and the Haymarket Affair 53
2. 'Pure Feelings, Noble Aspirations and Generous Ideas': Yellow Journalism, the Cuban War of Independence and *crónica modernista* 104
3. Manacled to Identity: Fugitive Aesthetics in Stephen Crane's Pluralistic Universe 142
4. Getting Some of the Way with Undine Spragg: Cosmopolitanism, Ethnography and War Work in the Novels of Edith Wharton 183
Coda: James Huneker, A Decadent Among Modernists 234

Bibliography 240
Index 249

FIGURES

1.1	Lithograph, 'The Haymarket Anarchists' (1886)	55
1.2	Cover, Michael Schaak, *Anarchy and Anarchists* (1889)	60
1.3	'8 Hours for Work, for Rest, for What We Will', artist unknown (1880s)	69
1.4	Cover image of Nina Van Zandt's edition of August Spies' speeches (1886)	88
3.1	Alfred Stieglitz, 'The Hand of Man' (1902, printed 1910)	152
4.1	Cover, *New York Tribune Illustrated Supplement* (Sunday 28 October 1900), 'New Relics and Fossils'	204
4.2	George Bellows, *The Cliff Dwellers* (1913)	219

ACKNOWLEDGEMENTS

So many people have a role to play in this book. I worked across a number of institutions while writing it (Nottingham, Kent, and now King's College, London) and conversations with my colleagues and friends in British Literary Studies have kept me afloat, even as British American Studies as a discipline in itself has often struggled: Will Norman, Hannah Murray (who finally got to Oz), Michelle Coghlan, Katie McGettigan, Graham Thompson, Judie Newman, Tom Wright, Emily Coit, Hilary Emmett, Xine Yao, Christopher Lloyd, Christine Okoth, Ed Sugden, Janet Floyd, Anna Snaith, Jon Ward, Alan Marshall, Sara Lyons, Natasha Periyan and countless others, have shaped how I thought about my work and made me laugh along the way, which is a thousand times better a thing to do than just to make someone smarter. I've travelled a lot to the US and met some wonderful minds whom I owe incalculable debts of gratitude. Among these are Brad Evans, Gavin Jones, Joe Shapiro, Nancy Bentley, Erica Fretwell, Priscilla Wald, and Meredith McGill. You have all be so generous and kind. Colleagues in Europe (which when I started writing this book was where England was) whom I have loved working with and learning from include Oliver Scheiding, Torsten Kathke and everyone at the Obama Institute in Mainz where I was invited to take up an Erasmus Lectureship, Cécile Roudeau at Université Paris Cité, and everyone in the American Literature group at The University of Vienna. Many thanks to The Universities of Kent and King's College, London for writing leave to complete this book.

I have learned from my graduate students about how to be a better scholar, and, frankly, person. I hope I have set you all up for the careers you richly deserve. I thank Hannah Huxley, Olga Ackroyd, Ellie Armon-Azoulay, Patrick Turner, Robyn Shooter, Samantha Seto, and George Kowalik.

I wish to thank Martin Halliwell, Mark Whalan, and everyone at Edinburgh University Press. You have brought grace, professionalism, and wisdom to this process. A delight to work with on every level.

I thank the Leverhulme Trust for the initial Early Career Fellowship that permitted me to begin work on this book. Material from this book has appeared in *Comparative American Studies*, *Radical Americas*, and *The Cambridge History of American Working-Class Literature* ed. Coles and Lauter.

This book took me a long time to write and like every book is not just a measure of the work that has gone into it intellectually but a monument to the phases of life that shaped it. I began in earnest to think about literature and time, culture and anarchy, realism and modernism all at once in the Autumn of 2011, the same time I married my wonderful and supportive wife Becky, whom this would not have been completed without. My son, the kind, sweet, and oddly-wise Sam, was born in 2013 and his sister, the excitable and inimitable Martha, in 2015. They are growing up so well and bring me endless joy and illumination. Kids, you are a source of such pride to me. This book about why we should think about how the world should be, rather than just about how it is right now, is dedicated to the future, which means it is dedicated to you. Do not worry though, you are not compelled to read it.

[E]ach of you is a creature which has never in all time existed before and which never in all time shall exist again and which is not quite like any other and which has the grand stature and natural warmth of every other and whose existence is measured upon a still mad and incurable time; how am I to speak of you as 'tenant' 'farmers,' as 'representatives' of your 'class', as social integers in a criminal economy, or as individuals, fathers, wives, sons, daughters, and as my friends and as I 'know' you?

James Agee, *Let Us Now Praise Famous Men*

Be Realistic – Demand the Impossible!

Slogan on a Wall, Paris 1968

Introduction: Modern Times; Or, Re-Reading the Progressive Era

> 'Let fiction cease to lie about life; let it portray men and women as they are, actuated by the motives and the passions in the measure we all know; let it leave off painting dolls and working them by springs and wires; let it show the different interests in their true proportions; let it forbear to preach pride and revenge, folly and insanity, egotism and prejudice, but frankly own these for what they are, in whatever figures and occasions they appear.'
>
> W. D. Howells, 'Editor's Study', May 1887 pp. 78–82

> 'To become "modern", that is to get rid of its dependency on the rules of social hierarchy, action simply must be faithful to what can be observed in the everyday life of any ordinary man ... It is not simply a matter of opposing the everyday to the long run. The everyday is the fictional framework inside which the truth of the experience of time must appear: the truth of the coexistence of the atoms, the multiplicity of micro-events which occur "at the same time" and penetrate each other without any hierarchy ...'
>
> Jacques Rancière, 'Fictions of Time', p. 35

This book is about turn-of-the-twentieth-century American literature's discovery that in the overwhelming complexity of everyday life was the key to imagining the future. More especially, it is about the way in which writing in the last decades of the nineteenth century and first decades of the twentieth sought to express the political possibilities that lay on the surface of the everyday in opposition to conservative forces that relied on historicising American experience by reifying difference so as to suppress a progressive imagination of the future. This new focus liberated American writing from its dependence on the *Event* as a key structuring principal of aesthetics and turned literary art towards questions of the *anti-evental*; the ongoing, unresolved, excessive and chronic quality of time. In contrast to the Romantic era's dependence upon the temporally organising principal of the spectacle, Progressive Era literature developed aesthetic practices that sought to find potential in the ongoing and immanent quality of lived experience. Crucially, 'modernism proper' from the 1910s onwards, then (exemplified in the international scene by works that drew on the quotidian as the resource for art, such as *Ulysses, Mrs. Dalloway, Manhattan Transfer*, etc.), did not constitute a wholesale rejection of the literature of the Gilded Age and Progressive Era (as has often been claimed by critics who have emphasised a decisive break of modernism with tradition around 1914) so much as an extension of its philosophical and formal commitments to exploring the possibilities, diversities and pluralities of everyday life. Nevertheless, much of what lies within this book remain 'roads not taken' on political and aesthetic questions; approaches undermined by institutional practices of academic critique and the mobilisation of scientific state power in the twentieth century. The late nineteenth century in literature (at least in the hands of the artists discussed in this book) represented a genuine attempt to establish a cosmopolitan art that America's later obsession with itself as a primary subject of attention corralled and undermined. Following the theories of Jacques Rancière concerning the necessity of aesthetics to the project of politics, my readings of the works under discussion in this book frequently highlight the extent to which late nineteenth-century literature issued a warning to the world that it remains our duty still to hear: that to develop a politics that is actually liveable in the present, society must develop forms of aesthetics that are generous enough to suggest possible futures without reducing them to the terms of present power relations. This should not imply a wholly autonomous position for literature (a position only certain individuals of privilege and power could ever truly claim for art), so much as suggest that the crises of the late nineteenth-century did not necessarily result in artists reducing their horizons to singular, present needs and concerns. Often it resulted in them opening them up. This was nothing less than an understanding of 'literature' itself as something that paid attention to the everyday, but whose politics exceeded the immediate. In short, literary complexity in this period (so often seen by later critics as a marker of elitism) was often the product of a desire for a perversely better means of imagining democracy than mimetic simplicity and directness, for even when times seemed bleak, as the philosopher and psychologist William James once aptly noted, 'Reality, life, experience, concreteness, immediacy, use what word you will, exceeds our logic, overflows and surrounds it'.[1] Taking this as the most discernible fact from their studies of everyday life, many significant writers and thinkers of the period (Franz Boas, Stephen Crane, José Martí, Edith Wharton, August Spies and others) showed how, to be ethical and to be democratic, one must live in knowledge of the limits of their knowledge and open to the possibilities of other worlds than their own.

One of the most memorable scenes in the canon of American literary realism comes towards the beginning of William Dean Howells's 1890 masterpiece *A Hazard of New Fortunes*. The protagonist Basil March and his wife Isabel, fresh from New England and searching for an apartment in the metropolis of New York, encounter a man on the street rifling through garbage. Described as 'decently-dressed' and 'decent-looking' but 'with the hard hands and broken nails of a workman' (70), he is 'hunting' 'like a hungry dog' (70). The combination of the archetypal exterior of the American middle class with apparent impoverishment and atavism troubles March's sensibilities concerning the appropriate modes of behaviour for the man's social position, instantiating an ontological crisis that elicits in him an empathetic response. March is compelled to chase after the man ('I must go after him') and finds that 'he could not speak English, monsieur' (70). In this moment, Howells's narrative departs from the free indirect discourse he has used up to this point, which has privileged Basil's and Isabel's interiority, and the reader is made to confront the voice of the French tramp as direct address ('monsieur'); a spatial gesture that crosses what Amy Kaplan has called the heavily policed 'line' (*The Social Construction of American Realism*, 48) of class and culture in the novel, and is one of Howells's few genuine attempts in fiction to inhabit fully the mind of the underclass. This empathetic narrative gesture is then continued by March, who switches out of American English, we are told, to address the man in French, asking 'are you in want – hungry' (70). The man's response to the question holds for a moment the class and cultural status of both himself and March in a state of suspension. Offering not a direct answer that would positively assert his relative inferiority but instead a 'pitiful, desperate shrug', the man says only 'Mais, monsieur' [*But*, mister]. This 'Mais' implies something like the famous 'Do you not see the reason for yourself?' uttered by the eponymous Bartleby of Herman Melville's 1854 short story. It is an acknowledgement that any decision taken from this moment forward comes with a caveat and invites different potential futures. Any action March now performs has some price, but also some affordance. The choice lies with him. In this way, the man's 'mais' is the aesthetic equivalent of the strike or the go-slow. It holds official time in suspension and demands of its interlocutor the rational contemplation of future possibility. Is the man a refugee from modern political upheavals in France – disturbing positions of status and culture through his global dislocation? A representative of a French-speaking immigrant section of New York with which the Marches are as yet unacquainted? Or is he a 'confidence' trickster, as March will later convince himself, in the precarious economic world of *fin-de-siècle* New York? How should March and he comport themselves in each case? What is the 'genre' of the man's identity and what demands does that make on us? Finally, does the question of one's comportment ultimately really matter if he appears in need?

Significantly, the scene holds easy systems of classification in suspense linguistically and narratively (*mais*, but) and compels March to confront what is right in front of his nose, an unjust economic system that imposes on all people a condition of radical uncertainty. March is engaged in what Emmanuel Levinas has read as the 'infinite responsibility' of the Self when encountering the moral authority of the face of the Other.[2] The recognition of confusion and disturbance creates for Basil, the Frenchman, and the reader together, a moment of egalitarian narrative time where all possibilities exist simultaneously; a precarity in the experience of everyday life that is felt and calls out in the instant of its expression to a sense of common humanity. This is because this aesthetic uncertainty forces the acknowledgement of a strangely appealing yet also unnerving doubleness that Howells locates at the centre of the modern world. The Frenchman is Basil's doppelgänger: a homeless, 'cosmopolitan' of sorts. After all, the encounter occurs in the context of a scene that involves Basil and Isabel's own, seemingly doomed, search for a home, and articulates Howells's thesis across the book that even as it creates marketable 'types' of people modern capitalism also erodes the certainties of class, culture and habit for all that come under its sway. The moment has power because it forces March to confront a possible future. He has, after all, gambled all on the move to New York. While it is unlikely that March will fall to destitution, the man is nonetheless a harbinger of possible fates, if not for himself, then for others whom his decisions affect. The moment expresses what Marshall Berman would extract famously from the writings of Karl Marx – a sense that 'modernity' is describable under capitalism as a phenomenon in which 'all that is solid melts into air'. It is, as Howells would term another of his novels, 'A Modern Instance' that requires no generic or disciplinary framework to understand, but invites a show of relationality. This precarity is of a piece with the vulnerabilities Judith Butler has emphasised as the essential quality of a new global politics in the twenty-first century, expressed when 'our ethical obligations ... are up against another person or group, [and we] find ourselves invariably joined to those we never chose, and must respond to solicitations in languages we may not understand or even wish to understand' ('Precarious Life, Vulnerability, and the Ethics of Cohabitation', 134).

Yet this show of relationality is accompanied by another impulse; an impulse framed as a question of *form*. Unlike the theatre performance Basil and his wife discuss, and following their encounter with the French tramp feel they no longer have the stomach to attend, this encounter is not a moment of melodramatic social organisation experienced at a distance in which everyone knows their generic place or role based on what history has dictated for them. What we have instead is a 'beggar' who will not beg, a bourgeois who is left unsure of his responses or his motives and a reader who is left momentarily in suspense. The moment generates an ethics of encounter that could lead to a new political future based in the recognition of a shared precarity. This sense of uncertainty and shared precarity is only really possible within the form of the 'new' realist novel of the nineteenth century, because the novel as it developed after Balzac and Tolstoy represents what Jacques Rancière calls the politics of 'Mute Speech'. This is a form of democratic, political speech that only becomes possible when art breaks from representative structures of meaning that define what kind of language is used to address what kind of subject (rhyme royal for kings, melodrama for the middle class, ballad for the working class, the social novel as etiquette manual in prose, etc.,) and in which the artist themselves makes meaning in a comparatively free space of expression. In so doing, the 'mute speech' of the novel expresses an aesthetic version of politics that

> does not allow itself to be compared to anything outside itself; it does not relate to its subject in terms of a representative system of decorum [but] builds, in the matter of words, a monument that must be appreciated purely in terms of the magnitude of its proportions and the profusion of its figures. (*Mute Speech*, 53–4)

Making its own meaning from its own specific use of symbols, as the Russian formalists had argued, the novel is political not through its representativeness alone in making visible certain communities or events, but through the creative sense it mobilises that all things – institutions among them – can and will be made and remade again. My argument here is that the politics of 'mute speech' is therefore a temporal politics that resides in the freeing of objects from certain accepted, contemporaneous modes of time (labour time, biological time, history itself even). This raises the question of how to frame a new sociality: a distinctly political question. If the moment of confused encounter March has with the beggar can be described in terms of an awakening and 'critique' of the existing social order, it does not do so without also simultaneously mobilising an affiliated urge to construct a new one. It is in this affect that the aesthetic politics of realism resides. This is what Anna Kornbluh has called the 'political formalism' of literary realism, which 'disclosed the ungroundedness of all socialities while building them up anyway' (*The Order of Forms*, 7). As it turns out in Howells's novel this promise is not to be realised, which is a tragedy more profound than the eventual deaths of the characters Conrad Dryfoos and Lindau. In 'put[ting] a coin in his hand' March quashes the promise of a new sociality and re-establishes normative social relations as both begin again to play their historically assigned roles:

> the man's face twisted up; he caught the hand of this alms-giver in both of his, and clung to it. 'Monsieur! monsieur!' he gasped, and the tears rained down his face . . . His benefactor pulled himself away, shocked and ashamed, as one is by such a chance . . . the man lapsed back into the *mystery of misery* [my italics] out of which he had emerged. (70)

After this initial moment of encounter, the re-instantiation of hierarchy by means of the coin triggers an equivalent reorganisation of the affective network of relations: the man cries out in a performance of gratitude that confirms his position of relative inferiority, and March runs from him in guilt and shame after confirmation of his own higher status. The coin as a symbol of power transforms the 'man' into something dramatic or theatrical – 'a mystery of misery' as Howells puts it – by establishing systems of depth and suspicion. There is a form of capitalist *enchantment* at play here. The coin disembodies social relations and transmogrifies the man into a commodity of sorts that comes to function for March, as Sianne Ngai has put it, as a puzzle: 'both wonder *and* trick' (Ngai, *Theory of the Gimmick*, 469). Or rather, the man becomes a 'wonder' and this, in turn, promotes the feeling in the disenchanted March that he may also be a 'trick'. Either he is not working or he is working very hard at the practice of deception. The financial exchange reinforces suspicion about the man's motives – was this just a confidence game after all? – and the feeling that March has just bought the response of gratitude he has received. At the heart of this aesthetic judgement (is the tramp 'correct' to be in this place, to act in this way?) is an affective valence that highlights a fundamental uncertainty about present forms of sociality, for, as Kant notes in the third *Critique*, aesthetic judgements index forms of social feeling.

What follows in the narrative shows the potency of March's active decision to behave in the manner he deems appropriate to his bourgeois status – something that the reader comes to doubt is the correct response and frees them to imagine alternative options and choices. The incident invigorates March's compulsion for 'deep reading' the New York world, and the novel's richest descriptions of spectacle, such as the famed scenes of voyeurism into 'domestic intensity ... with all its security and exclusiveness' (76) on board the elevated train from 'Third Avenue', follow hot on its heels in the narrative. The sense of the world as marked by spectacles or singular events gives birth to a desire to discover an underlying ontological condition to things. It is as if in handing the coin to the beggar and re-establishing hierarchy, March has transformed the frank into the furtive, the world of common humanity into a deceptive theatrical spectacle, made life into a static and lifeless form of art, and fashioned himself into a detective seeking to uncover underlying systems of meaning. Capitalism, for Howells, does not clarify social relations, but muddies them into mysteries. It actually promotes a prurient desire to peek beneath the surface world as if the wealthy are owed full knowledge of the underlying condition of the poor they make poor. The Progressive Era vogue for slum tourism that *A Hazard of New Fortunes* catches instantiates this entitled mode of inquiry. Following his exchange with the tramp, March becomes, in short, a vector for what Anna Kornbluh calls 'dissolutionism' and which we can see as a *non-constructive* mode of *critique*.[3] As Rita Felski has noted, the 'entrenching of suspicion ... intensifies the impulse to decipher and decode ... [t]he suspicious person is sharp-eyed and hyperalert; mistrustful of appearances, fearful of being duped, she is always on the lookout for concealed threats and discreditable moves ...' (Felski, *Limits*, 33). *A Hazard of New Fortunes* comes after this point to dramatise the hermeneutics of suspicion as a form of reading that actually *maintains* bourgeois decorousness by policing against deception and probing essences and ontologies, leaving us after 450+ pages with a haunting final sense of radical doubt about the validity of surfaces: 'Well, we must trust that look of hers' (496), says Basil in the final pages, as if trying, poorly, to convince himself. However, *A Hazard of New Fortunes* is not only a novel of urban detection – attempting to find out what drives one person to behave one way and another person another (the answers to which might be class based or follow the essentialist logics of race). It is also quite clearly a novel about the construction of the world; our active choices and responsibilities (political, social, aesthetic). From the opening of the novel Howells asks us to see Fulkerson's magazine *Every Other Week* as an America in synecdoche, but not just America *as it is* in terms of a fixed temporality. The repeated dialogues about what the magazine is and could be demonstrate that America is itself an object constantly under construction from an *excess* of possible options about which active choices must be made and active revisions undertaken.

The confusion of social hierarchy causes us to read what is on the surface of life and right in front of Basil's face (namely gross injustice and inequality), and this is no grand thing; it is almost beneath notice. The re-establishment of pre-existing genres of social performance implied by the subsequent references to the stage by contrast render the world, ironically, a place of darkness and incommunicability – of a mystery that brings a sense of grandeur. Handing over the coin leaves the two men incapable of communication about their shared conditions and across their class and cultural divides. As Howells would note in his own critical writings on realism's challenge to older forms of literary practice, the characters here have given up their autonomy and become so many 'paint[ed] dolls ... work[ed] ... by springs and wires' behind the scenes. Toys, played with by external powers. Howells's 1887 'Editor's Study' article (from where the line that serves as my epigraph derives) demonstrates the author's awareness that realism as an aesthetic practice depended upon a new narrative temporality that was activist and attempted to reorganise political life. '[C]eas[ing] to lie about life', as Howells understands it, means abandoning conventional forms of literature and their historically determined narratives: 'let it forebear to *preach* pride and revenge ... ' 'egotism and prejudice', he says – the genres of revenge narrative whose temporality is loaded by the actions of the past. For Howells, modern literature should move instead to a mode of time that highlights incidents 'in whatever figures or occasions they appear' (78–82). In this epoch prior to the Freudian revolution in psychology, when theories of trauma impacted character in a way as to make the past resurgent again as a force in present life, it was possible to imagine history as something that literature had the capacity to move beyond.

Consequently, the realist aesthetic of the everyday as Howells conceived it consciously courted a sense of uncertainty about fixed correspondences so as to express modern time and its potential freedoms. To state it plainly, American realism is a mode of critique and also a mode of social constructivism; the two do not exist in opposition to one another. In Howells's mind as he composed *A Hazard of New Fortunes* was the clear sense of the implications inherent in the generic and formal qualities of literature for the treatment and depiction of modern time. Instead of historical depth (revenge, prejudice, psychology) that locate a shaping force prior to the text, we have the world as it *appears*; a flattening of experience. Directed neither to the salvational religious future of the preacher, nor to a vengeful cycle of reciprocity that would have resonated deeply in the aftermath of a bloody Civil War, developing a modern politics for the novel as Howells understood it involved foregrounding aesthetic choice over pre-ordained forms of mastery.

Importantly, the next discussion March and Isabel have in the novel is shaped by the former's ironic comment about how 'we must go to the theatre' rather than 'change the conditions' (71). That is, March is caught in a vicious cycle of complicity that maintains structural inequality and is bound up in the question of form. He rearticulates the official political order through an act that establishes his superiority to the French man (handing him the coin), and then, so as to escape the feeling of shame he experiences at having performed his pre-ordained role within that order, he seeks out the theatre. More specifically, he seeks to re-inscribe the 'form' of the theatre and its structured social performances against the radical, everyday disorder of the street, for, as Caroline Levine has suggested, 'politics involves activities of ordering, patterning, and shaping [a]nd if the political is a matter of imposing and enforcing boundaries, temporal patterns, and hierarchies on experience, then there is no politics without form' (*Forms*, 7). Theatre becomes the genre that bourgeois life must perform at that moment to assert its authority and repress its uncertainties; an aesthetic politics.

Another option was always possible though. Another 'form' would, to paraphrase Levine, have a different 'affordance' and produced a different set of values and meanings.

By following this description of the radical state of potentiality felt in the encounter with the Other with a description of social forms and genres that produce a different, ostensibly less free, version of the future, Howells highlights the radicalism of his own realist aesthetic. While it is by no means a common gesture to see Howells's work as radical in the slightest (rather the opposite in fact), it is nonetheless so because of its 'modern' moves, which conform precisely with the definition of 'modern time' as deployed by Jacques Rancière. In 'Fictions of Time' Rancière notes,

> the abolition of the representative hierarchy in fiction does not simply consist in introducing common people and the prose of the everyday into the realm of high art. It entails something more radical which is the destruction of the representational form of the event and of the connection of events as an 'arrangement of actions' which was based on the division between active and passive human beings. The typically 'modern' time is thus the time 'disconnected' from the integration of its moments into either the temporality of intentional action or that of mechanical repetition . . . (Rancière, 'Fictions of Time', 34)

After seeing the man, March is unable to establish rational, 'intentional action' and unable also to understand the appropriate sets of sequential actions required of that moment. He is unable to establish the status of the 'event' according to a pre-existing hermeneutic code. The temporality of the narrative is disrupted and so is its form; and this is overtly political. In handing the coin to the French man it is as if he has empowered an automaton to perform a 'mechanical repetition', the man's subsequent behaviours as melodramatic and expected as a doll moved by strings. As such, the man becomes in the sense above 'passive' and disempowered; discharged of agential life. However, in momentarily suspending the appropriate forms of representation for a given class or culture through his realist aesthetic of everyday encounter, Howells can be seen to have performed an uncoupling of the 'event' from the established, normative sequence of events that sustains the capitalist and governmental orders of life. Intentionality is disturbed, translation occurs between languages, the narrative itself breaks down its own model of free indirect discourse, 'theatre' can no longer adequately represent or provide a salve to life, and so forth. In short, 'modern' time has been made and experienced through the aesthetic of the text. Read in this way Howells's famous realist mantras of 'Democracy in Literature' and 'common ground' seem less naive than critics have commonly implied. It may not be fully 'representative' of all the classes, cultures and groups alive at that one moment in true historical time (Howells undoubtedly fails on this account), but the realist aesthetic does nonetheless open up narrative to the limitless possibilities of time (and so to *hope*) by capturing the sense of uncertainty that lies at the affective core of democratic life. What Howells is suggesting with this scene is central to my argument in this book; that literature from the 1880s through to the early decades of the twentieth century developed new aesthetic concerns that uncoupled *expression* from the established and appropriate models of *representation* demanded by older regimes of power. By offering aesthetic moments when the traditional genres through which everyday life was lived are disturbed or overturned (suspensions, anti-structures, liminalities), this literature makes the potential futures contained in any modern, everyday occasion transparent to us. This sentiment was manifest in many major artistic works of the period. Alfred Stieglitz's photogravure work from the early twentieth century, 'A Dirigible' (included as the front cover of this book), represents precisely this sense of multiple futures always crossing through the present that I refer to as the 'aesthetic of the everyday'. In a moment when various forms of transportation and possible future forms of everyday life were present at any one moment, the dirigible becomes, to us, a Progressive Era future not taken that was there in the everyday world of 1910 as an option. Stieglitz's close attention to the everyday reveals a world interpenetrated always by potentiality and in this way it is 'modern' in the sense Rancière describes. Moreover, the photogravure 'A Dirigible' indexes this sentiment at a formal level, too, since the technology of photography was itself in a state of liminality or precarity in relation to more established hierarchies of art – as Stieglitz well knew and frequently decried. The photograph is like late nineteenth-century literary realism in the sense that it performs as what Rancière has called a 'genreless genre' – an aesthetic form that expressed 'democracy' by means of the fact that its formal features have not yet been organised by critical convention into established generic doxa. Given that genres are designed to function as means of address to specific audiences and commissioners, the 'genreless genre' of the realist novel – that underplays style in favour of a more fluid, context-specific approach to form – addresses an audience whose needs cannot be presumed and is, therefore, a democratic art. Stieglitz's image conveys a sense of possibility in the sphere of culture that was also present in the writing of this period, wherein one can discern a wish to move *beyond* or *past* the past of American life (most immediately that one shaped by slavery and by the Civil War) and find modes of expression that did not enslave authors to established mores and cultural norms.

The principal effect of this is that it establishes the 'modernity' of Progressive Era literature, which ceases to be describable only in terms of its presumed, aesthetic conservatism or latency relative to the more established doxa of 1920s 'Modernism'. Moreover, following the work of Michael Elliott, Brad Evans, Nancy Bentley, Susan Hegeman, Marc Manganero and others, it is now clear to critics that literature of the Progressive Era was actively engaged in exploring the meanings society attached to 'culture' in a way that brought it into the orbit of modern social scientific research. Yet, it is important to note that this social scientific research – ethnology, ethnography, sociology, demography, and so on – is also itself a branch of literature, particularly in the era before the official postwar professionalisation of disciplines standardised what it was appropriate for different literary forms to address and express as their specific field of knowledge, and does not yet stand superior to or in advance of literary expression in other fields, thereby leaving 'literature' with the task of 'representing' something outside, superior, or adjacent to it. To understand literary expression in the period before the mid-twentieth century it is worth keeping in mind that literature did not yet hold the secondary position to science it now finds itself in and could therefore be considered as its own legitimate field of knowledge. I would argue that social scientific *and* literary texts of this period engaged collectively with the question of aesthetics to liberate writing from an idea based upon a normative social division of labour and time (inexorably bound to a temporal conception of racialisation) that implied an 'industrial worker' must look and act one way, a 'native' another, a 'bourgeois' yet another, and so on, and that anything otherwise is a philosophical impossibility. This had far-reaching consequences in determining what was sayable within the public sphere and so what then might be made anew by it.

Jacques Rancière has called this idea of a new organisation of the relation of representation to social conditions the 'aesthetic regime' and notes how this way of understanding the world was largely a product of the late nineteenth- and early twentieth- century period of democratisation discussed in this book. This 'aesthetic regime' is an essential precondition for modern art, but is not synonymous with 'aestheticism' or 'modernism' as they are commonly defined. Indeed, it can be located just as easily in fictional works typically called 'realist' as in non-fictional 'life writing', journalism and other modes. For Rancière

> in the aesthetic regime of art, the property of being art is no longer given by the criteria of technical perfection . . . It is given in a specific experience, which suspends the ordinary connections not only between appearance and reality, but also between form and matter, activity and passivity, understanding and sensibility. (*Aesthetics and Its Discontents*, 30)

Within the 'aesthetic regime' – whose dominion begins ostensibly in the late nineteenth century – a work adopts an approach to its subject that is premised less centrally on rearticulating an established or official pattern of narrative time as encoded principally in the political and anthropological notion of the unitary, explanatory 'Event'. The 'aesthetic regime' is not an antirealist move, therefore, but operates through the production of an affective excess that makes present what is often contained in a moment but seldom acknowledged by the official structures of power. Moreover, 'technical perfection' is assessed less by means of a work's adherence to an external standard than through its expression of the requirements of the scene itself. This suggests that a work seeks to express its autonomy and so places pressure on 'representation' where that is defined as a mode of mimesis relying on something behind or adjacent to the work to define its meaning or value. Yet, crucially, this semi-autonomous art object is in no way apolitical. Because a work operating in the 'aesthetic regime' is engaged always with the presentation of potential, alternative temporalities beyond itself, and develops its own meaning through its particular use of symbols, it has political power to imagine different futures and worlds. In *Mute Speech* (2011), Rancière puts this another way:

> The passage from a poetics of representation to a poetics of expression [the aesthetic regime] overturns the hierarchy of relations ... [I]n opposition to language considered as an instrument of demonstration and exemplification, addressed to a qualified auditor, it promotes ... language as a living body of symbols ... expressions that do not so much show a particular determinate thing as the nature and history of language as a world-or-community-creating power. (63)

Aesthetics or 'a poetics of expression' have, therefore, a 'community-creating power' that transforms literature into a tool for the creation of the new possibilities, rather than just a means of reflecting its current organisation. This is not to say it does not engage in what we have come to call 'critique'. It certainly does. But the buck does not stop with the deconstruction of the Event. There is in the modernity of the everyday a call outwards to new systems of organisation and forms. The aesthetics of the everyday that is seen in the realist turn in American literature (that if not started then certainly galvanised by Howells) disrupts hierarchies of expression dependent upon certain proscribed versions of narrative time. This might include the lyric moment prized by Romanticism or the spectacles of Victorian melodrama. This new sense is there right from the opening of *A Hazard of New Fortunes* in the posture adopted by Fulkerson as he makes his request that Basil become the editor of his new magazine venture:

> He got up from the chair which he had been sitting astride, with his face to its back, and tilted toward March on its hind legs ... He put his leg up over the corner of March's table and gave himself a sharp cut on his thigh ... (7)

Fulkerson's aesthetic is a projection of a new world because nothing here is appropriate for its business according to a Victorian standard of decorousness. It is *off* somehow; an example of what Rancière has called a 'warped conjunction' (*Disagreement: Politics and Philosophy*, 14) to describe moments of democratic clash between residual forms of address and emerging modes of democratic association. It is also there in the moment with the French tramp, whose confused social status is unaccountable to the terms of March's regressive Boston Brahmin mind. Somehow the mode of address – the posture, the style – cannot be squared spatiotemporally with identity of the man.

This helps us to understand what Brad Evans has suggested in relation to Howells, that he developed a version of realist aesthetics that often embraced the 'chic', the decadent, and other categories of *fin-de-siècle* art regularly understood as 'realism's' natural foil.[4] What this aesthetic shows is that there is a great deal at stake beyond literature's capacity to 'represent' pre-existing social realities or to be a pseudoscientific carrier of information. It helps to imagine new realities, too, by opening up narrative time to the possibility of the condition I label here under the umbrella of 'the modern'. In a number of respects this approach helps one respond to one of the most pressing questions for the literary criticism of the political Left. As Gavin Jones sees it, this is the dilemma of seeking 'to recognize the aesthetic dimension of poverty, the complex ways that it has catalysed the forms and content of literary expression' in a way that does not 'merely dismiss [. . .] this aesthetic as an act of internal "colonization" or as a repressive, bourgeois appropriation of the poor' (Jones, *American Hungers*, 19).

The Prize Fight of Critique: Class *versus* Culture

This book is about the possibilities of modern, everyday life. It speaks in favour of uncertainty and against fixed positions, which I suggest is a crucial aspect of what it means to be 'modern' in America at the turn of the twentieth century. By emphasising the modern experience in the aesthetics of literary works that take as their subject everyday life, this book is concerned with putting pressure on two persistent and interrelated fictions held commonly by scholars proclaiming allegiance to the legacies of Marxism that have dominated literary studies of the late nineteenth- and early twentieth-century USA. The first assumption is that 'anthropological' narratives of 'cultures' as plural and non-hierarchical, whose greatest proponents began their work at Columbia at the end of the nineteenth century under the guidance of the American-German-Jewish ethnographer Franz Boas, stand somehow *in the way* of a radical challenge to capitalism; that the forms of 'multiculturalism' and 'relativism' that originated in the work of the Boasians in the USA and disciples of Bronislaw Malinowski in Britain led inexorably to a complacent collusion between literary studies and a frustratingly unimpeachable capitalist order. This assumption implies that a multicultural society transforms social class into an identitarian condition that one might wish to *preserve* rather than *abolish* or overcome through revolution. At its worst, the homeostatic impulses of the American culture concept are described as stilling the future orientations of Marxian class consciousness.

This thesis was espoused controversially by Walter Benn Michaels in 1995's *Our America: Nativism, Modernism, and Pluralism*, to be subsequently revised in 2006's *The Trouble with Diversity*. Numerous critics have sought to distance themselves from this position (even while grudgingly accepting much of its reasoning). Yet prefigurations of the argument lie in other works in the field, often enacted through critical method rather than stated outright. Before Michaels, Amy Kaplan's ground-breaking work *The Social Construction of American Realism* (1988) distilled many of the then current trends in critical discourse around the genre by 'explor[ing] the dynamic relationship between changing fictional and social forms in realistic representation' (Kaplan 8). Kaplan characterised the social life of symbols in realist literature in terms of their 'representative' force as markers of the numerous, specific, historical, social and political groupings of the epoch whose simultaneous appearance at the end of the nineteenth century 'produced fragmented and competing social realities' (9) that realist writing tried, usually in vain, to corral together for purposes of critique. Speaking of Howells's *A Hazard of New Fortunes*, Kaplan argues that

Howells's first novel about the modern metropolis both undercuts the common ground of his theory of realism and strives to reconstitute it. *Hazard* forges an urban community out of the debris of social conflict and molds a common language from a 'veritable Babel of confusion' (Riis, 87). On the 'largest canvas' he had 'yet allowed' himself, Howells struggled to contain the centrifugal force of his urban materials within a coherent narrative frame (Kapan, *The Social Construction of American Realism*, 46).

Kaplan's emphasis on Howells's 'struggle' to reconstitute the world here presumes the necessity of a project of holding together, of synthesising by force, and of pushing beneath the world as it appears to find a thread that makes all things connect up without remainder in order that we might in turn see systems of oppression that lie beneath the surfaces of the everyday. Yet while Kaplan proposes an alternative, her New Historicist methodology commonly shared with her reading of Howells a sense that the everyday world was an impediment. Even as it spoke to diversity, then, it still closed down what Bruce Robbins in his discussion of prolepsis in the fiction of Henry James calls 'the endlessness of social relations' in the service of 'authority in a totalizing impulse' and a 'social resolution' ('Many Years Later: Prolepsis in Deep Time,' 196). Moreover, for Kaplan, 'Realism in *Hazard* is a process of imagining and managing the threats of social change inscribed in the 'unreal city' (71). In Kaplan's conception, Howells's realist writing is doing the work of the police, as Michel Foucault and D. A. Miller would understand it, in disciplining unruly peoples and events and marshalling them to order by making the 'unreal' quotidian world solidly and consistently 'real'. Yet, living in cities in the late nineteenth century demanded confronting the very real presence of injustice and inequality on the surface of everyday life. In many ways, no digging down or marshalling – a method New Historicism would come to promote as the legitimate stance for confronting the unreal of everyday life – was required to be witness to cruelty. It was there on the surface.

Kaplan's New Historicist or New Americanist sense of the real is as so many comparatively static/passive historical objects that when combined give alchemical life and solidity to the text, and allow it to be comprehended and to 'speak' to us of its condition. The most famous example of this critical tendency is, of course, the founder of New Historicism Stephen Greenblatt's own desire to recreate the lived experience of the past by 'speaking with the dead'. As Greenblatt and Catherine Gallagher expressed this desire retrospectively in *Practicing New Historicism* (2000), it had the pseudo-religious frisson of a sacred resurrection or transubstantiation performed by a specially trained clerical elite:

> What we wanted was not social science but ethnographic realism, and we wanted it principally for literary purposes. That is, we had no interest in decisively leaving works of literature behind and turning our attention elsewhere; instead, we sought to put literature and literary criticism in touch with *that elsewhere* [my italics]. (28)

They continue:

> We wanted to recover in our literary criticism *a confident conviction of reality* [my italics], without giving up the power of literature to sidestep or evade the quotidian . . . We wanted the touch of the real in the way that in an earlier period people wanted the touch of the transcendent. (31)

In the hands of New Americanists and New Historicist critics, the desire to give renewed life to the past by 'touching the real' and stimulating a 'confident conviction of reality', was part of a project of celebrating literature's capacity to 'sidestep or evade the quotidian'. This 'quotidian' world of the text would, apparently, deceive us, because it was so very 'unreal'; thereby making our task one of aggressively uncovering a more useful, coherent, political truth that cannot be seen by all – usually by means of a singularly illuminating anecdote or archival object. In this criticism there was a certain kind of spectacular economy of revelation at play. This became married in the later twentieth century to a political will for 'representativeness' (in the senses both of what *is* there already, but unnoticed, and what *needs* to be there in greater abundance for different racial, sexual, gendered and class identities to have voice). Yet as the example from Howells above helps to show, the strategies of 'realist' texts can also exhibit their investment in the generative potentialities of anti-structure – moments when the aesthetic suspends the pull to fixed positions and reveals in the everyday the infinite possibilities of time.[5] In seeking to 'speak with the dead', New Historicism has frequently risked imposing its own ideological dominance on texts – a Romantic show of critical force – that closes down temporal potentialities and excess in its desire for 'confident conviction' and 'representativeness'. It desires to be *right* about history, rather than to wonder what might be useful to the future.

A variant of the New Americanist thesis outlined above characterises the highly significant anthropological turn away from evolutionary theories of 'race' and towards 'culture' effected by the Boasians and cultural relativists of the pragmatic school from the 1890s onwards as an outright failure that suspiciously rearticulated the underlying logic of racial difference as an essential category (in Michael's thesis *relies* actively upon it), rather than moving for its overthrow. The critique commonly points attention to how, in the words of Richard Handler, 'racist notions' either exist as traces, or 'seem to be *reborn* [my italics] in discourses ostensibly about culture' (Handler, 'Raymond Williams, George Stocking, and *Fin-de-siècle* U.S. Anthropology', 459) after the 1880s. Handler's understanding of the racist notions that exist as residue in discourses of culture reflects a particular moment of late twentieth-century Deconstruction. The 'trace' is a principle in Derrida's formulation of the deconstructive project that appears in his *Of Grammatology*, implying that the linguistic sign includes within it the presence of its other. In this sense, 'culture' contains within it that which it ostensibly denies – namely, race – and so keeps alive existence of race in its denial. This notion of trace is key to Theory as it developed in the European and US academy in the years after 1968. It contributes to a sense of language as saturated with the logic of the oppressive environment and ideology that surrounds it, but does little in accounting for the potency of the performative act of speaking from an anti-racist position against that world – that is, the exoteric politics of expression and not the esoteric politics of the sign. In fact, the concept of 'the trace' offers a pessimistic take on the possibly of a new aesthetic or politics, since by its logic every work of art is always and forever haunted, dragged inexorably into the past. Moreover, Susan Hegeman has argued in her survey of Boasianism in American Studies that Boas's 'culture concept' has been taken commonly to have 'implied something too rigid: a spatially and temporally bounded entity that served to reify differences between peoples' (*The Oxford History of the Novel in English*, 411) rather than a system to precipitate diffusion, exchange and possibility. Later in this introduction I will take up Boas's own writing to argue from a different stance. I suggest that 'culture', as Boas first formulated it in his earlier career prior to the institutionalisation of the 'culture concept' proper by his students, is seldom 'rigid' and is, rather, impressively plastic.

New Americanist reading practices enact a process by which historical Boasian and adjacent anthropological traditions and literary styles of the turn of the century are afforded vicarious blame for the failings of our neoliberal present, and doubt is called on significant claims by practitioners of the American 'culture concept' to have challenged or supplanted race as a temporal and biologically essential marker of absolute difference. This frequently means casting aspersions on the leftism and pluralism of cultural relativists generally, including questioning the sincerity of Boas's own socialism, or highlighting the assimilationist strands of his thought, as Lee Baker has done. Baker has argued that

> The anthropological concept of culture made it possible to promote the idea that regardless of race, Indians, Negros, and Orientals could and should learn to think, behave and act like good white Protestants – white privilege would follow colored respectability, or so was the expectation. (7)

As I will show later in this chapter, Boas's own understanding of how culture operated was not designed to be exclusive in this sense since even as it argued that a given culture or race would not be understood as that alone for all time, a conception of culture that might be seen to permit assimilation, it also undermined the validity of Anglo-Saxonism's claims to autonomy or historical superiority since whiteness too existed under a condition of inevitable collapse or reconstitution by historical forces. In this sense, Boasianism took a non-committal view of all race, and a pessimistic one about the survival of the US under present conditions of white supremacy. On the one hand this might appear blithe, but it also placed white supremacy under a death sentence. History, and the historical interpenetration of cultures that are its dominant fact, would never permit it to exist indefinitely. Contrarily, and taken as a broad tendency, New Americanist reading practices often proceed under a misreading of Boasianism that leads them to subscribe to a narrative of the 'culture concept's' natural impediment to progressive 'class' thinking. It is something that gets in the way.

* * *

The second major assumption in studies of late nineteenth- and early twentieth-century literature with which I take issue in this book is a corollary of the first. It argues that to foreground an 'aesthetic' stance in any work of literature serves, at best, to reassert the artist's (or the critic's) position within a rigid but often opaque class *habitus* and, at worst, performs an ideological sleight-of-hand designed to mask (and so tacitly permit or endorse) underlying injustices. This mode of reasoning identifies something that is at the core of the cultural relativist method from Boas onwards, with its important inheritances from German Romantic and Counter-Enlightenment thought that critics such as Matti Bunzl and Eric Aronoff have ably discussed: 'culture' is primarily an 'aesthetic' – a style and means for attributing value to objects in the world.

This method of reading class and culture charges aesthetics with being the system that maintains such an immoveable order (is a repressive force and part of the Police as Rancière would describe it), and aestheticism as a morally and politically dubious kind of enterprise, rather than finding within it a means of disturbing the hierarchical patterns that render the world static and one's position within it always already fixed. It supposes that a given text has an ideal and definite pre-ordained reader whose position is largely solidified within a social, cultural and political order and that a literary style responds to it directly. More insidiously, perhaps, it supposes that the scholar recreates this sense of intransigence by reading texts according to a prior knowledge of whom that ideal reader may be. What is at play here is the notion that the 'cultural relativist' project is simply, *merely* aesthetic; that it is a flat description that addresses content to a reader (a kind of label or flag) in a way that supports a project of identity politics, but lacks value as a resource with which to really change the world. It, in short, is an anti-literary/anti-art theoretical orientation that sees little difference between the goals of literature and institutional social science and the mechanics of modern statecraft.

Rooted in the work of the French thinker Pierre Bourdieu, this second thesis grew out of the 1980s Culture Wars in the field and describes literature in terms of a sociological topography that envisions the aesthetics of literary works as just so many weapons in the war of all against all that is the post-Civil War American 'cultural field'. For critics inspired by Bourdieu, class differences and systems of 'habitus' are as fundamental to the social order as they are frequently opaque to all but the group to whom a work is nominally 'addressed'. The Bourdieusian cultural field analysis envisages the subject as always inevitably walking into walls they never even knew were there; and then positions the critic as a master who shows their acolyte where they will meet an obstacle and how to navigate it. Moreover, as Phillip Barrish argues in his influential *American Literary Realism, Critical Theory and Intellectual Prestige, 1880–1995*, this battle for distinction extends to realism's later critics, taking form in poststructuralist debates about how well a given critic's work analyses historical materialist realities in a manner that replayed middle-class debates in the age of high realism about intellectual prestige and taste. Barrish suggests that '"my real is more genuinely material than your real" one-upmanship . . create[d] a certain effect of wheelspinning' that was deeply ironic given that 'any assumption that one can be "right" about materiality seems to run counter to some of recent critical theory's own most crucial insights' (155). This criticism calls out the age of high 'Theory' as little more than a game of 'Keeping up with the Jones's', whereby rather than being the sites for genuine learning and humanistic growth, university Humanities departments are characterised as the pre-eminent site for the reproduction of middle-class *habitus* alone. Overall, this pattern of reading might be described as a narrative emphasising 'class's' dominance over, or hijacking of, 'culture'.

To recap, the first model of reading class and culture makes history essentially static by asking readers to rebuild the social conditions of the past so as to know definitively what a text wants to 'say' to them: to speak with the dead as if they lived among us and we could be clear about what it is they *really* mean or they could offer up to us the 'key' to the past. The second method outlines a stance whereby the present becomes immutable. One's interpretation of a text becomes merely a reflection of the underlying class conditions that shape it. 'Culture' in these two variants of Marxian critique is a *trompe l'oeil* that has disturbing effects: either too 'deep' a description – haunted incessantly by the racial essentialism it nominally rejects – or too 'shallow' somehow; merely a gloss on, or a distraction from, the really *real* material of economic conditions. The 'aesthetic' (the very stuff of our discipline that makes literary studies different and valuable as more than a *mere* descriptive history) emerges within these twinned mindsets as a *problem* to be worked around, an illusory 'representation' where one facet of life (culture) always somehow masks another (class) and vice versa.

Stating it outright, Americanist criticism has been given all too often to a disavowal or self-loathing of its own activist content and purpose, as well as a *hatred* of the democratic, radical potential of the literary (a term I use as a translation of Rancière's term *la haine* from his 2005 broadside against Chirac's presidency *La Haine de la Démocratie*). The compelling, pluralistic diversity of American experience in the age of Great Migrations (Europe, Asia, Latin America to the USA, The South to the North), which in our own age of ever-sharpening hostility towards immigrants and growing inequality a more progressive American Studies should be placing its power behind endorsing, is frequently called out for tacitly stopping America being just to its poor. Gavin Jones expresses this in *American Hungers: The Problem of Poverty in U.S. Literature, 1840–1945* as 'an imbalance, or a series of biases, in recent critical discourse ... a failure, put simply, to harmonise the competing claims of "class" and "cultural identity" in a way necessary to illuminate poverty as a category or a concept' (Jones 4). Yet, I would go further to suggest that in highlighting the birth of what would later be called 'multiculturalism' as an origin point for post-Civil War American class injustices we are not only misrepresenting the aims of much Progressive Era Literature and of the Boasian culture concept (something to which I will return shortly), but have often also played into the hands of the political Right in making it seem that the analytic category of class is intrinsically incompatible with cultural diversity. This is, after all, precisely the argument of the Trumpian and other 'new' Rights of our global political scene; that 'multiculturalism' and 'cultural relativism' are a conspiracy against the masses. The later Boasians can be dealt some of the share of blame for this attitude, especially in their development and utilisation of 'national character' studies in the postwar period. Indeed, it is the primary argument of Margaret Mead (an avowedly *liberal* critic in many significant ways) in *And Keep Your Powder Dry: An Anthropologist Looks at America* (1942), whose influence on Cold War American Studies methods and assumptions about the 'classlessness' of the national scene is abundantly clear. Mead writes blithely that

> It is possible to describe the American system without mentioning class, to talk instead of the premium on success, and to go directly to the dynamics of character formation which lie back of the American will to succeed. If our European observer, who has haunted these pages [talking of Alexis de Tocqueville, Marx and numerous other famous America-watchers as well as the eye of America's own immigrant past] could be eliminated, I think that is the way it would be done. An observer from a country without a feudal past, or an observer from a country still in a feudal state would find our whole bewildering network of pecking orders and temporary crystallizations of status to have so little form as to be unworthy of primary mention. (41–2)

Mead sees class as a feudal structure alone (she states outright that 'class is not dynamic') and not as shifting patterns of behaviour, demeanour, expectation and the like. Indeed, the fluid nature of class relations in America, for Mead, renders class 'unworthy of primary attention', and notes that race obscures or overwhelms class as a subject of analysis in the USA. As I will show later, this is quite far from Boas's original vision for the culture concept, yet by the 1940s it had become a standard thesis. A little of this legacy can still be perceived in contemporary American criticism. Indeed, it is the primary thesis of *The Trouble With Diversity*; if you want to talk about class you cannot also pay attention to race or culture, and vice versa.

This sense of class and culture as engaged perpetually in a game of pulling the wool over each other's eyes is exacerbated by the stance of suspicion that criticism has frequently adopted in relation to them. This stance of suspicion casts readers in an imperial position and invites a test of force that one of the two primary combatants – class or culture – must *win*. The battle between class and culture has often been of our own construction because we have proceeded from an assumption of their incompatibility and presumed an either/or position that undergirds an implicit narrative of domination or supremacy. Somehow, we in American Studies have come to believe that celebrating diversity and cultural autonomy *and* moving towards a greater economic equality is to have our cake and eat it, or that we do not have *time*, somehow, for both. This equivocation leads by degrees to a method of enquiry whereby, as Rancière has compellingly put it, 'one searches for the hidden beneath the apparent, [and] a position of mastery is established' (*The Politics of Aesthetics*, 46). Like Ahab in *Moby-Dick* we must punch through the aesthetic world's 'pasteboard masks' to come to the essence of truth. The 'mastery' described here is twofold. First, it charges the scholar with a special power of deduction and so reckons their intelligence as functionally higher than the common reader (like we have an x-ray vision that lets us see what others do not below the surface). Second, it supposes that class and culture cannot hold weight equally or work together in the textual present, so that one narrative must be dominant or else both pull apart.

I am here approaching ground covered recently and controversially by Rita Felski in *The Limits of Critique* (2015) and Sharon Marcus and Stephen Best in their work on 'Surface Reading'. These stances have come to influence an emerging tradition known as 'postcritique'. Felski argues that 'critique' and 'suspicion' are methods for rendering complete and interconnected every element of a system without remainder. In seeking totalities, critique exercises undue force on the material world by presupposing either that what is there is invalid, or that something *truly* meaningful lies behind it, if only it were accessed by a suitably gifted interpreter. As a method, *critique* unites the New Historicists with their 'cultural field' colleagues by means of shared feelings of contempt for aesthetic experience, a proclivity for peeking round corners, under the objects of their analysis, for cramming dead parts together to breathe new life into history, or else for weaponising the surface world. Felski argues that

> [t]he scholar-turned-sleuth broods over matters of fault and complicity; she pieces together a causal sequence that allows her to identify a crime, impute a motive, interpret clues, and track down a guilty party. (Even the deconstructive critic who clears the literary text of wrongdoing seeks . . . to expose the shameful culpability of criticism). Rather than being a weightless, disembodied, freewheeling dance of the intellect, critique turns out to be a quite stable repertoire of stories, similes, tropes, verbal gambits, and rhetorical ploys. (Felski 7)

Of course, this is not the only system of thought within American literary studies, as Felski herself has noted and critics such as Lee Konstantinou have argued more forcibly.[6] I am also not convinced that literary studies as a whole is necessarily stultified by this mood of suspicion. Indeed, it has essential value in thinking through how the sometimes unconscious, more often conscious, logic of race and capital motivate certain literary works of the period. Nonetheless, the mood of suspicion does exist as a strong, mobilising tendency in New Historical and New Americanist approaches to realism. With it comes a will to mastery. Opposing this method of domination, shaming, fault-finding, locating complicity and so forth, I argue in *Exoteric Modernisms* that the balancing act of competing claims to mastery might be avoided – and so awareness of the inequalities of class united with the project of multicultural or culturally relative reading – if we endeavour to proceed from a position of radical equality and 'conceive of a topography that does not presuppose this position of mastery' from the get-go, using attention to aesthetics as tools by which we might 'try to reconstruct the conceptual network that makes it possible to conceive of a statement, that causes a painting or a piece of music to make an impression, that causes reality to appear transformable or inalterable' (Rancière, *The Politics of Aesthetics*, 46). By truly considering the possibility of an equality (by which I mean the idea that a style, genre or form is a matter of a 'choice' that the writer is comparatively 'free' to make and that there are a multiplicity of audience interpretations of any given aesthetic event), and by performing our readings as if such equality existed, we are permitted to take aesthetics (and the 'literariness' of literature) seriously as a means for capturing the potential political futurities that lie always on the surface of everyday life and in what the pragmatic philosophical tradition would consider to be the common pool of experience. Importantly, the 'network' of texts that I collect here to produce this topography is widely distributed, diverse, transnational and intrinsically plural at root. It does not presuppose that a 'working-class' text, for example, must use idioms from or speak only to a 'working-class culture' as Raymond Williams would have seen it, or that middle-class writers have value only to those seeking to shore up middle-class status, as the Bourdieusian position would presuppose. Rather, something truly radical is at play, a desire for equality (that any and all worlds could be available to any and all subjects at any time) that finds its expression in the aesthetics of literary texts that are not targeted to an absolutely recognisable class/culture group.

In the words of Paul K. Saint-Amour in a 2018 issue of *Modernism/ Modernity*, the bonds between individual texts or people in this literary topography are 'weak'. Indeed, the works I am exploring here have in common a commitment to a 'weak theory' stance that performs, in turn, a decisive 'weakening' of representation and its force – punching so many holes in the fabric of a solid and coherent cultural or racial 'reality'. This 'prompt[s] us to revisit, in both our critical practices and our pedagogy', says Saint-Amour, 'the gender[ed] politics of yielding and force, of all-or-nothing arguments with their forgotten middles and superseded alternatives, of agency and its relinquishment' (Saint-Amour 438). This 'weak network' is not resolved or crystallised in an institutional framework of coterie. In periods of strange transitions and uncertainties such as were the late nineteenth and early twentieth centuries, when new democratising forces emerged to challenge the older orders even as those older orders doubled down on violence to maintain control, the radicalism of any given text did not lie in its claim to speak perfectly as an unsullied representative of the forms of expression and thought appropriate to a pre-ordained 'strong' in-group, but in its references and connections outside of appropriate behavioural norms and fixed spatio-temporal loci: its 'forgotten middles and superseded alternatives'. The world I describe in this book is one that includes such figures as August Spies, the working-class anarchist aesthete; José Martí, the journalist who writes like an avant-gardist; Edith Wharton, the modernist who writes like a realist, and so on. People, simply, who just do not know the rules, or choose actively to ignore them. These are also often works whose status, genre or aesthetic is self-consciously 'minor' and which exhibit few desires towards the totalities or majoritarian authority of a more official 'Modernism'.[7] Indeed, my reading practice here is aimed at de-spectacularising the advent of 'Modernism', which becomes not an 'Event' as such – even if it was curated by many of its practitioners as though it were – but the instantiation of a method of insubordination that begins with the aesthetic and intellectual practices of nineteenth-century realism. To read modernism as Event is to presume its status as the reification of a set of ideals (in and around 1922) rather than regarding it as part of an ongoing and continuing process of democratisation in the realm of the arts that weakens the hold of a particular spatio-temporal regime of narrative upon experience. The aesthetic practices at play in this method of insubordination are similar to what in anthropology has been celebrated recently by Lars Rodseth as 'reckless empiricism' – a ranging over fields of enquiry and genres that was first noticeable in Boas and has re-emerged in a new and somewhat less appealing form, in Bruno Latour's new 'ontological turn'.[8] For Rodseth, as for me, Franz Boas's work is a significant progenitor of this method of 'reckless empiricism' because of the premium he attached to culture as a means of mobilising, and, too, a product of, interaction and diffusion. Moreover, I see Boas's ideas as comprehensible alongside the work of writers in other professions and genres who saw their work as rebelling against a class-bound rigidity of method through a renewed aestheticism.

As with Saint-Amour's sense of 'weak theory', seeing the new aesthetics of the period as a weakening of the structural bonds of temporality by means of a rendering of everyday life as shot through with non-hierarchical 'micro-events' and disturbances of fixed correspondences between behaviour and social position also has implicit feminist and queer dimensions. Michael Davitt Bell's famous thesis concerning the gendered logics of American literary realism and naturalism argued that its opposition to the language of sentimentalism and romance was a means to assert the masculinity of many its authors and their projects as they faced the 'feminising' conditions of late nineteenth-century professional authorship.[9] Yet, by taking seriously everyday life as they did, the writers in this book were also constantly undermining the presumed solidity of social processes and performances in ways that had differently gendered effects. *Exoteric Modernisms* attempts to read with the texts and according to what appears in them rather than through the many protestations or claims that lie behind it. This is a surprisingly revelatory exercise that allows texts not often placed alongside one another or understood not to be cut from the same cloth in gendered and other political terms to be stitched together, and serve to build a more egalitarian society.

In this book, I suggest that the shifts of the period are part of a collective endeavour that might not even have recognised itself as such. In other words, my project is to invert the story of class and culture at the turn of the twentieth century so that we can consider not how aesthetic practices divert our attention from some underlying political truth that it then becomes the task of the critic to elucidate and define, but rather how aesthetics (including 'culture' as defined in the anthropological sense) permits objects to be read *as* affirmatively political and so participate in the making of a new social world. Reading this way produces an empowerment of the subject to inhabit multiple positions that is not reliant necessarily on the diminishment of one or another comparable category of identity so that the square peg of the literary object can be made to fit the round hole of its ideal group referent. The simple fact of diversity as described by Boas and others is valuable for its own sake in legitimating as forms of *political* expression objects that were previously outside of the purview of the official-political and its concordant demarcations of space and time. This includes the work of people previously regarded as 'primitive' or other, as much as those of lower-class or immigrant status relative to the white symbolic order of the period, who are given after Boasian anthropology and literary realism the right to possess selves that Victorian, temporally locked ideas of race and evolution had historically denied them. It also causes us to recognise the precarity of experience in modernity as a potential condition for the emergence of a radical, reinventive politics.

This will inevitably raise the question of 'cultural appropriation' (which I will turn to directly in Chapter 4). I would argue that this question turns on the stance we take as critics on the relation of the political to the aesthetic. In my method, it is not implied that the politics of the new aesthetic world that these texts make through their attention to the everyday is identical with an official political order of republican representation, constitutions, congressional debates and the like. To imply that would be to fall back on a Bourdieusian synthesis of class and *habitus* in assuming that aesthetic ideas are mere representations of underlying social structure. Yet, my working definition of politics is (re: Rancière) that it is the creation of a space (often by means of an art object or work of literature) that permits an ongoing conversation about the distribution and organisation of social resources in complex societies. I suggest that this discussion can be energised and directed by a work of literature and its realist aesthetic of disorder and dissensus; its re-organisations of the perceptual world. This does not mean that the aesthetic answers fully the needs of the officially political. It strikes me as a different issue, for example, to imagine the possibility that at any moment class, culture, and even racial systems of social organisation could be switched, inverted and played with in an egalitarian field, to the marketisation and exploitation of indigenous resources solely for the benefit of non-indigenous peoples. Literature, after all, is not the same as real politics, but an aesthetic and expressive space for trying out different variations of experience. The moment exploitation occurs the right of access to those resources by the people with whom a given sub-culture 'originated' has been impeded and the desire for egalitarianism quashed by the hegemonic exercise of power. We should not, however, abandon the hope of democracy before we even begin to have the discussion about how best to distribute resources in the most equitable manner possible. This debate can begin with the aesthetics of the everyday developed strongly in Progressive Era writing and thought.

Rather than rearticulating one or other of the dominant tendencies I have described above by setting class and culture at loggerheads, in challenging these methods of reading literature from the period between the close of the American Civil War and the 1920s I take up the ideas of Jacques Rancière to point to how texts written in this period by a diverse body of authors (working-class activists, anthropologists, native and subaltern peoples, professional middle-class novelists, bohemian avant-gardists), who may not have occupied anything like the same locus on a Bourdieusian map of the 'cultural field', performed collectively something of a quiet revolution or apostasy in the name of the modern. While this 'revolution' happened, as it were, in the open field of the aesthetic, it did not always proclaim itself loudly as such. Consequently, it differs in several respects from somewhat more bombastic claims to newness made by the works that literary history has seen fit to term 'Modernism' proper; embodied most forcibly in Ezra Pound's mantra 'Make it New'. Indeed, this quiet revolution comprised many texts that literary histories regularly badged under the term 'realism' to isolate them for numerous reasons from that narrative of radical newness whose temporal markers are situated conveniently around the First World War. Yet, I argue, in their simple discovery and aesthetic rendering of the socio-temporal possibilities of everyday life in the modern world, literary practitioners of all stripes effected collectively what Rancière has termed a 're-distribution of the sensible' that gave quiddity to the works of 'high modernism' that followed them, allowing them to be perceivable by the public as forms of expression with genuine gravity and political import, and not excluded *a priori* as so many forms of neutral, or apolitical, *noise*. I show where the statements of American modernism came from; what preceded them to make them possible, and what alternative models of the future reside in realist worlds, by showing how Progressive Era literature 'weakened' structures of correspondence and made modern time feel porous and undecided.

The writers I discuss in this book performed 'the modern' not by rendering events as cleaving doggedly to one preferred status position or group, or by forcing the submission of one to another, but by creating fluidity in experience and permitting innumerable positions to be occupied simultaneously in any given moment without intrinsic hierarchy. Both of the dominant modes of reasoning about class and culture in nineteenth-century literature that I have outlined above – a Bourdieusian sociology that takes class position as the dominant in all social relations, and the New Historicist method whose critical power rests on the spectacular revelation of an anecdote that can correct our view of history by restoring what we deem to be missing from the visible picture – turn on the production of certainty and the construction of a monadic 'key' that unlocks the world. Yet they have missed, to some extent, the pluralism that was emergent in the period, and in whose presence we experience time as an ongoing, evolving encounter with micro-events that do not always cohere. An encounter, that is, with democracy understood as a chronic affect of persistent instability. As Rancière has remarked, the intellectual turn to realism in the late nineteenth century allowed producers and critics to conceive of an aesthetic that is

> the thought of the new *disorder* [my emphasis] . . . artworks no longer refer to those who commissioned them, to those whose image they established and grandeur they celebrated. Artworks henceforth relate to the 'genius' of peoples and present themselves, at least in principle, to the gaze of anyone at all. (Rancière, *Aesthetics and its Discontents*, 13)

This, indeed, is one of the very important achievements of Progressive Era literature (incorporating literary, philosophical, anthropological, life-writing, and overtly political texts) and it runs counter to the Bourdieusian 'distinction' paradigm, with its mapping of the cultural field. American realism is not just, as Kaplan first suggested, 'socially constructed' in the sense of being the result of past or contemporaneous histories of representation. It is also involved in the construction of the social. Consequently, I offer here a reading of the aesthetico-onto-political micro-events that makes the 'modern' thinkable, actionable and potent; the result of an accumulation of frequently neglected speech acts in the public sphere of the Progressive Era USA.

If the primary thesis of this book seems counterintuitive it is so only in the sense that it suggests that the aesthetic practices of authors working at the end of the nineteenth and beginning of the twentieth centuries that tried to capture the everyday rendered the operation of politics transparent and readable and do not necessarily impede politics by binding our sensory encounters with a text to an inward fold that refers it back to the existing group affiliation or the status position of the speaker only. I suggest that in order that the possibilities of class and cultural consciousness be described ethically, and encountered simultaneously, the scholar must not ask of the writer that their work conform to simple representations that lead into incapacitating discussions about whether or not a certain figure got it 'right' from the perspective of an assumed, pre-ordained cultural or ethical field. The question of 'representation' is typically a matter not only of art creating a resemblance to reality, but of attempting to create an alignment between a type of subject matter and a particular, discrete form of address; an exercise that is bound to a moral regime of power. The form of address chosen affects what can be said about a subject and so how that subject exists in space and time – its value to the political order. Contrarily, I hold that in such an era of uncertainty as the late nineteenth and early twentieth century (perhaps also our own), the future was always up for grabs, and this becomes all the more apparent when instead of debating relative positions in a cultural field we choose to explore what is revealed to us when we try to embrace what Herman Melville called in *Moby-Dick* a strange 'bedfellow', so as to meet as equals and make the modern world in the imaginative realm of the aesthetic.

For the 'Common People': Franz Boas and Exotericism

Rethinking the relationship between the 'culture concept', class and literature in the Progressive Era necessitates first extricating Franz Boas from a dominant description of his work that characterises his ideas as a system for establishing and reifying *stasis* and cultural difference as a fundamental human fact. This involves taking seriously his calls to grace, humility and hospitality in the ethnographic method, as well as his socialistic advocacy for what he called 'the common people' ('The Ethnological Significance of Esoteric Doctrines', 874), which has often been forgotten in American Studies, even as his concept of 'culture' has informed our own understanding of 'multiculturalism' and identity politics methodologies. Essentially, Boas's theory of 'cultures' in the plural, which are the origin point for our own conception of American society as a mosaic of group differences, is also, implicitly, a theory of class, such that it is inaccurate to draw a distinction between these things. To think about class is to think at once about the cosmopolitan origins of a culture. Rethinking Boas's work, then, is required in part because analysis of 'culture' (as a pluralistic concept) has often been a master theme of American Studies, especially after the turn to multiculturalism in the 1980s, in a way that has often seen class analysis as its other when, in fact, Boas drew no distinctions between them and undertook to study both simultaneously by means of his understanding of 'esoteric' and 'exoteric' 'doctrines'. These 'doctrines' were regimes of power that were permanently and continuously interacting in the present. In addition, as Brad Evans has argued, it is important to differentiate between a younger Boas who is part of an earlier phase that emphasised diffusion, change, chance and contingency, and a later phase characterised by the more reifying impulses of the 'culture concept' proper as it was taken up by his students – that is, by the cultures understood not as interpenetrating and fluid, but as homeostatic and coherent.[10] 'Boas' is not identical to 'Boasianism' as a school or tradition. By accounting once again for the serious interventions made by Boas in the earlier phase (when he was part of a Gilded Age and Progressive Era 'aesthetic regime' such as I have described above), I will offer a grounding for understanding the 'modern' as I use it in this book: an impulse that is crushed by the conservative intellectual impulses of the 1920s and beyond.

In 1902, American social science was in the grip of a debate about the origins of complex ritual cultures that had been precipitated by the anthropological research of the Bureau of American Ethnology and the large Jesup North Pacific Expedition to the Bering Strait. As Franz Boas described it in a short article in *Science* on 28 November of that year, entitled 'The Ethnological Significance of Esoteric Doctrines', discoveries concerning 'the symbolic significance of complex rites, and the philosophic views of nature they reveal' came 'as a surprise' to ethnologists because they 'suggest[ed] a higher development of Indian culture than is ordinarily assumed' (872). How was it, American anthropologists asked, that a 'primitive people' like the Southwestern Puebloans were capable of developing complex rites such as were usually seen only in the lifeways of more 'advanced' or 'civilized' Eastern tribal cultures? Citing work by 'Miss Fletcher' on 'Mescal ceremonies', the Bureau's work on the 'Sun Dance', and in the context of a discipline still reckoning with the effects of the Ghost Dance and the Massacre at Wounded Knee (when a 'new', radical and unifying native cultural practice was rapidly developed and diffused among a range of peoples and tribes), Boas noted that the ongoing debate was not just about the disturbance of longstanding hierarchies of civilisational progress (Lewis Henry Morgan and E. B. Tylor's models of 'savagery' to 'civilization' and various tribes' position on it) but about how the diffusion of ideas and practices occurred.

In considering this question Boas divided the social life of societies into an 'esoteric' doctrine (based on the hierarchical superiority of a definable 'in' group or priesthood) and 'exoteric doctrines' that represented the group life of the remainder of people. Crucially, though, Boas came to a fascinating conclusion about how these differences of social class operated in native societies. Rather than argue that 'complex rites' were the product of the elite mind of a clerisy or intellectual vanguard (as his forebears Tylor and Morgan had) that then filtered down their symbolic meaning to the rest of a society and so gave 'birth' to a social order, Boas argued instead that the elites performed a kind of theft from a common pool of cultural symbols within the mental life of a society so as to develop and reinforce their status and position. In the terms Rancière has laid out, Boas's 'esoteric doctrine' would be synonymous with the repressive regime of the Police. At any given moment, a 'culture' or society is full of any number of rituals, practices, traditions and so forth, none of which are coherent or unified, but the powerful exert undue influence over that plurality, reducing it to a monad for the purposes of societal control. 'Whenever a certain ceremonial came to be placed in charge of a small social group', notes Boas, 'were they chiefs, priests or simply men of influence, the conditions must have been favorable for the development of an esoteric doctrine' (873). Historical readings that have seen 'elites' as the originators of an aesthetic purity and perfection – of the synthetic 'whole' of a culture – have had the effect of uniting the Boasian 'culture concept' in its pluralism with the aims and principals of 'culture' in the sense

Matthew Arnold used it (and that might be seen as its functional opposite) as a system of 'a strict hierarchy of aesthetic, moral, and political value' (Hegeman 15). As Susan Hegeman has suggested, the 'modernist' sensibilities of the 1920s and 1930s permitted the unification of these two competing impulses, arguing that 'cultures', albeit plural, were still governed by an elite hierarchy of values and, to borrow a term from the arts, an 'avant-garde'.

Importantly, however, in 'The Ethnographic Significance of Esoteric Doctrines', Boas suggests that the operation of power in the creation of a given 'culture' did not occur in secret, but out in the open in full view of the 'exoteric' forces of the wider society and its 'common people'. Boas writes:

> It seems worthwhile to consider briefly the conditions under which these esoteric doctrines may have developed. Two theories regarding their origin suggest themselves: the esoteric doctrine may have originated among a select social group, and the exoteric doctrine may represent that part of it that leaked out and became known, or was made known, to the rest of the community; but it may also be that the esoteric doctrine developed among a select social group from the current beliefs of the tribe ... It seems to my mind that the second theory is the more plausible one (872).

In Boas's important rewriting of the origins of ethnic group life, the social elites were not described as active producers of the cultural resources of a group but, rather, unashamed and unapologetic extractors of them. In Boas's version of the culture concept (as it would later come to be known), then, class consciousness of a radical kind was implicit and foundational. It was, too, for Boas's forebear in American anthropology, Lewis Henry Morgan, whose ideas motivated the philosophies of such influential early anthropological collectors as the Bureau of American Ethnology's Director John Wesley Powell or W. H. R Rivers in England. However, in Morgan's version of cultural development and transfusion, the operation of power ran in the opposite direction to that of Boas. In the 1877 work *Ancient Society*, Morgan argued that the early stages of human development were communal and, importantly, frequently also matriarchal. Advancement through stages of evolution commonly meant the development of patriarchal social structures and secret societies that protected the laws and ethnos of a group. This focus on 'progress' meant that 'advancement' through stages was dependent upon accepting patriarchal social structures and secretive codes of law and order. As Thomas Trautmann has suggested, Morgan's vision of '"communism in living" in the early stages of evolution gave an appeal to socialists' (*Lewis Henry Morgan and the Invention of Kinship*, vi) such as Friedrich Engels, who saw in Morgan's work a justification for seeking the abolition of the bourgeois state and a return to an earlier stage of human evolutionary development in the service of social justice. However, to embrace Morgan as the basis for a socialistic reinvention of society meant undergoing a revolution against the progressive narrative of Western temporality; rejecting 'evolution' to, in a sense, devolve to a state of more perfect union. It also necessitated the development of a hermeneutics of suspicion that sought to find the key to unlocking the secrets of a given society, normally by understanding the operations of a more-or-less covert elite within that group. Contrarily, Boas's model of 'esoteric' and 'exoteric' doctrines suggested that no such reversal of progressive temporality was necessary for two reasons. First, because there was no golden age or Rousseauist 'noble savagery' and all opportunities and futurities could be seen to lie in a rich, common pool of cultural resources that were theoretically available to all at the same time. Second, that there may in reality be no secret that had 'leaked out' and gave structure to society or required decoding from within in an attitude of doubt and suspicion. Moreover, in upending ethnological time in such a way, Boas turned the continued existence of powerful cults into products of repeated and ongoing appropriations and usurpations of power in the present. For Hegeman and other critics '[Boas's] crucial intervention might be . . . described as a *spatial* reorganization of human differences' (33). I contend this claim, seeing the reorganisation of power implicit in his attention to the 'common people' rather than the elites as an opening up of the potentiality of everyday life in a way that suggests his primary intervention is at least as much temporal as spatial. This was anthropology without a master narrative or an assumed relationship between culture and the deep time of historic power; an anthropology that politicised everyday life and that through the new focus on participant observation and the anthropologist's reading of the quotidian life was poised to be active in the present. This was an aesthetic vision of culture that was also deeply politicised.

A now established and commonly cited incident in the development of the Boasian mode of reasoning about culture is the public battle he engaged in in the pages of *Science* in 1887 with Otis T. Mason, the first curator of ethnology at the National Museum of Natural History. The story runs that Mason sought to organise the human exhibits in a way that charted a developmental trajectory for humanity in Morgan's terms: from savagery to civilisation. The marker of this progress would be the 'invention' of different tools at different stages of development, from the simplest multipurpose stick to refined and specialised technologies. According to Elliott and Hegeman, this argument turned on a spatial question solely. Contra Mason's 'strong' armchair theorising, Boas argued that there was no generalisable rule about cultural development and so objects could be understood only in the context of their use. This is undoubtedly the case. Yet, there is crucially also an essentially 'aesthetic' question at play; one that invites us to consider a secondary question of time. Transferring the decision-making power from the evolutionary theory and 'data' to decide the shape and form of the displays onto the curator themselves (what constitutes valid 'contexts' for certain objects, what looks 'right') mobilises the artistic sensibilities of that curator. It also invites the possibility of there being a potentially different organisation of form, and therefore, a different sense of meaningful contextual factors based on individual preference and experience. The Boasian solution to the problem of organisation was to produce a plasticity in time and empower the viewer as a 'maker' of historic meaning, rather than just a 'reader' of it. That is to say, he regarded the surface world of aesthetic encounter as a site of potentiality, plurality and what Rancière calls 'dissensus'. It also revalued the anthropologist's work, from the use of one's expertise to confirm existing arrangements in time to using their knowledge essentially expressively; the curator as artist. This was of a piece with his later comments on the 'exoteric doctrine'.

The criticism that anthropology as a science trapped its objects in a singular space-time to the exclusion of the ongoing life of the subject is commonly traced to Johannes Fabian's notorious 1983 text, *Time and the Other: How Anthropology Makes its Object*. However, as Lars Rodseth has noted, acknowledgement of the dangers of confining an ethnographic group to the static space-time of evolutionary or racialised subjecthood was present in the foundational 1900s work of Boas. For Boas, the project of criticising the principle of race was inexorably tied to the project of undermining the standard logic that 'culture' was a unified and singular force. It meant, instead, highlighting how constantly and continuously a group was subject to 'foreign' material and influence, incorporating it into itself and shifting its doctrines and behaviours in relation to changing historical circumstances that might be quite immediate.

In his time, Boas was criticised for lacking a unified method. Fellow ethnographers Alfred Kroeber (his student) and, more so, his enemy Leslie White, were among the critics that accused him of being unwilling, or unable, to develop his insights into a structurally unified, *strong*, theory of culture. George Stocking has remarked that Leslie White found that

> Boas was so 'obsessed with particulars' that he 'could not see general outlines or forms'. White finds the key to Boas's mind and work in the latter's suggestion that once the 'beautiful simple order' of evolutionary ethnology had been shattered, 'the student stood aghast before the multitude and complexity of facts that belie the symmetry of the edifice he had laboriously erected'. In this situation, Boas, according to White, was left with little more than the 'chaos of beliefs and customs' that he found in the data of his field studies. (212)

This characterisation captures something that later accounts of his anthropology would miss, a sense in his early work that 'culture' was a weak force rather than totalising structure that wholly shaped those who existed in its field. To look at Boas from a perspective that assumes the necessity of a 'strong' theory is precisely to miss the point. The achievements of the Boasian model, which was frequently lamented by anthropologists that followed him in the twentieth century such as White for the tension under which it placed the discipline and profession by undermining its status as a cult with elite knowledge and the power to decode, were its structural weakenings of synthetic theoretical models and narrative temporalities. At core, Boas's work belongs with the American pragmatists and the pluralists (whom he is surprisingly seldom grouped among, in part because he had little direct correspondence with William James or Charles Peirce in particular) in the deliberate instability of its methodology. Boas's resistance to unified theory at the macroscopic scale was reflected in his approach to discrete cultural groups at the microscopic. Rather than there being a key principle that could unlock the whole value system of a given culture or tribe that was held in reserve by an esoteric cult or priesthood within a group, for Boas, 'the esoteric doctrine must have been evolved on the foundation of the general culture of the tribe'. This suggests that there is a political principal at play in his thought. Some form of agreement, or if not an agreement then a violent schism or coup, must occur for the 'esoteric doctrine' to take shape out of the 'general culture of the tribe'. There must be some form of politics that happens for one to transform into the other – a radical supposition given the widespread belief that some forms of group life were 'pre-political'. Reading Boas through the insights of Rancière as I have done above highlights how Boasianism is a practice contemporaneous with the emergence of the 'aesthetic regime' in late nineteenth-century society and arts; with, that is, the 'thought of a new disorder'. For Boas, anthropology was a creative discipline that operated in what Rancière calls 'aesthetic regime', because it could describe how resources could, at least in theory, belong to anyone and be, again in *theory*, endlessly reorganised.

Without the need for an external standard of evolutionary time against which to judge an event or ritual practice, Boas argued that the justification and meaning of a particular expression of a culture was made through an ever-evolving encounter with it. In this way, the younger Boas shared much with the pragmatist William James (with whom the Boas archive has no extant correspondence). In particular, this applied to James's sense of a 'Pluralistic Universe', a theory he had long held but finally defined and published in 1909 based on Hibbert Lectures he had given in Oxford. In *A Pluralistic Universe*, James took issue with Hegel's definition of 'the aim of knowledge' as being 'to divest the objective world of its strangeness, and to make us more at home in it'.[11] For James, this definition of philosophy was 'sovereignly unjust' and created a master role for the philosopher, who imposed too readily their will upon 'the individual', or undermined and 'chastised' them for their view of the world. Crucially, the difference of the individual's world to that of the philosopher may be only 'propensities to emphasize differently' or not to speak in the 'correct' 'clerical vocabulary ... a technical or professorial one'. That is to say, the critic or philosopher was too often aligned with the work of power, in Boas's terms 'the esoteric' doctrine, and this removed possibility from the world and closed down potential futures if they could not be reduced to the method of the philosopher's technical vocabulary.

For Boas, the 'technical precision' of the ethnographer (or writer) – or what for James was only a 'clerical vocabulary' and nothing more – became a matter not of making a 'culture' conform to an external model of narrative time (savagery to civilisation), or of developing a particular 'grammar' or appropriate mode of address that described that culture for all time, but of how far the ethnographer described the society according to how it appeared. A self-consciousness about time is present in the concept of the 'exoteric' and 'esoteric' doctrines, which presume that in certain moments shifts occur that change a culture and that they are not therefore bound by evolutionary stages. Susan Hegeman and others have noted that the Boasian revolution generated a distinctly spatialised meaning for culture that turned on a 'modernist fascination with the estranging possibilities of the other' (Hegeman 13). Yet, its greatest achievement might be described as a reconfiguration on the temporal axis that aligns it with the aims of a future-led pragmatism such as James's. Reading culture in a Boasian manner demanded considering the 'esoteric' 'as a secondary phenomenon the character of which depends upon the *exoteric* doctrine ... It may, therefore, be said that the exoteric doctrine is the more general ethnic phenomenon, the investigation of which is a necessary foundation for the study of the problems of esoteric teaching' (my emphasis, 874).

As Michael Elliott has remarked, accounting for this whole exoteric system of culture was practically impossible; mainly because of its absolute excess and abundance of material and so possible modes of reading it. He notes, 'one can ... understand Boas's publishing practices as a testament to his belief in the complexity of all cultures. For while he pushed for the discovery of scientific truths about culture, he also insisted that one could not arrive at such conclusions until one accumulated all the necessary evidence (11). Collecting a body of evidence significant enough to describe accurately the exoteric doctrine (which could, in turn, explain the esoteric) was a task that was seemingly beyond the reach of any single field or fieldworker. This pushed anthropology away from a search for a singular, unified 'truth' claim and towards a pragmatic mode of operation whereby describing a culture was a synchronic process, designed to serve the primary needs of the moment, and textual objects had value in and of themselves – even where they existed outside of a clearly recognisable and diachronic pattern of behaviour. The effect of this was radical as it rendered all group life a structure *within* the present and not an evolutionary throwback or what E. B. Tylor would think of as a 'survival'. By removing forms of tool, and so the forms of labour they were meant to serve, from an evolutionary hierarchy (as was implied by Boas's rejection of independent invention), the individuals who used those tools were themselves liberated from an association between forms of work and diachronic patterns of time. Boas's vision of exoteric culture was an understanding of labour (by means of the objects of labour) that was also a conception of culture. Moreover, because of the rejection of 'independent invention' there was no primitive strictly speaking, so if a culture operated among us in the modern world it was modern. Yet, anthropology focused on the endlessly moving space of the exoteric surface world was also anthropology that self-consciously admitted the inevitability of its own failure to establish universal descriptions of a culture. No 'eureka' moment – the discovery of a particular tool and its associated mode of labour – could explain historical time because the speed of change always exceeded the capacities of the observer; leaving the observer in a constant process of reconfiguration and reinterpretation.

In fashioning anthropology as a tool of and for the 'common people', Boas also implied something that he would take up later in his ground-breaking book *The Mind of Primitive Man* (1911). This was the idea that prior to the appropriation and refinement of ritual practices by elite power structures the 'exoteric doctrine' was cosmopolitan at core and recognisable in its diversity and hybridity. Boas stated that as a widely shared pool of common resources, the 'exoteric doctrine' 'contain[s] many elements that can proved to be of foreign origin' (872), so that paying attention to the 'more general ethnic phenomenon' meant also paying attention to diversity, multiplicity and exchange, rather than offering a reading of society that moved out from a primitive core of unity and purity and towards eventual dissolution or chaos. The common people, Boas implied, are the hybridising, pluralising, diversifying forces in any society; and it is here where the analysis of a social order should begin. Applying this method to a Marxian reading of Progressive Era writing more generally suggests that aesthetics, and so politics, should begin with the multiplicity, diversity and cosmopolitanism of the working classes, or 'base', and this is what I have attempted in this book. Reading for the meaning of a complex text, art object or ritual meant reading for and with plurality. In a sense, the Boasian method after 'The Ethnological Significance of Esoteric Doctrines' was intrinsically 'intersectional'. This fact was lost as the culture concept in the twentieth century became synonymous with *habitus*, or a euphemism for 'race'. In highlighting that those under the yoke of power were far from ethnically, ideologically or racially 'pure', he helped to show that resisting oppression and the appropriation of common resources meant engaging simultaneously with class and with the behavioural patterns we have come to term 'culture'. This occurred not through focusing on elites as the fountainhead of social meaning and value, or undertaking a 'suspicious reading' of cultural objects, but by looking to the cosmopolitan 'common people' and their exoteric world as the primary locus of cultural meaning. Discovering the meaning of everyday life meant discovering a plural universe of non-hierarchical, temporal matter.

It is not hard to see the impact of Boas's socialist politics on his understanding of cultural diffusion, which allowed for anthropology to move past the fixed logic and temporality of 'race' while also being inclusive of the experience of the common man and woman in society. Returning to Rancière, it is possible to see Boas's subversion of the hierarchical patterns of culture as a significant facet of a wider intellectual refashioning of the experience of 'modern time' in the late nineteenth century that is the subject of this book. By 'get[ting] rid of its dependency on the rules of social hierarchy' (Rancière, 'Fictions of Time', 35) (in which something must be addressed to a particular recipient with a special place in the pecking order), Boas's culture concept was 'faithful to what can be observed in the everyday life of any ordinary man . . .' (35), rendering that 'everyday life' as charged up with potentiality, dynamism, and plural futurities, but also contingent and provisional. Eric Aronoff has also taken the Boasian sense of culture as 'provisional, momentary, [and] not the only possible compositional order' (*Composing Cultures*, 193) as an invite to develop a new discipline of 'critical culturalism' in American Studies scholarship. This book is perhaps a response to that invite, but sets the clock back on the project of 'critical culturalism' from being a discipline rooted in American 'modernism' proper to an earlier moment incorporating 'realism'.

The Boasian culture concept was conceived as a method for accessing the everyday, and resisting the pull to the 'Event' as the only means to generate a definitive description of group life. This was something that Boas's students Elsie Clews Parsons and Alfred Kroeber in particular took extremely seriously. In the introduction to her 1922 edited collection of short fictions by leading anthropologists, *American Indian Life*, Parsons remarked that the aims of her anthropology were essentially liberatory and rooted in a desire for an exoteric mode of reasoning and public education to challenge the esotericism of academic knowledge. Parsons writes:

> Appearances to the contrary, anthropologists have no wish to keep their science or any part of it esoteric. They are too well-aware, for one thing, that facilities for the pursuit of anthropology are dependent more or less on popular interest, and that only too often tribal cultures have disappeared in America as elsewhere before people became interested enough in them to learn about them. (1)

She goes on to note that focusing on the synthetic whole of a 'culture' and understanding this to be accessed by means of a key within a specific esoteric ritual practice leads to problems of association and sympathy that establishes life on the basis not of commonality but of racial difference.

> [We] fail to see the foreign culture as a whole, noting only the aspects which happen to interest us. Commonly, the interesting aspects are those which differ markedly from our own culture or those in which we see relations to the other foreign cultures we have studied. Hence our classified data give the impression that the native life is one unbroken round, let us say, of curing or weather-control ceremonials, of prophylaxis against bad luck, of hunting, or of war. The commonplaces of behaviour are overlooked, the amount of 'common sense' is underrated, and the proportion of knowledge to credulity is greatly underestimated. In other words the impression we give of the daily life of the people may be quite misleading, somewhat as if we described our own society in terms of Christmas and the Fourth of July, of beliefs about the new moon or ground hogs in February, of city streets in blizzards and after, of strikes and battleships. (2)

For Parsons, the anthropologist's eye (like the New Historicist's) overlooked similar materials in the exoteric doctrine in the favour of a fixed mode of difference observable in the esoteric. It was a selective epistemology whose aim was to reify by focusing on the spectacular Event – the ritual or ceremonial that was markedly different from the anthropologist's own worldview. Yet in so doing, anthropology affected a double move in reifying the ethnographer's own 'culture' in the acknowledgement of the difference of a 'foreign' Other. The implication of this is an anti-racist version of the ethnographic method that is not rooted in difference but in what is shared from the common pool of human resources, but not necessarily conceptualised in the same way by each subject.

In reflections on the changing meaning of the term 'culture', Brad Evans has noted that the Boasian culture concept was rendered insufficient by the cosmopolitan, diasporic and hybridising moves of late twentieth and early twenty-first century Theory. Evans suggests that, 'In place of "culture", "diaspora" and "cosmopolitanism"' became the new buzzwords, and circulation emerged as a kind of antidote to culture's conceptual stasis in place and time, such that one now spoke instead of routes and flows ('Rethinking The Disciplinary Confluence of Anthropology and Literature', 435). However, I would suggest that in some clear respects, for Boas, attending to 'diaspora', 'cosmopolitanism' and other terms that opposed the principle of cultural stasis was always a key concern of his thought. It is, after all, notable that Boas in his second or third language of English was not always a clear writer or communicator. The word 'Cultures', for Boas, was only ever really a placeholder for precisely the forces that Theory would come in time to describe. Along with the contemporary anthropologist Lars Rodseth, I would argue that 'the reputation of Boas and other "anthropological codgers" for theorising simplistically about cultures as bounded, organic wholes is largely undeserved' (Rodseth, 'Back to Boas', 873). Boas was quite specific about how 'messy', 'complex' and 'mongrel' he aimed for 'culture' to be. The faults found in Boas were for the most part the products of a specifically literary method of reading for representativeness; of hooking texts into patterns of group behaviour that served either the needs of a nationalist American Studies in the creation of a distinctive, shared 'American culture' or '70s and '80s multicultural critique. Looking at culture at its messiest – where it belongs to the 'common people' – invites us to consider instead what appropriations or acts of power have occurred to make it *seem* solid and bounded, regressive and ossified. These acts might be formal (in the sense of literary form and convention shaping what can and cannot be said about a tribe or group), or they might be symptomatic (in the sense of a text's positioning within a wider structure of feeling). Boas remarks that

> there remain many ideas that are not coordinated with the general system, and that may be out of accord with it . . . [i]n such cases the contradiction between the general scheme and special ideas often escapes entirely the notice of native philosophers. (873)

This implies an excess of exoteric content to societies that it becomes the task of the anthropologist to account for, placing the fieldworker and critic in a constructivist space of meaning-making and not in an objective space that points beyond everyday life and pragmatic need.

Consequently, the Boasian method pre-empts in crucial respects the 'linguistic' and 'self-reflexive' turns in anthropology that are generally understood as the products of the 1980s work of Marshall Sahlins, James Clifford, Clifford Geertz and others, as Rodseth has noted. This is not really a surprise if we situate Boas in his 'literary' context. After all, writing was very clearly having an 'aesthetic moment' around 1900 when formal and stylistic considerations were understood as absolutely central to the production of meaning. In opening up what can be known and said about a 'culture' and showing how 'class' and literary form operated in that dynamic, Boas (along with other writers and thinkers of the Progressive Era discussed in this book) performed a 'redistribution of the sensible'; a re-description of social processes and imaginaries that had historically depended upon a far more rigid sense of narrative time.[12]

Taking Boas at his word has implications for reading Progressive Era literature. For starters, it assumes that there is no conspiracy behind a text (no key to unlock the complex symbols of a particular event or object that is held in reserve by elites), just a fragmented social order that refines, modifies and reconstitutes collective resources in different ways. Whereas the Morganian evolutionary model reified hierarchy by suggesting that anything one might presume to be a 'common culture' of a group is an effect of the operation of 'secrets' and conspiracy (a 'leak' that trickles down from elite power 'on high'), Boas suggested that it is not the minority that creates the culture of the majority, but a mass or multitude that has its objects appropriated from a common pool. Boas's vision for the culture concept as it developed, therefore, challenged a presumptive hermeneutics of suspicion in the service of a version of political populism. It is in this spirit that my reading of Progressive Era literature will proceed.

***

In Chapter 1 I consider more fully the question of the function of 'conspiracy' or 'suspicion' for a conservative rendering of culture in the Progressive Era, by presenting a new reading of the Haymarket Affair (an 1886 bombing in Chicago and the subsequent executions of four 'anarchists' that is a major moment in the history of the modern American left) that highlights this event as an important node in the development of the aesthetics of modern time for American literature. In the chapter I consider how the noted liberal William Dean Howells's public support for clemency for the Haymarket anarchists impacted his approach to questions of 'representation' in his later work, which did not depart from 'realism' so much as truly embrace its political potential as a means for expressing the multiplicity of sub-events that constitute everyday life. Moreover, I demonstrate how Howells' increasing awareness of the existence of class conflict in the USA led to his development of a complex, 'modern' approach to the aesthetics of the novel. Crucial to this argument are my readings of the autobiographies of a number of the Haymarket 'martyrs' (especially of the German immigrant August Spies, written in prison awaiting execution) as works that attempt to perform a 'redistribution of the sensible' that lays claim to the world of 'high culture' as the legitimate possession of a working-class subject. This reading moves beyond seeing their engagement with high art and ideas as either merely an 'ironic' disruption of what Pierre Bourdieu formulated as the cultural field imaginary, or as an act of simple 'representation'. I show how the Eight-Hour Movement that was blamed for the agitation that led to the Haymarket Affair, in seeking a reorganisation of everyday life destabilised fixed correspondences between class culture, and time, and precipitated the development of these new aesthetic practices.

Chapter 2 considers the friendship between the Cuban leader José Martí and the US journalist Charles Anderson Dana in relation to questions of transnationalism, print culture, modernist aesthetics and the politics of dissent during the era of the Cuban War of Independence (1895–1898). It investigates the radical potential and aesthetic difficulties of rendering genuine affection in print at a time when American friendliness towards Cuba often served to mask imperialist intentions. Yet it also shows the potential of the work of the newspaperman as a site through which in rendering the everyday a shared space of affection might also be created. I offer a reading of Charles Dana's obituary for José Martí as a text that destabilises assumptions about Cuban–American relations in the late nineteenth century by presenting an alternative political vision that imagined the possibility of an autonomous Cuban subjectivity alongside several of Martí's modernist 'chronicles' and writings for English-language publications. In doing this, I resurrect Charles Dana's work as a proto-modernist alternative vision of US culture that mobilised the history of American Transcendentalism within the forms of late nineteenth-century print media to register his opposition to the rise of modern press magnates such as W. R. Hearst and Joseph Pulitzer. This chapter thereby seeks to challenge dominant narratives on three fronts: first, by suggesting an alternative to normative accounts of the development of the late nineteenth-century commercial press; second, by exploring the mutual interpenetration of Latin American and US American radical histories; and third, by disrupting periodisations of the development of literary modernism in the USA by expanding the spatial frame to include transnational actors.

Chapter 3 begins with a close reading of Stephen Crane's short story 'Manacled' from 1900, which situates this rarely considered short work within the context of contemporary debates about realism. I then proceed to argue that many of the debates raised by the tale have an afterlife in our own era of American literary studies, which has frequently focused on questions of 'identity' and 'culture' in its reading of realism and naturalism to the exclusion of the importance of cosmopolitan discourses of diffusion and exchange across national borders. In the second half of the chapter I offer a new reading of Crane's novel *George's Mother*, which challenges commonplace suggestions in recent criticism that particularities of cultural difference in Progressive Era literature have come to conflate ideas of class and social position with ideas of culture in ways that have ultimately obscured the presence of genuine historical inequalities in US society. In order to challenge this critical commonplace, I situate Crane's work within a history of transatlantic cosmopolitanism associated with the ideas of Franz Boas and Matthew Arnold, to demonstrate the ways in which Crane's narratives sought out an experience of the universal within their treatments of the particular, illustrating how his radical use of modernist aesthetics served to promote his readers' affective engagements with the problem of social class, rather than deflect attention from them. The chapter contextualises Stephen Crane's work within the transnational space of US, UK and French literary publishing at the turn of the century and also alongside Progressive Era writing around immigration, such as Hamilton Holt's 'lifelets' or *Life Stories of Undistinguished Americans*.

Chapter 4 closes the book and considers how Edith Wharton drew on her understanding of American ethnography, gleaned from her extensive reading and contributions to the Scribner's syndicate magazines, in her treatment of divorce as a means to allow the flow of goods and capital around the globe in the age of American imperial encounter, cultural appropriation and modern aesthetic experimentation. Starting with a reading of *The Custom of the Country*, I show how Wharton's narrative of the rising status of an American serial divorcee served not only as a satire on the 'conspicuous consumption' of the 'leisure class' (Thorstein Veblen) (material that has been well-trodden in Wharton studies), but as a comment on the changing understanding of tradition and performance mobilised by the emergence of early versions of the American culture concept. Reading the heroine's Apex City, North Dakota origins and the narrator's frequent references to Native American performance cultures as a response to the recent Sioux War, I consider how Wharton weaves critiques of US cultural pluralism into her vision of capitalist excess, raising questions of the complicity of American anthropology in the very processes of imperialist acquisition it sought frequently to criticise. In the final part of the chapter I consider how Wharton relates to divisions in the political culture of the US around questions of cosmopolitanism and class politics at the time of the USA's entry into the First World War. Reading *A Son at the Front* in relation to debates in American literary circles over entry into the war, I show how the perceived 'split' in the political Left between 'ethnic particularism' or 'cultural pluralism' and collective action has its roots in this period.

Notes

1. 'Lecture 5', *A Pluralistic Universe*. <https://www.gutenberg.org/cache/epub/11984/pg11984.html> (accessed 15 May 2022).
2. See Levinas *(Entre Nous)*, p. 74.
3. See Kornbluh, 'Extinct Critique'.
4. See Evans, *Before Cultures*.

5. It is possible at this point to begin to think with ritual and performance theory in the tradition of the British social anthropologist Victor Turner whose late career was spent largely working through the implications of his own thesis concerning the dramatic potential of liminal states in the ritual process when a figure is in transition from one symbolic order to another – the 'anti-structure' between two orders of being. I consider this topic more fully in relation to literary form in an earlier book, *The Drama of the American Short Story, 1800–1865*.
6. See Konstantinou, 'The Hangman of Critique'.
7. See Deleuze and Guattari, *Kafka*.
8. See Rodseth, 'Back to Boas'.
9. Bell, *The Problem of American Realism*.
10. See Evans, 'Where Was Boas During the Renaissance in Harlem?'
11. *A Pluralistic Universe*, <https://www.gutenberg.org/cache/epub/11984/pg11984.html> (accessed 15 July 2022).
12. Boas's critique was not just directed against the Morgan school and its linear model of narrative time, it also implicitly took aim at earlier models of 'diffusionism', particularly that of the 'dean of comparative anthropology' J. G. Frazer. These models of 'diffusion' presumed a ritual core common to all cultures that spread out from particular centres of power – Hellenic Greece, Christian Rome – to become the loam from which diverse civilisations sprang. For Boas, diffusion was more specifically an effect of contact and exchange that was not so predictable. This is not to say he had no theory of hegemony, merely that the 'inclusion of foreign material' was not unproblematically bound up in empire and colonialism and included space for resistant or subaltern inclusions into the 'general ethnic phenomenon' of a 'culture'.

CHAPTER 1

Culture and Anarchy: Time, Narrative and the Haymarket Affair

> 'To put the events of these days into a newspaper chronicle is like trying to gather lava from a volcano into a coffee cup.'
> José Martí, in 'Correspondencia particular del *Partido Liberal*' (19)

> 'When realism becomes false to itself, when it heaps up facts merely, and maps life instead of picturing it, realism will perish . . .'
> William Dean Howells, *Criticism and Fiction*

On 4 May 1886, an anonymous individual threw a dynamite bomb at advancing police who had begun to violently disperse a crowd of labourers in Haymarket Square on Chicago's West Side. The group had assembled to protest police brutality in response to a recent strike at McCormick's Reaper Factory, a large producer of agricultural machinery for the Mid-West. The strike had been part of a far-larger campaign by a variety of trade union and workers' societies in Chicago for fairer pay and conditions, called the Eight-Hour Movement. The bomb killed one policeman, Mattias Degan, instantly and twenty-three officers were injured enough to disable them. Six policeman died of injuries in the following weeks and months – though it is not known whether these were sustained from the bomb or friendly fire in the chaos following the explosion. The police response to the bomb was panicked and disorganised. They shot into the crowd with live ammunition, failed to identify participants from by-standers, and reports exist suggesting they even fired into their own lines. Accounts vary quite widely as to the number of civilians killed, as no official count was taken by police or the newspaper syndicates, although the historian Timothy Messer-Kruse suggests 'three civilians were killed near Haymarket that night of May the Fourth' and 'several dozen' sustained bullet wounds (3). The lack of an accurate headcount was likely because the workingmen and women involved were unwilling to reveal themselves as present at the time and so face a potential death penalty for conspiracy or other forms of extrajudicial violence that were promoted in the press as legitimate responses to what was framed as, but did not always refer to itself as, 'anarchism'. The panic and conspiracism that came to surround the event created a foreclosure of care, as militarisation forced on the public a suspicion that prevented access to hospitals and public services by the oppressed citizens facing reprisals and aggression by the state. As Shelley Streeby and others have shown, the press response to the bombing marked anarchism as a discrete 'culture' with a specific and continuing relationship to the exceptional event of the bombing. Anarchism, moreover, was specifically racialised so as to render the defendants part of an alien race whose presence disrupted the normative features of 'American' everyday life and not, in fact, as they were, a multiethnic, multinational workforce whose cultural proximity to one another was established because of, not in spite of, American labour conditions.

In the aftermath of the riot, seven men (who were proved to have not thrown the bomb themselves and whom the prosecution did not indict under that suspicion) were captured, placed on trial and eventually sentenced to death. Their names were Albert Parsons, August Spies, Samuel Fielden, Michael Schwab, Adolph Fischer, George Engels and Louis Lingg. On 11 November 1887, four of the men were hanged. Another, Oscar Neebe, faced fifteen years' imprisonment. All of these men were active in the anarchist and trades union movement in Chicago, as writers, orators and organisers. Only two, Samuel Fielden and August Spies, were present at the time the bomb was thrown.

This moment is a well-known tragedy in the history of American labour relations, inaugurating a 'string of legal decisions that served to restrict the civil rights of workers and empower the federal government against them' (Messer-Kruse 4). As with many

Figure 1.1 Lithograph, 'The Haymarket Anarchists' (1886).

acts in history given by kneejerk reaction the name of 'terrorism', Haymarket ultimately permitted an authoritarian armament of the US police that suppressed the burgeoning labour movement in Chicago and nationally, as well as a counter-response from the American Left that came to deify as 'martyrs' the men who died at the gallows.[1] Yet, my point here is not so much to restate the immorality of their treatment, or even make yet another case for the innocence of the Haymarket 'martyrs'. Indeed, as Messer-Kruse has meticulously demonstrated in his powerful re-reading of the case, *The Trial of the Haymarket Anarchists* (2011), there was considerable evidence testifying that the Haymarket anarchists were guilty of what they were charged with, according to contemporary Illinois statutes; namely, the appallingly catchall crime of being an 'Accessory': '[H]e who stands by, and aids, abets, or who, not being present, aiding and abetting, hath advised, encouraged, aided or abetted the perpetration of a crime . . .' (as reported in the *Chicago Journal*, 5 May 1886). The Haymarket 'anarchists' certainly did seek to arm themselves in preparation for violent clashes with the police at some future point, even if they could not be proven to have lit the fuse in this instance, and they encouraged arming themselves as a response to capitalist violence. Several, including Spies, were active members of an anti-capitalist militia in Chicago, the Lehr-und-Wehr Verein, which was stockpiling weapons for a future class war.

The legal loophole of 'Accessory' status did not, so the prosecution argued, require them to find the murderer whom the 'Accessory' abetted, merely demonstrate that they possessed a common anarchist 'culture' and shared sympathies. Indeed, the law of 'Accessory' is a system for establishing the complicity and conspiracy of a second-person actor by means of an ideology critique of sorts. 'Accessory' has a unique time signature that makes it essential to the prosecution of behaviours that by the 'official' speech acts of the juro-political order are made 'terrorism'. It effectively transforms a huge body of cultural expression in the exoteric field into the *a priori* product of a subsequent event: the act of terrorism or violence itself. To label a thing 'Terror' is a speech act that organises a situation into a narrative form. It reads backwards and this is, of course, a paradox. In the courtroom, a sequence of various, extraneous and more-or-less meaningless objects were presented to the jury (a set of what Alain Badiou has called 'situations' to mean 'any presented multiplicity') (*Being and Event*, 26) and were transmogrified by the rituals of the law from multiples into One. Moreover, objects which came before the act of terror (the Event) are made relevant as the expression of a particular 'culture' and set of sympathies that are made a unified 'thing' only in light of that which followed. The 'event' of the crime, as captured by the purview of the law, allows for the construction of the 'culture' as an ontology that supposedly created the 'event' of the crime. By this legal practice the circle is closed, and exoteric cultural expression can be made proof of a conspiracy motivated, in Boas's terms, by the ideas and actions of an esoteric sub-group that controlled affairs for a whole assemblage of people in secret from within. Put another way, the construction of culture as an ontology (a hard and fast *thing* rather than a constantly shifting and evolving set of practices) depends first on the creation by power of a conspiratorial sub-culture.

The transformation of exoteric cultural expression into an 'esoteric culture' also depends therefore upon the temporal condition of the 'Event' – as distinguished from the pluralities that are possible within any given 'situation'. This is why anthropology prior to the Boasian revolution focused so centrally on ritual practices as the system from which a wider sociality was born, and why, too, this temporality was a means of Othering. Ritual, including the law, is a form of assemblage that reduces the Many to the One through the creation of an Event. Indeed, the principal of the terrorist act as Event is also at the core of the concept of the *coup d'état* and frequently haunts societies born of revolution (like the USA) as its dark doppelgänger: both its originating act and the alternative to its official rule of law. Moreover, according to Jens Bartelson, the *coup d'état* constitutes a 'more general problem within political philosophy, one that concerns the relationship between the regular and the exceptional in political theory and practice' (Bartelson 323). For Bartelson,

> A coup d'état does not only by definition constitute an exceptional event, but must also invariably be justified with reference to exceptional circumstances to be successful. At a minimum, therefore, the practice of coup d'état is the technique of *making* exceptions from old rules and creating new rules out of these exceptions. (323)

In the case of the Haymarket prosecution, the bombing – whose provenance and purpose was not definitively established – was a situation (it was the performance of something in the world) that was turned into an exceptional Event – a political ontology – that could allow for the subsequent expansion by the state of its security apparatus and justified according to the logic of what the Nazi jurist Carl Schmitt called the 'state of exception'. The 'state of exception' is a condition with a deliberately unclear temporal frontier of action (it can go on for as long as the sovereign wishes it to), and where the whole of the law is permitted to be embodied in the sovereign such that any act by them is automatically justified by the law. In radical distinction to the Left revolutionary Event as theorised by Badiou, which is the production of an excess that allows for the inclusion of subaltern voices into the political order, the characterisation of the Haymarket bomb as an act of 'terror' by the state, and the deployment of the law of 'Accessory' to fashion a conspiracy, constituted the performance of a specifically capitalist version of the Event. From the perspective of the juro-political order, terrorism, like the *coup d'état*, must be made exceptional, as this allows for the construction of a discrete, esoteric and conspiratorial culture that can be used to justify state violence against unwanted groups; leftists, Germans, Jews, POC and the like. Incidents, causes and objects that were part of the exoteric fabric of a wider, pluralised social life were transformed by a process of law and media into evidence of a specific Other culture or exception to the norm so as to permit the exceptional response that followed from the police.

The deployment of the law of 'Accessory' during the Haymarket Affair permitted the police to tie the complex and multifarious social life of Chicago workers into the Event of Terror. It also allowed, indeed relied upon, an excess of 'evidence' – including false leads, red herrings and other miscellaneous content – to be utilised in the construction of a narrative of exceptional conspiracy that could criminalise a whole group, permit the execution of 'ringleaders' wherever and whenever they were found, and compensate in the eyes of society for the absence of the real bomb-thrower. The subsequent late nineteenth-century expansion of anti-immigrant sentiment seen in such moments as the passage of anti-immigration laws like the Anarchist Exclusion Act of 1903 (which fused anti-Eastern European and anti-Semitic racial animosity to political affiliation) were made possible by the creation of 'anarchism' as an alien 'culture' that was understood to exist perpetually in a time-locked state relative to the Event of Terror at Haymarket in 1886. After Haymarket, the category of 'Terrorism' racialised and excluded people by labelling them as bound up in an Event with a single point of origin but without a horizon or end point (an ontology in other words), thereby fashioning any encounter with the Other as one marked by the peculiar effect of temporal dislocation. When labelled part of a Terrorist group or culture, the Other does not inhabit the present when encountered by a representative of the law or the dominant group it serves, but is bound forever to a historic Event.

In this chapter I show how the Haymarket Affair served as a focal point for a hermeneutic crisis in late nineteenth-century writing that caused a shift in the 'distribution of the sensible' and helped make thinkable a later literary modernism. This occurred when 'realism', such as that practised by Howells in A *Hazard of New Fortunes*, sought to highlight the excesses on the surface of everyday life that could be mobilised against the temporal and representational logic of what I called earlier, after Franz Boas, 'esoteric' cultural determinism, and the reduction of all possibilities in the exoteric space of culture to a conspiratorial core through the production of the capitalist form of the Event. In response to a perceived terrorist threat, the Haymarket prosecutors developed a right-wing form of cultural critique and used this to justify a state of exception that was deployed in the service of the status quo, white power, and anti-labour sentiment. It did this, in part, by declaring a time war on individuals and ideas; expelling 'anarchism' from its claims to the future, by using the law to construct an Event that tied a culture forevermore into the past, and making it unacceptable as an expression of modernity.

The evidence the prosecution offered to the jury in the trial was not of a forensic kind. They were not attempting to prove that the Haymarket defendants were murderers themselves. Indeed, forensic science did not really exist at this point in 1886. In the aftermath of the riot, the police focused on militarising their presence on the streets in the service of protecting the populace (or so they claimed), while the juridical order turned towards proving a far-reaching conspiracy of culture. It is worth noting the extent to which the production of a fascistic state of exception that permits persecution of minorities relies therefore upon a double movement: a legal process of exclusion through the construction of an Event that reassembles social relations on one hand, and an ongoing 'culture war' that seeks to delegitimate certain speech acts as conspiratorial on the other.

As Messer-Kruse notes,

> Almost every prisoner incarcerated in this era had been convicted solely on the basis of some witness's or victim's testimony. Circumstantial or physical evidence of any kind was rarely brought into courtrooms, except

where a torn skirt or a bloody knife could arouse the disgust, anger, or sympathy of a jury. (9)

Haymarket was different though. Lacking direct evidence tying the defendants unequivocally to the deaths, what the prosecution sought to create was a discrete, esoteric culture to be blamed for the crimes. This was achieved by evoking an excess of sentiment in the jury by presenting a steady stream of vaguely suspicious objects that allowed discrete things to be tied together in sympathy: a paranoiac form of ideology and cultural critique. Moreover, this process was not confined to the courtroom, but was bolstered by a whole publication industry based around highly illustrated guides to identifying and fighting anarchism. In 1889 the Captain of the Chicago Police, Michael Schaack, produced a book of almost 700 pages, containing approximately 190 original, high-quality illustrations – many of them of objects found and seized by police during the investigation that followed the bombing.

Figure 1.2 Cover, Michael Schaak, *Anarchy and Anarchists* (1889).

As Sara Ahmed has usefully noted, emotions shape the relations of proximity we have to objects and this might, in turn, affect our desired proximity to the people and events for whom these objects are made to stand metonymically. She writes that 'Orientations register the proximity of objects, as well as shape what is proximate to the body ... We move toward and away from objects through how we are affected by them' (*The Promise of Happiness*, 24). The melodrama staged by the courts and the press produced through its own excess of objects an excess of feeling (a kind of terroristic gothic sublime) with the purpose of utilising that affective excess for the production of a unified juridical response to an Event defined as singular and exceptional and thereby requiring an 'exceptional' response. In several respects the genre of the court's performance here was crucial. I use the term 'melodrama' above very specifically for the sense it conveys of being 'realism's' antithesis, and as a description of the specific mode of excess deployed by the state. Melodrama as a genre is a form of spectacular economy that communicates with an excess that gives the impression of liberatory release or catharsis, except that the feelings called for are unidirectional, immanent, and galvanise the spectacle presented to the audience into the form of an official politics. Melodrama's spectacles ask that the audience feel deeply and suggest that they do so spontaneously, but this is really a phantasmagoric effect, because their feelings are put to a particular unified end – the transformation of a 'situation' where multiple futures exist simultaneously – into the reified form of the Event. The genre's reliance on tableaux and cliffhanger is the self-conscious aesthetic embodiment of this form of politics and temporality; fixing potentiality as image so as to transform affective multiplicity into structural unity. This makes melodrama closest in kind among the dramatic arts to ritual itself. It also places melodrama at the furthest point among genres from the abstract production of zeitgeist or tone. Melodrama frequently mobilises the sublime as a tool of speech-suppressing awe rather than evoking its power to awaken the audience to a new shared sociality. This twin effect of the sublime was present initially in Kant's consideration of aesthetic judgement in the *Critique of Judgement*, where it is noted that the wonder and terror of the sublime is that it both forces us to relate to other minds and imagine ourselves as part of something greater, even as it closes down our capacity for speech. It is for this reason that melodrama has in American life such a specific history in relation to the process of racialisation.[2] As a genre it is a recessive form forever dragging spontaneous emotionality in the present back into the past. This is partly why it so often seems corny, especially by the late nineteenth century when it becomes a specific object of attack for the upcoming generation of realists and modernists, wedded as they were so fundamentally to the aesthetic value and political urgency of the present. As Fred Moten has remarked of Saidiya Hartman's understanding of the repeated spectacle of black bodies in antebellum culture, melodramatic schemes of violence and suffering frequently diverted attention away from the everyday and ongoing presence of African Americans in modern life and rendered racial identity into a historical condition shaped by the Event of slavery. At the extreme end this historicised injustice, too, absolved the present of complicity in ongoing cruelty by projecting trauma backwards.[3] The further an affected individual is from an Event such as slavery, or individual or collective trauma, the more able the current political order is to pass the buck onto their ancestors and expel that trauma from what it signifies in the present.

In the Haymarket prosecution and the media circus that followed, people and situations associated with 'anarchism' by the trial lawyers were made, under a barrage of spectacular sentiment, into something exceptional so as to effect a rejection of certain groups from the accepted temporal rhythms of present everyday life. Jesse W. Schwartz has usefully suggested that

> By sentencing the Haymarket radicals to death, the prosecution . . . legitimated an innovative framework for what we might think of as a legal theory of literary complicity: a juridical reconciliation of the conceptual space between words and deeds that allowed potentially all writers to be held liable for the social lives of their texts. (523)

The First Red Scare that emerged in the wake of Haymarket expanded on this mode of paranoid historicist reading. In several respects, the Haymarket prosecutors pre-empted the conclusions of Franz Boas's students in the field of anthropology – though not, crucially, of Boas himself – in focusing on authenticity, unity and consistency as modes that would permit the construction of a discrete culture.

In 1924, in his famous essay 'Culture, Genuine and Spurious' from the January 1924 edition of *The American Journal of Sociology*, Edward Sapir gave the most fulsome definition of what was becoming solidified by that point as the 'American culture concept', dividing that which might be understood as 'authentic' from all the elements of aesthetic and social expression that he regarded as inauthentic trash. In that essay, Sapir defined an authentic culture in terms of the sympathy and sentiment felt by the observer, anthropologist or curator:

> inherently harmonious, balanced, self-satisfactory . . . richly varied and yet somehow unified and consistent . . . an attitude which sees the significance of any one element of civilization in its relation to all others . . . in which no important part of the genuine functioning brings with it a sense of frustration, of misdirected, or unsympathetic effort. (410)

Ideally, this aesthetic sense of harmony and balance would have been informed by a prior experience of the viewer's embeddedness (participant observation) within the cultural group under discussion. Culture, for Sapir, regulated the appropriateness of feelings and expressions and smoothed out the snags. Defining a culture relied on an aesthetic sense in the viewer that somehow everything belonged together. This is not, in point of fact, that far from an Arnoldian argument about the best and most beautiful; things that seem to belong together in some transcendent sense. At the Haymarket trial (indeed, too, in subsequent attempts by critics on the political Left to use Haymarket as an originating source for a unified workers' culture by cultivating uncritical sympathy for the victims put to death by the state), a similarly enormous body of discrete objects (clothing, texts, shell cases) was called upon to give the jury the impression of a unified, directed and sympathetic effort; a culture constructed from within for the purpose of the Event of Terror and bound ever after to it.

The Haymarket Affair has been considered from a variety of perspectives, literary and political, including most recently Shelley

Streeby's Foucauldian reading of the print culture around the Haymarket bombing and trial as staging a 'drama' that served as a cruel form of compensation for the late nineteenth-century 'removal of state-sponsored executions from public spaces . . . [and] promised access to forbidden scenes of punishment (35)'; thereby regulating and controlling public feeling in favour of the police and prosecutors' version of events. I agree, of course, with the sense that the media and courtroom drama was serving here as compensation for an invisible presence or void – in this case the bomb-thrower themselves. Yet, I would challenge the claim that the spectacularity of the workers' movement necessarily provided an effective radical alternative to the spectacular economies of state violence, since it presumes that spectacle must be met with spectacle; an escalation that reproduces in dissent the originary logic of state violence. Streeby's argument serves to reify an alternative collective sympathy and sentiment across a wide geopolitical space and time so as to present an image of a transnational 'worker's culture' that might resist the 'terrorist assemblage' (Puar) created by the panoptic State. It is still, therefore, an esoteric form of culture that raises the problem of authenticity and is conditioned by the temporality of the Event. By contrast, I would suggest that it is more the case with Haymarket that its significance lay in how the prosecution created a model for future racist and bourgeois anti-terrorism legislation by creating first a collective that could then be used to define certain individuals (Spies, Parsons, Lingg et al.) and situations as the fountainheads of a dangerous set of ideals and practices. This collectivisation was very clearly also a process of racialisation and drew on the white supremacist legacies of pro-slavery activism and it is not easily answered by the performance spectacle of the alternative. Indeed, it is crucial that the motion to try the defendants separately was denied undoubtedly in part because it would have substantially weakened the grounds of the prosecution's case in the establishment of collective 'Accessory' status and been less effective in the production of the mode of sentimental excess required to suture discrete acts and situations together into one singular Event and 'culture'.

In what follows, I will explore how in response to Haymarket, William Dean Howells (who against the norms of genteel bourgeois society fought for clemency for the defendants) and August Spies himself registered aesthetically their dissatisfaction with forms of writing and thought that posited a static relationship between literature, culture and the political sphere. They did this by rejecting the reductive logics of 'sentiment' and sympathy, and through the mobilisation of an alternative mode of excess, frequently ironic or detached, that could generate multiple potential futures and produce 'dissensus'; seeing this as central to the project of imagining a new progressive politics for the twentieth century. Howells positioned himself as an outlier to the Genteel Tradition in his defence of the Chicago workers, and Spies frequently also performed a kind of decadent individualism that pushed him, in the eyes of many of his fellow workers and activists, outside the fold of acceptability and sympathy.

Reading this way challenges the last two decades or so of Foucauldian-inspired scholarship that has sought to elevate sympathy and sentiment as necessary forms of resistance to the operations of state power, frequently describing the liberal state as cold, utilitarian and unfeeling in its deliberations. At Haymarket this was far from true. The state ran very hot, and relied upon the sentimentalism of its people to mobilise sufficient anger to persecute the innocent. In Howells's and Spies' work, modelling a resistant politics for the Progressive Era relied upon a rejection of these affective economies, such that realism's rejection of sentimentalism and romanticism might open up, rather than close down, the possibilities of the future.

In their distinctive ways, and from their differing perspectives, Howells and Spies argued that literary sympathy had been misapplied in order to suture techniques of representation to the politics of the US state in ways that would render it untenable as a genre for radical political engagement. This was a particular problem in the context of growing state violence against populations both domestic and foreign. The claims by realism's founders (including Howells) to the 'Americanness' of the genre has left it over the years exposed to criticism for its implicit conservativism at times when the American state's cruelty was so apparent, such as the with Haymarket trial. In the case of Howellsian realism this was because when seen as a genre that was merely 'representative' of social conditions, it fashioned as immoveable the position of individuals and groups within a cultural field whose topography was already established *a priori* – a practice that became in this period a readily available tool for claiming literary texts as complicit and 'cultures' unified and singular. As Howells noted in the quotation from *Criticism and Fiction* that serves as one of the epigraphs to this chapter, realism was for him not a collection of fictional occurrences mapped onto reality and verified by factual data, but a looser formulation that included space for alternative versions of life: 'When realism becomes false to itself, when it heaps up facts merely, and maps life instead of picturing it, realism will perish . . .' (15). Anna Kornbluh sees this problem with realism being characterised as a purely mimetic genre as a contemporary critical 'conceit' that 'bolsters today's hegemonic consensus that literature is information, that the task of the critic is to tabulate information, correlating work to cause, word to referent, with ever more granularity' (*The Order of Forms*, 16). By contrast to this conceit, it is my claim that in the hands of these writers, realist literature did not mobilise a politics of representation, and fix identities in ways that reproduced the racialisations conducted for the purpose of the exclusion of individuals by the state – that it was not mere 'information' like so much legal evidence – so much as challenge the hermeneutics of suspicion by opening up new potentialities of experience within the historical present.

In the hands of Howells and Spies, literature performed a mode of excess that redistributed 'the sensible' – the sensory and affective responses to an experience grounding one's impression of the meaning of an event – and so allowed the authors to imagine a new politics. This excess of exoteric, synchronous content was especially valuable as a response to the Haymarket trial because of the close relationship between the incident itself and the radical reorganisation of modern time promised for the working classes by the Eight-Hour Movement – a movement that among other things sought to permit workers' 'free' time for self-transformation and growth beyond the confines of a singular 'workers' culture'. The reorganisation of the relationship between workers and time sought by the Eight-Hour Movement, which brought freedom and diversity into the experience of modern life, can be seen as in clear distinction to the claims of the Haymarket prosecutors for a unified single 'culture' of the defendants that could stand as evidence of their conspiracy against the United States.

8 Hours for What We Will

To understand the Haymarket Affair and its aftermath, it is useful to turn to its original spur, which escalated Labour's challenge to Capital in Chicago (and to which the Haymarket defendants were variously committed), The Eight-Hour Movement. To interpret the movement, I will look to Rancière's writings on the relationship between labour and philosophy, as outlined first in *The Philosopher and His Poor* (1983) and developed in *The Politics of Aesthetics* (2004). In these works, he considers the question of poverty and class in philosophy as foremost an expression of temporality. Prior to the nineteenth century, he reasons, workers were excluded from the public sphere, and so from the field of official 'politics', because of a pre-eminent 'distribution of the sensible' (an account of what can be known and understood by a community as a legitimate act and/or work of reason) that saw the worker as only ever existing in relation to their labour, 'the private space-time of their occupation' (*The Politics of Aesthetics*, 40). He notes that since Plato's rejection of the artisans from the Republic, philosophy has been understood to be a product of the 'free time' of the philosopher to think, and so prefaced on a privileged exclusion of the philosopher from hard 'labour'. This makes any claim to reasonable speech emerging from the mouth of the worker immediately negated. The idea of the 'worker' as thinker is therefore an 'impossibility' for a philosophy that demands the workers' 'exclusion from participation in what is common to the community' (40). Put another way, in the Platonic philosophical traditions of the West, the worker is commonly understood as a 'private' entity (in Greek, *idios*, which translates into Latin as *idiota* and English as *idiot*) who is not part of the communal world and incapable of the form of discourse that is proper to it. In this way, any thought emerging from the workers is, prior to the democratisation movements of the nineteenth century, by definition, *noise* or unreasonable speech. This is why Rancière's term 'distribution of the sensible' (a translation from the French 'le partage du sensible') is so effective as a description of the aesthetic-ontological-political systems that keep certain groups welded to a certain place and time in the organisation of social life. 'Sensible' evokes rationality, intelligence and acceptability at once, and makes these things conditional on a presumed relationship between a certain group and the sensory world. It is such a distribution of the sensible that explains Cartesian classed distinctions between the rough labour of the working body and the sentimental affections of the elite. For Cartesians, bodily labour and mental labour inhabit different positions in the political order, and so, too, an incompatible sensorium. Labour movements such as the Eight-Hour Movement performed a redistribution of the sensible because they sought to elevate to the status of legitimacy and intelligence the responses of a subaltern group to their own lived experience. The workers' movement confers a prefigurative condition of citizenship upon a community previously known to bourgeois society only by their privacy or 'idiocy'. It then uses that elevated status as the basis upon which to effect change in the legal positioning and protection of workers in the juro-political order.

Along with other workers' reform movements of the period, the Eight-Hour Movement sought to give the workers 'free time' separate from the 'private' space of their labour in which to think and so to participate in a common culture and engage exoterically with the world. In this way, it violated the fundamental compact under which labour had existed in relation to community; namely, one of exclusion and invisibility. We can see this dream of the Chicago workers in one of the more famous images to emerge from the Eight-Hour Movement, an anonymously produced engraving entitled '8 Hours for Work, for Rest, for What We Will'.

This engraving performs a careful diagnosis of the relationship between space and time that organises labour. On the left-hand panel a woman works alone at a loom. This was clearly not an accurate rendering of work in the late nineteenth century, where labour conditions were commonly overpopulated. Yet through the verticality of the framing of the image and the focus on a single individual it does demonstrate the sensibility that work is a 'private' enterprise in the sense Rancière uses it above – disconnected from community. The second panel displays an individual asleep

Figure 1.3 '8 Hours for Work, for Rest, for What We Will', artist unknown (1880s).

in bed. The caption below reads 'for Rest' and is suggestive of both a conservative morality – it communicates that bed is understood to be for sleeping alone – and, once more, a sense of privacy. The final panel, however, does three distinct things. First, it opens up the spatiality of the drawing to include the outside world; the characters appear to be engaged in the bourgeois pastime of boating on a lake. Second, it displays the worker, presumably liberated from the confines of their private dyad (workplace or bed), reading a newspaper, and thereby participating in the processes Benedict Anderson famously attributed to the construction of an imagined national community. It also, therefore, displays the worker's literacy and ability to think – an emancipation from their status as 'private' or *idios*. Yet the image is also distinct from the others in displaying two figures, indicating both a sense of community from which the worker has traditionally been excluded by a fixed relationship between labour and time, and, because they appear to be a heterosexual courting couple (the boat suggests, perhaps, a date), the possibility of reproductive futurity. Across the three panels there is a narrative, which uses a spatial imaginary as an adjunct for individual freedom. In the first panel, there is no extraneous space. In the second there is an open window, which, since the figure is asleep, may also indicate the 'dream' of the worker to liberty. This is further enforced by the pensive position of the head of the woman in the first panel. Reading across panels her gaze is oriented towards the open window of the second frame in a way that suggests she may be in a dream, reverie, experiencing desire for the possibilities represented by the outside world, or otherwise thinking of home and her bed. The third panel represents actual leisure, symbolised by the open lake, and the sense of a dream fulfilled.

By framing each image of the worker within a time-based structure, 'Eight Hours' for each of the activities, the artist implies that there has been an expansion not only of spatiality but of time (even beyond that of the specific eight-hour period symbolised). The eight-hour period of leisure pays dividends far greater than the sum of its investment of time by the capitalist boss. The single working woman of the first image has a 'future' by the last (conceptualised in a heteronormative sense) that allows them to exceed their identity as 'worker' and be opened up to the condition of potentiality. In this way, the engraving shows how the key difference between the subject permitted to be political and that permitted not to speak is of a temporal nature. Plato opposed the artisans from entering his republic because to be a political entity and a worker would constitute a narrative deception. It would mean they were permitted the time to be two discrete things – thinkers and workers. However, the Eight-Hour Movement that the anarchists were lobbying for in Chicago was an important moment in the development of the modern aesthetico-political regime because it conferred upon the worker the 'time' to do other things, to perform an *excess* or double-function in being thinker and worker whose identity was not defined solely in relation to the labour theory of value.

At this point it is briefly worth returning once more to William Dean Howells's dramatisation of a peculiarly modern incident in Basil March's encounter with the well-dressed tramp in *A Hazard of New Fortunes* that I discussed in the introduction. It is significant that in this moment March's bourgeois mind (that of the idle philosopher or man of letters) regards the dual or multiple appearance of the French man – his divergence from the specifics of a typical, generic representation of homelessness or joblessness as March understands it – as indication that he must therefore be a deceiver, a phony, a confidence trickster. This is an expression of the residual, Platonic mode of theorising that considers the presence of the underclass within the agora as evidence of a deception or conspiracy; the will to inhabit two mutually exclusive positions that is a violation of the workers' pact with privacy. It is modern, like the demands of the Eight-Hour Movement, because of its spatio-temporal apostasy.

Strictly speaking, the Eight-Hour Movement's mode of solidarity across cultural lines was not a consensus-building exercise, but a *dissensus*-building process that opened up new configurations in the political regime by disrupting the ligaments that bound working life to a particular, strategic organisation of time and to a singular workers' 'culture'. The demands of the Eight-Hour Movement uncoupled speech from a particular regime of action, rendering it effectively 'free' to circulate across whatever spaces it chose. The '8 Hours for What We Will' engraving abandons the vertical confinement of the first image for the flat plane of the boating lake in the last; an image of lateral potentiality that is mirrored in the open form of the newspaper – the lake and paper open out simultaneously. Moreover, the first frame possesses a religious *tone* not unlike the treatment of the saints in stained glass. This implies that even when subject to a reification and deification at the hands of the workers' movement, or in the religious rhetoric of the Christian Sermon on the Mount, the worker inhabits a residual genre or form of life that demands a certain mode of expression and action. Yet, holiness is not synonymous with the freedom of the worker (or more pointedly of women) in modernity. Various forms of leftist praxis, feminism, and psychoanalysis have revealed for us how inhibiting the genre of the religious can be. By the last engraving sexuality, secularity and the profane are presented as the ideal future of the modern subject: one that is not reified, and so isolated in a private space-time away from the everyday, but wholly a citizen and part of the exoteric expression of public life.

This move from private to public is further demonstrated by the figure's changing stance. In the first image, she is facing away from us, and so we are unable to discern an individuality that Western societies frequently see carried by the face. We are able, though, to discern the tools of the worker's labour – the loom. This loom has a gothic tone as the strands of thread seem like webs, confining and binding her to her singular status as labourer. This is reinforced by the shabbiness of the second image. Returning to posture, in the second panel, we have only the feet, which is both endearing and also evocative of empathy for the toil and stress of the workday, since we must imagine that 10–12 hours standing at a loom would be enormously painful upon the feet of the worker. The third panel reorients the female figure to face the viewer, to meet our eye level but not necessarily our gaze. She is not hailed by us, but she occupies nonetheless the same plane as us. She is entitled to her thoughts, but they are of the level of the viewer. They are her own, as is her possession of the social world, which constitutes a definition of legitimate political speech. The personal, but level, gaze resembles the sense in which Levinas spoke of the face of the Other as a performance of a nominal equality. In meeting our eyeline as she does, the woman challenges the Platonic sense that for workers to be thinkers – directing their thought to the future – would constitute a deception. Here, the engraver implies, is a person who is undeceiving and whose openness is a product of the dissensus built by the Eight-Hour Movement's challenge to unfair working hours.

The final figure's placid occupation of space is reflective of a general need on behalf of the workers for the time for leisure and contemplation, but would have had a still deeper and particular resonance in the context of 1880s Chicago. Following the Great Fire of 1871, the city was undergoing a large-scale rebuild that was designed to transform it from an industrial boomtown of the immediate post-Civil War period into one of the jewels of the modern, cosmopolitan world. The expansion of beaux arts building design combined with the flowering of a homegrown American Arts and Crafts movement in the form of Louis Sullivan's 'Chicago, or Prairie School' (who were also responsible in part for the introduction of steel-frame skyscrapers that would make the city's name internationally) placed the question of the aesthetic and the question of physical space on the same intellectual plane.[4] The key concern was that Chicago – much like Baron Hausmann's renovations of mid-century Paris – was being rebuilt for the bourgeoisie alone, and in the embrace of a new beautifying aesthetic would effect an exclusion of the workers who had built the city and were responsible for its wealth from the sightlines of the other residents. The demands of the Haymarket anarchists and the Eight-Hour movement in Chicago were partly related to having access to that public space that was under construction in the 1880s, which they regarded as synonymous with the right of access to 'modernity' in more general terms. To picture a man and woman sitting in the public space of the park was confrontational across several temporal registers: the civilisational time of Western philosophy that spoke to the Platonic exclusion of the workers from the Republic; and a more immediate present in which the construction of aesthetic space by the bourgeoisie of Chicago threatened to make the 'aesthetic' and 'the modern' comprehensible only as the possession of that group. The lateral moves, panel to panel, of the 'Eight-Hours' engraving dramatise a 'renovation' of their own that seems like a move through evolutionary stages of development: from the gothic first image; to the shabby second; to the almost 'clean', hygienic space of the last panel.

In my reading of the engraving above I have applied a formal analysis of aesthetics to reveal how the Eight-Hour Movement was itself bound to a vision of modern everyday life as a specific reorganisation of the forms of time. Even as I have argued that a Rancièrian dissensus is produced by the exploration of the possibilities of modern freedom, this is not to suggest that the Eight-Hour Movement argued for a formlessness to life. In the specific imaginary of Progressive Era modernity, form and freedom do not operate as countervalent forces. Indeed, as I argued in the introduction, one enables the other. The engraving formalises the ideal time signature of the day and presents freedoms of thought, of access, and of community, as reliant upon this form. In this way, through its combined representation of everyday life and its projection of potential futures, it constitutes a model of what Anna Kornbluh calls 'political formalism' and describes in terms of generic 'realism'. Kornbluh notes

> Theorizing realism as model dispenses with the problematic of mimetic fidelity to the single world, privileging realism's drafting and projecting of

worlds: realism fundamentally designs and erects socialities, imagines the grounds of collectivities, probes the mystique of materialism, modulates institutions and productions beyond the scope of the given (*The Order of Forms*, 16).

Consequently, The Eight-Hour Movement performed a redistribution of the sensible that challenged the fixing of legitimate speech to certain performative acts, of culture to class position, and militated against the temporal assumption that doing 'anything else' than work was an impossibility. The Eight-Hour Movement had innumerable other effects in pointing the way forward to a modern conception of life and time. Importantly, as William A. Mirola has noted, the movement facilitated a reworking of the ethnic and cultural lines of difference that bisected Gilded Age Chicago:

> Shortening the workday and reducing the workweek were umbrella issues for the American labor movement. Reducing the hours of labor linked a host of other industrial reforms and spawned a class-based consciousness among American workers that no other issue had done previously or since. The eight-hour day was salient to native-born and immigrant workers, to labor radicals and conservatives, to the skilled and unskilled, and to men and women, and Chicago's workers were at the center of it all. (Mirola 2)

According to Mirola, the effort to effect a reorganisation of the temporal regime under which workers laboured facilitated the construction of a multiethnic labour force that had seldom existed before in the history of Chicago politics. The fight over *time* was a fight that redrew the lines of the political world. A new distribution of the sensible was born that in the process of placing labour within the frame of rational discourse reorganised the relationship between ethnicity and social class. If the classical Platonic synthesis of class and culture, described above, relied upon a political ontology that fashioned work and ethnicity as immobile identities operating together to impede access to the world-making power of the public sphere, then the Eight-Hour Movement represented a new, modern form of action-oriented, performative politics whose reorganisation of the temporal demands of everyday life effected a de-essentialisation of identity. By contrast, in prosecuting the Haymarket defendants by means of a legal process that essentialised identities by characterising them as rooted in the fixed, homogenous time of the 'Event', the juro-political order sought to crush the workers' dream of the future, by returning that distribution to its original organisation. It did this by elevating ethnicity as the 'cause' that motivated terrorism and thereby breaking the solidarity that had been born out of the attempt to create a new temporality of working life.

'August Spies' 'Autobiographical Sketch'

It is with this discussion of formalism and time that I move to the writings of August Spies, whose work constitutes a specific reflection on the problem of the reification of identity as a tool of state power in the wake of the Haymarket bombing.

Until the emergence of the New Working-Class Studies in the 1990s, there was a tendency towards viewing working-class life writing as a documentary form alone, of concern to scholarship solely for its 'representative' value. This came at the expense of critical work attendant to the pluralities and inconsistencies peculiar to the experience of living memory. According to Tim Strangleman, the communitarian impulse of much twentieth-century working-class literary study revealed a lack of 'sensitivity and critical respect for its object of study, working-class life' (147). In order to renovate the study of working-class literature, and open up the field to new subject positions, scholars and activists must be attuned to the complex, historical valencies of the texts within our archive. This renewed respect comes when working-class life writing is seen less as an authentic expression of a 'culture', an entity understood to exist objectively in the world free from the shaping influence of institutions and genres, and more as a series or cluster of literary *performances* that operate within, and against, generic expectations. In the words of Lynn Abrams, we must move our focus 'from what is said to how it is said ... [t]his means that we ought to be conscious of how performance shapes forms ... we should acknowledge that any narrative cannot be separated from its form – from its performance' (130). The ethnographic urge that predominated in Progressive and New Deal Era literary practices focused on preserving historical cultures by emphasising the authenticity of literary texts as curated historical artefacts. Focusing our critical work on considerations of the performance of the speaker and their understanding of the genre in which they are writing, instead of on the ethnographical urge towards the representative, we can consider class in relation to the localised, historical and particular demands of a certain space and time, the *locus* of action, and so renovate the agency of the writer.

Resurrecting the 'sensitivity and critical respect' (Strangleman 147) for working-class life writing that Strangleman calls for demands critical readings to pay closer attention to the question of literary form and performance. August Spies' autobiography from 1887, written in the wake of his arrest and trial as one of eight men wrongly charged with conspiring to throw a dynamite bomb at police in Chicago's Haymarket Square on 4 May 1886, is an especially rich instance of anarchist life writing because of its engagement with the very problem of the representational value of literary texts that the New Working-Class Studies has made an important subject of inquiry.

Because the trial of the eight Haymarket anarchists was conducted by 'extensively using speeches and publications as evidence' (Messer-Kruse 181), the event exposes the ambivalent politics of working-class life writing more generally. Spies' work indicates how the activity of the state disciplinary apparatus during his imprisonment and trial offered him a larger platform on which to speak about his life (something he ordinarily would have been denied) and at the same time served to condemn him in the eyes of the jury. Spies' 'Autobiography' is expressly theatrical, performing an excess that serves to criticise the fixing of working-class voices as the products of a historical 'culture', or as artefacts of larger political groupings, seeing such appropriations as tools of authoritarian state power.

The autobiography was first published along with those of the other condemned men in serial form in the official paper of the fraternity and Trade Union *The Knights of Labor* in the weeks leading up to his execution. Spies, writing in English, begins his narrative with an archly satiric declaration of his identity: 'Barbarians, savages, illiterate, ignorant Anarchists from Central Europe, men who cannot comprehend the spirit of our free American institutions, – of these I am one. My name is August Vincent Theodore Spies (pronounced Spees)' (59). There is a good deal of humour in this line, not least from a man who was facing imminent execution with little chance of clemency. The strategy taken by the mainstream press to the treatment of the anarchists was satirised by José Martí in his article on Haymarket, claiming 'Every newspaper from San Francisco to New York misrepresents the trial, depicting the seven accused men as noxious beasts, putting the image of the policeman ripped apart by the bomb on every breakfast table' (212). From this position of ironic self-identification Spies moves on to adopt a variety of theatrical postures that playfully subvert dominant nineteenth-century literary styles. First, Spies challenges anthropological and naturalistic narratives of culture that reified birthplace as an index of expected behaviours. Spies writes,

> Viewed from a historic standpoint my birthplace is quite an interesting spot. And this is the only excuse I can offer for my selection of the place for said purpose. I admit I ought not to have made the mistake, ought not to have been born a *foreigner*, but little children, particularly unborn children, will make mistakes. (60)

As I noted above, at the time of Spies' writing there were numerous exposés of 'anarchist culture' in the popular press, contributing to '[t]he drama of Haymarket, as [José] Martí called it, which included the anarchists' imprisonment, trial, appeals, and execution crucially mediated by the late nineteenth-century expansion of the pictorial marketplace and the transformation of visual culture' (Streeby 35). According to Shelley Streeby, the Haymarket affair was a defining moment for the development of the late nineteenth-century's new print media. The numerous reports on the events deployed new technologies of printing to render everything in minute detail for their audiences, who wished to understand the motivations and demands of the anarchists. The saturation of print media with racist and misleading imagery contributed to a perception of anarchism as the project of a foreign, 'barbarian' culture existing in parallel to civilised peoples within American cities. The spectacular nature of the accounts of Haymarket were aided by an assimilationist institutional and juro-political framework that sought to transform anarchism into a 'culture' or 'sub-culture' that had to be eradicated in order to preserve the sanctity of the American symbolic order. In other words, what was sought (even by the trade unionist *Knights of Labor* periodical in which the text first appeared) was an approach to life writing that created a *representation* of 'anarchist culture' for the readership. However, this very process of being given a platform from which to speak was a mixed blessing, since it also subjected anarchists like Spies to the purview of the state apparatus.

The defence attorney for the eight Haymarket defendants himself raised the problem of representation for the politics of labour during the trial. In an article that appeared in the 8 October 1887 edition of the *Knights of Labor* (one day after the guilty verdict had been passed and one day before sentencing), collected by Eric Foner, Captain William Black wrote:

> The theory of past reforms in administration . . . ha[s] been that the only panacea for existing disorder was political liberty. But . . . the highest types of republican government, with universal enfranchizement and substantially absolute political [e]quality, serve only to show that political liberty does not insure a prosperous, happy, or advancing condition of society as a whole. The most that can be said is that political liberty may prove favorable for the application of the true remedy for the social disorder. (20)

Captain Black's statement warned against transforming the political speech of the Haymarket defendants during the trial and subsequently in their written autobiographical sketches into the acts of a 'social type' or cultural sub-group that might eventually be afforded political representation within a pre-existent, unreconstructed republican system; a representation that may also take the form of a ritualised expulsion or exclusion from that order. In this way, Black renders the problem of representation distinctly as a question of genre and of time: genre, because individual speech in American letters has frequently served as the expression of a form of liberal subjectivity that seeks recourse and acknowledgement by power; and time, because of the presumption that the temporality of the autobiography is retrospective – closing down the ongoing dissent of that speaker. In effect, the generic traditions of autobiography always raise the threat of a social death (the closure of futurity and potentiality) that comes with inclusion within the 'representative regime' of power. This is especially true in the case of Spies, whose autobiographical writings emerged within the context of potential execution by the state.

In traditions of political anarchism in the USA subsequent to Spies, this problem of autobiography's pre-ordained containment within traditions of American liberalism was raised repeatedly, often as a means of criticising the values of one's own *side*. In the first part of her huge, two-volume memoir, *Living My Life* (1931 and 1934), the famed anarchist orator, writer and working-class activist Emma Goldman remarked that many of her 'closest comrades' had seen the writer's political 'duty' to act as proxy for a collectively disenfranchised and voiceless underclass as incommensurate with her own commitment to the 'beautiful ideal': a life suffused with individual human passion, exuberance and joy. Goldman describes an important moment in her political development when a fellow anarchist chastises her for dancing, suggesting, 'it did not behoove an agitator to dance . . . certainly not with such reckless abandon anyway . . . [i]t was undignified . . . frivolity would only hurt the Cause' (42). In response, Goldman remarks.

> I want freedom, the right to self-expression, everybody's right to beautiful, radiant things . . . Anarchism meant that to me, and I would live it in spite of the whole world – prisons, persecution, everything. Yes, even in spite of the condemnation of my own closest comrades I would live my beautiful ideal. (42)

The memoir is full of such instances, when fellow activists or critics take issue with the theatricality of Goldman's oratory, her supposed subordination of 'public' activism to 'private' feeling, her enjoyment of the 'elite' or 'bourgeois' theatre of Ibsen and Chekov, or her associations with the self-fashioning, modernist bohemians of *fin-de-siècle* Greenwich Village.[5] What Goldman returns to repeatedly in the memoir is an ongoing conflict between working-class activists who considered her actions in terms of their representative value as an expression of the 'culture' of the working classes and her insistence that her own life (and her rendering of it in prose) be an exercise in the expression of a private selfhood to which she was entitled. We are reminded here of the unincorporated gaze of the woman in the '8 Hours for What We Will' etching – level with us but not hailed by us – as a metonym for this exoteric form of engagement with the world. In effect, Goldman called out a complicity between seeing 'anarchist culture' as a discreet and unified force and the goals of the liberal state anarchists actively opposed.

The problem is crucial to any understanding of radical life writing: the speeches, personal narratives, oral histories, autoethnographies and published diaries that take the 'real life' of the proletariat as their intended object. These forms of working-class literary expression frequently find themselves marked by the conflicting pressures of numerous forces and intentions. How does a working-class writer express their relationship to a group identity, while still adequately and fully representing feelings and perspectives that are personal to that individual? This is especially pertinent in the context of genres of life writing – for two reasons. First, the genres that comprise it are usually rooted in living memory and so frequently demand a personal perspective that is not a necessary requirement in poetry or the novel. Second, because, as Paul John Eakin, G. Thomas Couser and others have noted, the genre is frequently judged according to ethical standards of 'truth' (evoking a sense of 'reality' and also of 'evidence'), yet also risks the exposure of private details that could endanger or expose other, unwilling, friends and associates to the public eye.[6]

Goldman considered this problem repeatedly when composing *Living My Life*, and was conflicted from the outset about the very exercise of writing her memoirs. Her relationship to collectivist forms of working-class activism trained her to see autobiography as the product of an essentially bourgeois, liberal version of self-fashioning that she regarded as an indulgent and elitist product of unequal social relations. She was concerned about what effects the exposure of personal details of her life might have on the security and reputations of her fellow anarchists (especially given her involvement in Alexander Berkman's assassination attempt on

Henry Frick). Additionally, she also questioned whether the cost of the two-volume work would be prohibitive for working-class readers in the depressed 1930s. Yet her anarchist impulses meant that she also regarded the individual as central to all forms of literary and political praxis. The exercise was made even more problematic by the fact that after a lifetime of radical activism '[a]lmost everything in the way of books, correspondence, and similar material ... had been confiscated by the Department of Justice' (Goldman lxix).

Goldman's memoir highlights the fact that expressions of working-class life are usually constructed in the shadow of government, party or culture, and the concept of a fully autonomous working-class literary subject under liberalism, free to write their life in their own manner, is seldom more than a political fantasy. Indeed, for working-class people the need for the free time and opportunity to write and publish has often meant that their life writing has required negotiating the intervention of some institutional frame. These tensions were crucial to the aesthetic of Goldman's autobiography, which appeared in the 1930s when government-sponsored liberal reform movements were mandating the collection and publication of working-class life writing in the service of a project of national renewal. The memoir is characterised by its wilful performance of uncertainty, its refusal to present life as if it were marked by fully consistent political, emotional or erotic sensibilities leading to a final reconciliation or settlement. Even the title resisted any claims to objectivity. *Living My Life* implied an ongoing project, a sense of being, as the author referred to it, always 'in the very torrent of it' (lxix) and so unable to create the critical distance required by more traditional memoirs in order that one be able to reflect back on the trajectory of one's life. Grammatically, Goldman's narrative was in the past tense, yet included few reflections from the older writer on the feelings of her youth. Goldman exhibits no urge to historicise or revise because, for her, all affect was legitimate and the project of anarchism not bound, like autobiography commonly must be, to a historical past or singular Event status.

Returning to Haymarket, it is notable that the space of a trial or of incarceration time-locks speech into a retrospective mode, in a manner that makes the freely expressive articulations of the speaker in the present evidence either *for* or *against* a particular situation made by those in power. In calling for the recognition of a situation as the Event of Terror and pinning it by circumstantial evidence to a racialised sub-culture, the state generates a situation whereby liberal traditions of 'freedom of speech' and *habeas corpus* can be evoked to demand the appointment of individuals to speak as political 'representatives' of a whole discontented and oppressed 'class' that has been created by the public sphere in the present (and does not exist simply prior to its summons by the law), thereby allowing the State to retroactively reify as *real* the groups it wishes to expel from the political order. William Black's statement argues that true freedom and prosperity would only come when class and race themselves were abolished as categories, not when members of that class were merely afforded the right to speak as representatives of a group. In the case of the Haymarket defendants, where, unlike a normal criminal trial, for the charge of conspiracy to stick the men could not be tried individually, a burden of proof lay upon the prosecution to render the eight men as a collective – committed to the same exact aims and objectives. Haymarket reveals how the charge of complicity upon which the prosecution of terrorism relies is itself reliant upon forms of racialisation that turn on the appointment of a speaker as a representative of a wider group. When the Event of Terror is inaugurated, the individual does not speak as an individual; they are denied the right to free expression and to the production of political dissensus. Crucially, this practice does not lie outside the rules of political liberalism, with its dependence on *habeas corpus*, but is central to it. To be summoned by the State in the context of conspiracy is always already to invite racialisation.[7] Even more, so dominant was the relationship between racialisation and violence, that the racialisation that occurred as a precondition of extrajudicial violence in the case of the lynching of black people during Reconstruction became a dominant mode of action performed by the State in the case of other subjects too; subjects that might in other circumstances have been considered 'White'.

In his 'Address Delivered to Judge Gary', made during the trial and collected by Nina Van Zandt in *August Spies' Autobiography*,

Spies challenged the court to prove the existence of just such a collective. He said:

> It has been charged that we (the eight here) constituted a conspiracy. I would reply to that, that my friend Lingg I had seen but twice at meetings of the Central Labor Union . . . Never spoke to him . . . Engel I have not been on speaking terms with for at least a year. And Fischer, 'my lieutenant' (?), used to go round and make speeches against me. So much for that. (65)

Well before ethnography and literary studies underwent their self-reflexive turns in the 1980s, anarchism and its defenders were already discussing the complicity of power in the creation of the idea of 'culture', by suggesting that the very liberal systems that generate the imperative for an individual to speak as a representative of a group invariably also render that group subject to discipline by the state.

In his autobiography, following his attack on the assumption that he is an anarchist because of his national origin and his class, Spies takes the tone of a genteel travel writer in a picturesque version of the European landscape – a dominant literary style in Gilded Age journalism – complete with the direct address and inviting tour-guide persona. At this point, Spies is clearly evoking a cosmopolitan sensibility frequently associated with the middle classes so as to challenge the fixation on his cultural or ethnic identity:

> But speaking of castle Landeck. Follow me there, reader, on a bright and clear day. We make our way up the old tower. Take care, or you will stumble over the debris. That? Oh, that is a piece of an old torture rack . . . So, now take my hand, I'll help you on top of the ruin. Look out for bats! (60)

In addition to various asides condemning the history of police brutality, Spies offers hyperbolic statements and black humour that reveal his attention to bathos as a strategy of dissent. In one instance he describes an area near where he was born in Germany in absurdly specific, scientific, geological detail only to immediately undercut this by referencing medieval folklore:

> Not more than 200 feet from where we stand there is a perpendicular (chasm) hole of volcanic origin; it is about 8 feet in length and breadth; its depth has never been ascertained. The saying goes that scores of girls were cast into this terrible abyss by the valiant Knights during their reign of peace and good order! (61)

The 'Knights' here evoke the Chicago Police Department, of course, through Spies' equation of 'peace and good order' with medievalism, and by which he implies that the expansion of police powers that were called upon to address the disturbances the Haymarket bombing revealed represents a regression into a feudal past; an expulsion from a claim to the modern.

Spies' use of irony serves two distinct functions. The first, as I have suggested, is bathos – puncturing the pompous tone of newspaper writing and the trial lawyers. Second, it is a self-conscious performance of intellect, literacy, learning and craft (something that might be encompassed by the term 'high culture') that functions to undermine the argument made by the press and the prosecuting lawyers in the trial that a lack of education might be used to explain the appeal of anarchism. Instead, Spies uses his narrative to demonstrate his learning. His knowing and ironic use of a variety of literary styles (exposé, travel narrative, autobiography, slave narrative, Marxian history, the Gothic) demonstrates his virtuosic command of the arts of 'civilisation' against the perception of him and his comrades as representative examples of a barbarian culture. Additionally, though, the narrative also functions as a form of working-class braggadocio and confrontational emulation; taking the snobs on at their own game. As Andrew Lawson has noted, 'emulation evolves from the desire to imitate another person with the aim of equalling or excelling him or her. Emulation is imitation with a competitive edge, a paradoxical engagement with another identity in the pursuit of difference'(598).

Spies's obsession with displaying his intellect is present throughout the narrative, which is peppered with quotes from Shelley, Emerson, Goethe, Paine, Jefferson and others. Spies even goes as far as to claim that his education in Germany was better preparation for a life of cultivated learning than would have been possible in America – a view that would not have been out of keeping with that of many of the transcendentalists of the 1840s and 1850s or liberals in the genteel traditions of American letters. 'In my native land,' Spies writes, 'children *must* attend school daily from the age of 6 to that of 14; every child in that "Barbarian country" is thus compelled to attend school for 8 years, and cannot therefore be "utilized and made to pay" by either their parents or factory lords' (63). He also makes the case that his father was a government employee on a fairly good salary and that at one point in his life in Germany he was middle class and even had education from private tutors. His claims as to his intellect and social value are therefore made to depend upon, and not to be made in spite of, his birth outside of the US state's jurisdiction and power, thereby revealing the contradiction that the ideal 'American' citizen (according to nationalist values) might have been born outside of its territorial space. Yet his autobiography is more than just a display of cosmopolitan autodidactism. 'The study of French, German and English economists and social scientists', Spies writes, 'soon made me view things differently . . . Buckle's History of Civilization, Karl Marx's 'Kapital', and Morgan's 'Ancient Society' have probably the greatest influence over me of any – I now became an attentive observer of the various social phenomena . . .' (68).

As Jesse Cohn has noted of classical anarchism, its individualist orientation and focus on human flourishing served as a rejection of the social Darwinist and Naturalist impulses that characterised dominant styles of Gilded Age class critique. Cohn writes that anarchism is

> not [. . .] naturalist, founding . . . [its] hopes on the assumption that human behavior is driven by unvarying natural drives and instincts but . . . constructivist . . . anarchy is not a 'state of nature', but something that must be collectively willed, struggled for, built, achieved, produced – in a word constructed. (57)

Spies' narrative voice is that of an educated and 'cultured' observer of modern life, well in control of his terms of engagement with the world. Spies constructs 'anarchy' by wilfully playing against the demands of the institutional forms imposed upon him by literary tradition and social convention and so performs a prefigurative political gesture by acting as though he were entirely free to manipulate reality as he saw fit.

In the 'Autobiography' Spies casts himself as an 'attentive observer of the various social phenomena' so as to deliberately, and ironically, evoke a position of detached critique and observation that he could not in reality inhabit (being imprisoned at the time of writing), yet performs as his right nonetheless. For the extended second edition of the 'Autobiography', included in the collection of Spies' work published in 1887 by his wife Nina Van Zandt, the decision was taken to refer to his life story as an 'Autobiographical Sketch'. This, too, was a deliberately ludic gesture in relation to literary form. As Kristie Hamilton has noted, the term 'Sketch' carried heavy class associations in nineteenth-century society since the sketch writer was understood to be 'doubly detached — above a scene ... and purportedly independent of society's prejudices as Romantic poets sought to be' (21) in a way that aligned the form with a middle-class writer like Washington Irving or, later, the writings of Henry James, with leisure time and privacy to wander the world, observe social phenomena and comment objectively upon them. By referring to his life writing as a 'sketch', Nina Van Zandt continued the legacy of Spies' inversion of the class hierarchies at play in the exercise of literary form and its claims to objectivity and oversight. The middle-class writers, lawyers and readers to whose institutionalised gaze Spies was the unwilling subject are parodied by the author's ironic position of identification as 'an attentive observer' of his own life and his world. According to Rancière's rendering of class as a temporal and spatial condition of exclusion based on Platonic conceptions of the ontological privacy of work and its difference from the free time of philosophy and art, to write one's life as a worker is not a neutral act, because the author performs a 'doubleness' that is at the heart of a new political order in being both worker and philosopher. Spies' claim to be an 'attentive observer' is a practice of laying claim to public life that is redolent of the aim of the Eight-Hour Movement to permit workers to practise as full citizens laying claim to the legitimacy of their voice and their vision of everyday life. By writing, or taking the time to write, there is an act of political reorganisation. Consequently, life writing might be understood as a fiction of time: a performance of the creative and reflective actions that the worker-subject had been excluded from by traditions of political philosophy. The irony is that this time is given to Spies as a result of incarceration in a way that further emphasises the tie of liberal individualism and selfhood to the repressive operations of State power.

The Haymarket trial and the publications that emerged from it blurred the lines between life writing and legal oral testimony so as to expose a paradox at the core of modern liberalism. By printing Spies' 'Address Delivered Before Judge Gary' immediately after his 'Autobiographical Sketch', Nina Van Zandt showed how the genre of working-class life writing operated in the Gilded Age in relation to power. Many of the ideas are replicated across both texts, which function as intertexts, and demonstrate how the demand that Spies write his life shared crucial and destabilising parallels with the demand that he testify before the court. Both texts constitute narratives of Spies' life and both directly and self-consciously refer to the conditions of their production. Yet, additionally, both are also marked by their literary style of excess. Spies' style is self-consciously ornate and affected. This was carried over in the production of the collection of his work by Nina Van Zandt. The title page (Figure 1.4) displayed the author's name, title, and publication information in a font style that obviously flirted with European *fin-de-siècle* bibelot typography, even including a knowingly cute key design that reflected synecdochally the radical chic persona Spies cultivated in his political and personal life. International observers picked up on this element of the Haymarket anarchists to the extent that William Morris himself spoke in favour of their clemency, and Walter Crane – the Aesthetic Movement designer – drew wildly circulated imagery in support of the same.

Indeed, the Haymarket anarchists lived and worked in spaces well-aware of the cultural work of European and American aestheticism. Aestheticism was not a wholly middle-class pursuit or interest and should not be read as such. Spies' primary trade prior to, and alongside, his journalism was as an upholsterer in the Chicago furniture trade, a profession that permitted him acquaintance with some of the emerging avant-garde and Arts and Crafts styles of European and American interior decoration. Additionally, by

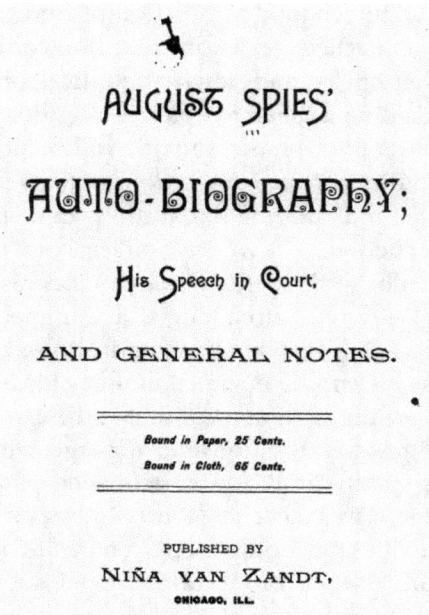

Figure 1.4 Cover image of Nina van Zandt's edition of August Spies' speeches (1886).

1886 Chicago was well established as a centre for the burgeoning American schools of design. Writing of Spies in his 13 November 1887 chronicle of the trial and execution, José Martí stated that he 'walks in all serenity where a more solid intellect senses that he has no footing . . . [t]his somber Narcissus is astonished and well pleased with his own greatness' (203). That is to say, he was arrogant, and went intellectually to places in his writing and speeches where, according to Martí's own ironic rendering of the public voice, a working-class radical was presumed to have no right to go.

Spies' mode of rendering everyday life might better be understood as consciously and deliberately 'aesthetic', which is to say it is a mode of expression whose articulation mobilises the possibility of future socialities and is not bound inexorably to the expression of that life as mere empirical evidence of the *now* or, indeed, of the past. Strictly speaking, Spies' aestheticism is of a Kantian character in its speculative dimension, parsed by Sianne Ngai as a 'judgement or experience – for Kant they are one and the same – [that] involves thinking the social in abstract' (*Theory of the Gimmick*, 18). If for the jury of the Haymarket trial the evidence presented was the expression of a toxic form of sociality that belonged to a group they were being trained to hate, then for Spies the accoutrements of his everyday experience testified to a projective will for a different sociality that mobilised a different judgement of value to that of the official account of events. The 'aesthetic' for Kant is always an experience that calls out to others to be verified and discussed. There is no purely private form of aesthetic experience, in fact, just versions of the public which may or may not be present to the thinker at the time of their encounter with the object. The aesthetic is therefore a rendering of experience that generates competing forms of temporality. In Spies' case, this was a different sense of the modern.

It would be tempting to see Spies' play with the expectations of class and race *habitus* in Chicago as being a war of position fought on the immoveable court of Bourdieusian distinction – where aesthetic values are just so many forms of address to others existing in a flat plane of time. Yet, as I have argued, to do so would be to miss how in the era of the Eight-Hour Movement working-class life could be presented as wholly central to the expression of a modern sensibility that turned both on the value of the workers' minds and their multicultural origins. It is not a contradiction to see Spies' outward performance of, and control over, ostensibly 'middle-class' pursuits and systems of thought as signs of a historical moment where markers were not so much blurred as existed in a state prior to their reification by the reactionary forces of the Gilded Age State.[8] José Martí's claim that Spies 'walks in all serenity where a more solid intellect senses that he has no footing' is a subtle account of the man and his time in many ways. In the pairing of 'solid intellect' with the lack of 'footing', Martí evokes the spectre of Spies' eventual drop on the gallows at the behest of the people in possession of a 'solid intellect' [we might read in here synonyms such as 'rigid', 'unyielding' and so forth, people who mean to see things, 'precisely as they are'] who sought to establish their control over history by the interpolation of a man whose life did not require their endorsement or values so as to be part of the 'modern' world. Spies was not so much indecorous to the modern world as he was envied for the claims he made on the modern; he was made a racial and political Other in order to bury his mode of futurity in a model of the past, and expel him for an official order of things that was itself born in the Event of, and response to, Haymarket.

'[A]pt to take ourselves a little too objectively, and to feel ourselves rather more representative than we need': *A Hazard of New Fortunes* and Exoteric Reading

The Haymarket Affair and the Eight-Hour Movement, then, were moments when US society was forced to contend with the present as a space of stressed temporality; where competing claims to the future – and to modernity itself – played off against one another in the realm of aesthetics, which was centrally involved in the shaping of political community. It is significant that William Dean Howells's major work to engage actively with the effects of the Haymarket Affair on Gilded Age society begins with a discussion of time and the representative power, or lack thereof, of older regimes of authority – namely, the white, male Bostonian Brahmin class. In contending with the challenge to normative models of power in the Gilded Age USA, *A Hazard of New Fortunes* develops its critique of representativeness and racialisation within and through a discussion of time and literary form.

Much has been written about the early scenes of house-hunting as an index of the novel's desire to locate a solid and unchangeable 'identity' for the main characters – expressed through an ethnological language that highlights the proper 'place' for a culture, race or species in the 'natural' order and hierarchy. This 'natural order' might also be understood through Rancière's terminology as a 'representative regime'. In this famous sequence of Howells's novel, housing is connecting distinctly to racialisation, and so to slavery, when the Marches encounter the black janitor of one of the buildings and decide they want to take the place, or else buy him, because, as Mrs March remarks, 'If I had such a creature, nothing but death should part us . . .' (46). Later, March confirms the relationship between New York real estate and the slave trade when he notes that 'There seems to be something in the human habitation that corrupts the natures of those who deal in it, to buy or sell it, to hire or let it . . .' (51). Yet, to focus on these elements to the exclusion of all else would be to miss that the opening chapters of *A Hazard of New Fortunes* develop two primary leitmotifs: the slipperiness of the present for the modern artist, and the tendency of the symbolic order to overstate their representative value to society at large. The first of these themes is established through March's poetic ruminations on the modern world, such as when he rides on the train to New York and notices that

> the foreground next the train rushes from us and the background keeps abreast of us, while the middle distance seems stationary? I don't think I ever noticed that effect before. There ought to be something literary in it: retreating past and advancing future, and deceitfully permanent present: something like that? (40).

The second comes with the discussion of the magazine and its purposes. These two primary themes come together in the discussion between Fulkerson and March about what to name their publishing venture. Their argument explores the temporalities of magazine publishing, which exploits an interstitial space between the ongoing present and the consolidating force of the 'Event' (the moment of publication). The name they settle on, 'Every Other Week', is a compromise that indexes a confused and complex form of time. It is not every week. It is not every day. It is not a monthly. What the magazine is, primarily, is a slightly off-beat or inconsistent version of the present. March even remarks that the name they settle on somehow indicates that the magazine – for all its other virtues – misses out on the present: 'I wish Mr. Fulkerson hadn't called it that! It always makes me think of "jam yesterday and jam t-morrow, but never jam today," in *Through the Looking Glass* . . .' (43). March's evocation of the warped space-time of Lewis Carroll's *Alice in Wonderland* novels shows how the magazine deploys a non-verisimilar aesthetic so as to represent the confused temporalities and anachronisms of the Gilded Age present. To be truly realistic the aesthetic of *realism* must capture the uncertainty that characterises a present shot through with microscopic moments that are never wholly reconcilable to a single vision of the state or of its political temporality. We might read this uncomfortable compromise as foreshadowing the magazine's eventual struggles within the marketplace – the tragic failure, as it were, to find its identity (just as the Marches never find their ideal dwelling place). It is more the case, however, that this conception of the magazine as existing in a complex relationship to time is synonymous with the novel's engagement with the blindnesses and misreadings that come when one group's view of the present is elevated over another. This is a consequence of Howells's increasing sense in the wake of Haymarket that the problems of American democracy were, at least in part, of a temporal nature.

In his now classic reading of the newspaper and the realist novel, Benedict Anderson proposed that both literary forms existed to render an experience of simultaneity and 'homogenous, empty time' that was the necessary corollary of a mission to project a shared 'imagined community' of the nation-state. As postcolonial scholars such as Homi K. Bhabha, Partha Chatterjee and, in a slightly different way Wai-Chee Dimock, have all noted, this homogeneity and simultaneity was implicitly racialised and gendered, and elevated white, male temporality and subjectivity as a proxy for national unity.[9] Yet in Howells's novel, the discussion of the release schedule and naming of the magazine occurs in the same scene in which March notes, and Fulkerson agrees, that 'we Western men who've come East are apt to take ourselves a little too objectively, and to feel ourselves rather more representative than we need' (9). March here is clearly holding the Western man 'come East' as a representative 'American' subject, only to then suggest that there is an arrogance in that conflation of one group with the entire symbolic order. New York, as March will come to learn, is a society with an increasingly important place for immigrants, such that white Mid-Westerners do not 'represent' the American world any more successfully or universally than the magazine itself will be able to represent an homogenous empty time synonymous with the nation-state. Indeed, through the metaphor of a magazine that exists in an uneasy relationship to time Howells's novel characterises the concept of the nation-state as a universal, coherent, bordered enterprise committed to the same shared goals as a fantasy that has probably never truly existed; an effect of a lopsided narrative of representativeness that has consequently skewed the perception of national space-time. Instead, we are posed a series of ongoing questions about how we build the future, or cope ethically with the demands of the present.

Scholars of later- nineteenth century American literature have developed something of a consensus on one major point: the challenge posed to the unifying aesthetic of realism as understood by Howells by the era's many divisive instances of class conflict. In a time of increasing social inequality and division Howells's well-known definition of literary realism as 'democracy in literature' seemed outdated; a voice not of freedom from the constraints of an aristocratic social order, but an altered version of that order – a 'genteel', 'civilized' literary convention that captured none of the energy of contemporary politics. This reading presupposes that the novel dramatises a deviation from a normative and normalised 'imagined community' based on Anderson's conception of homogenous empty time. Yet, in drawing attention to the manner by which any intervention into the literary marketplace of the Gilded Age would, in some fundamental respect, be unable to capture the modalities of the present, Howells calls attention to the impossibility, and mythical status of, homogenous empty time. What I see as a misreading of the moment of the 1880s leads to a tragic inflection entering interpretations of Howells's work. In particular, Howells's 1888 letter to his friend and confidant Henry James, in which he confessed that 'After fifty years of optimistic content with civilization . . . I now abhor it, and I feel that it is coming out all wrong in the end, unless it bases itself anew on a real equality' (qtd. in Bartel 661) has been used as an index of the authors' increasing sense of frustration with his own aesthetic project. This frustration, so it has been claimed by Kim Bartel, Paul Abeln and others, took form in *A Hazard of New Fortunes*, which is for many a problematic text; both Howells's masterpiece and his most noble aesthetic failure. Indeed, it is true that Haymarket was clearly a turning point; a moment in which Howells began to investigate more fully the premises upon which his aesthetic practices depended. Yet it is also a novel that is wholly transparent about the inability of the realist novel – represented in the text through the magazine – to be representative of all the multiplicities that punctuate the present moment (to be, in effect, a national form) in the aftermath of such events as Haymarket and the subsequent Red Scare. This experience of crisis was shared by many in the years following the 1886 bombing. The Cuban journalist and future martyr to the cause of *Cuba Libre*, José Martí, noted of the Haymarket Affair that it had an apocalyptic temporality that seemed somehow to exceed the limits of extant, genteel, literary forms like the high realist novel or the morning newspaper, remarking: 'To put the events of these days into a newspaper chronicle is like trying to gather lava from a volcano into a coffee cup' (José Martí in Laura Lomas, 25).

Critics of Howells's work have been remarkably prone to a narrative of decline and fall that draws attention to how his novels after 1886 are marked by what Paul Abeln has called a 'fundamental inability to locate a 'common ground' for his emotional, political, imaginative and professional personas . . . [and] are dominated by tropes of miscommunication, misunderstanding and misperception' (Abeln 3). In other words, critics have often deployed a hermeneutics of suspicion that renders Howells's work a failure and an evolutionary throwback that the rise of modernism replaced, where it is, rather, a self-reflexive work with distinctly modernist sensibilities; even, or perhaps especially, when these exist as small fragmentary moments. The image of Howells as a fusty conservative holds strong in criticism, but does not cling to a figure like Stephen Crane whom Howells supported and encouraged and whose own work is frequently spoken of in terms of a proto-modernism. It is not necessary, though, to read *A Hazard of New Fortunes* with such a tragic sensibility. Pointing out the inadequacy of Howellsian realism, even actively seeking to bury it in order that modernism might be permitted to rise in his stead, has become something of an obsession for scholars; an instance of a wider tendency to characterise modernism as forged through Oedipal violence against the values and aesthetics of the previous generation. In effect, the tendency to read Howells's initial definition of realism as positing an unproblematic relationship between artistic representation and the sphere of political debate casts the author as an exemplar of a privileged, elite mode of authorship that utilised the social power of sympathy to bind difference within a unifying whole that mirrored the assimilationist project of the US state. This reads backwards through modernism's eventual triumph, rather than seeing the novel as a genuine attempt to explore the complexity of the present in a way that aligns with the aspirations of modernism.

Following the trial and subsequent execution of four men who were quite openly judged for their ideas rather than their acts, and whom even the State's Attorney Grinnell admitted 'are no more guilty than the thousands who follow them' (Foner 8), Howells was unable to conduct his own literary practice in quite the same way and so laid the groundwork for the emergence of a non-verisimilar realism in US literary culture that in turn laid the groundwork for modernism. Howells's decision to openly defend these anarchists in the press and lead an ill-fated national clemency movement is often seen as the moment at which the so-called 'Dean of American Letters', Editor of the *Atlantic Monthly* and among the most esteemed American literary voices of his age, failed to serve his much-vaunted representative function for the American people – committing a radical act of sympathy with so-called 'terrorists' that was utterly out of keeping with the bloody and vengeful tenor of the debate as it was carried out in the courtroom and in the press. Howells, whom Nancy Bentley has noted was committed even at this point in his career to 'mak[ing] fiction an instrument of cultural pedagogy that would turn the popularity of the novel to the work of cultivating higher tastes in a broad national public' (*Frantic Panoramas*, 12), pointed to a disagreeable alignment in responses to Haymarket between the punitive and regressive culture of the juro-political order and the spectacular economies of Gilded Age mass culture. This alignment asked of serious fiction that it widen its gaze to the inclusion of new voices and aesthetic forms so as to serve the function as an arbiter of a higher moral order. This, in turn, placed the realist author within an aesthetic regime that would eventually be reified in the figure of the alienated modernist artist – a figure that literary criticism, operating from a Bourdieusian model for the last twenty years or so, has been keen to dismiss as politically suspect. Indeed, Jesse Swartz has argued that

> Howells's sense of obligation to the radicals came neither from Tolstoy [that is from an established 'Christian socialist' position] nor from the voluminous front-page coverage in the newspapers but, . . . 'through reading their trial' by way of two texts in particular: August Spies'

Auto-Biography (1887) . . . and Dyer Lum's sympathetic 1886 'history' of the trial. (Schwartz 534)

This indicates that a direct aesthetic and political influence was exerted by August Spies – who embodied this proto-modernist alienated aesthete – on the thinking and writing of the famous literary luminary commonly conceptualised as a political centrist.

The problem for Howellsian realism was this: if the realist novel had at its core an identifying function that justified its claim to 'democracy in literature' by means of its ability to depict diverse individuals or groups previously denied or excluded from political agency, how different is this from the legal function of a liberal state that identified, essentialised and brought to trial representatives of a sub-group and executed them for their ideals? After all, a 'liberal' state roots its own sense of justice in similar techniques of representation as the realist novel; that is, a liberal state locates subjects that can speak of their own condition and inversely also face trial in the event that such speech constitutes a 'clear and present danger' to civic order. Indeed, the liberal principle of the 'rule of law' and the aesthetics of literary realism arguably rest on similar premises, those of ritual and representation, which is embodied in law as *habeas corpus* or in the novel through diverse, representative speaking characters that function as surrogates or scapegoats. The empathy and aggression of the state is therefore mirrored in the aesthetic of pure verisimilitude, since an individual can only be empathised with if they can first be represented and thereby placed, too, within the purview of the state's disciplinary apparatus. When, as in the case of the Haymarket trial, the jurors and police have no idea who threw the bomb (and so there was no 'real' representative), in order for justice to be seen to function the law had to invent one or eight. As I stated earlier, this process was effected through the mobilisation of the law of 'Accessory' and its creation of a discrete, internally coherent 'anarchist culture' for whom a representative (or set of representatives) could be found to speak. Howells found this, rightly, abhorrent, and was unwilling to write novels that consistently supported a liberal order that he had come to find suspicious by reproducing its underlying representative logics when these very logics were built upon a system of fundamental inequality. Techniques of representation can be tools of inclusion into the liberal public sphere, but might also otherwise serve as techniques of exclusion. This is bound up in Haymarket, where a rejection of the politics of anarchism and its refusal to buy in to the liberalism of the US nation-state drove an urge for representation as newspapers and court reports began to render the defendants racially as dangerous, and crucially, foreign, Others. For this reason, in the absence of the real face of the Haymarket bomber Howells had to couch his criticisms of the handling of the trial as an abstraction.

Throughout *A Hazard of New Fortunes* Howells lays clues to the form of reading he asks of his audience. It is notable that, like August Spies whom he read during the ill-fated clemency campaign prior to the composition of the novel, it is the form of the sketch and what Brad Evans calls attention to as the 'chic' that is central to Alma Leighton's success as an artist in the novel and which March settles on as an appropriate form for the depiction cf working-class New York life. It has been variously noted, notably by Amy Kaplan in her famous essay 'The Knowledge on the Line: Realism and the City in Howells's *A Hazard of New Fortunes,*' that March's pull towards the 'picturesque' and wish to 'view [. . .] New York as a foreign country' in his literary sketches for the magazine represent a simultaneous intimacy with and rejection of the heterogenous population of the city that reflects a certain middle-class desire to aestheticise reality so that the present conditions of the working class might be knowable but also controllable. For Kaplan, March's sketches also perform a voyeuristic violation in their transformation of real, everyday life into the detached form of art. This reading proceeds from an assumption that the 'sketch' form is, by necessity, synonymous with middle-class subjectivity and the whimsicality of its will to power. Detached, complacent and privileged, the sketch is the embodiment of a positionality only those in possession of a degree of security and without precarity would adopt in relation to the world. The narrator's comments about March's *flâneurie* as a practice of serendipitous accident in which we 'never entered a car without encountering some interesting shape of shabby adversity, which was always adversity of foreign birth' (183) has more than a little of the character of a touristic engagement with an ethnographic exhibition. Yet, the sketch form can also be differentiated from the thick descriptiveness of ethnology in the sense the aesthetic conveys of the mutability and plasticity of the present. The narrator also notes that thinking aesthetically – that is, picturesquely – also motivates March to stand somewhat outside or to rethink his own self-involvement. Howells writes:

> Accident and exigency seemed the forces at work to this extraordinary effect; the play of energies as free and planless as those that force the forest from the soil to the sky; and then the fierce struggle for survival, with the stronger life persisting over the deformity, the mutilation, the destruction of the weaker. The whole at moments seemed to him lawless, Godless; the absence of intelligent, comprehensive purpose in the huge disorder, and the violent struggle to subordinate the result to the greater good, penetrated with its dumb appeal the consciousness of a man who had always been too self-enrapt to perceive the chaos to which the individual selfishness must always lead. (184)

On first reading, this description of the energies March attempts to capture with his sketches seem to partake of a popular Social Darwinism in its account of the 'natural' processes by which the 'weaker' are destroyed by the power of the 'stronger'. Indeed, we might expect to see this in the passage if we read Rooseveltian Progressive Era eugenically inspired Neo-Darwinism or Chicago School sociology into Howells work; problematically conflating the eventual power of the state and the social sciences with the aesthetics of Gilded Age realist literature. Yet, the second sentence of the passage reverses the meaning of the first sentence. It is after all the 'violent struggle to subordinate' 'accident and exigency' to 'the greater good' [an entirely socially constructed concept] that results in 'the destruction of the weaker'. In Howells's rendering of March's thought, 'individual selfishness' is equated with a conservative moral vision of the 'greater good' – a utilitarian concept, of course, but also evoked here as something universalist and repressive, like the Rousseauist 'general will' – in a way that sees the existing moral order as a force not for good, but for violence against the 'weak' or unprotected. The task of generating sympathy, for

March here, involves keeping open a heterogenous version of time; a presentism that does not retrospectively subordinate '[a]ccident and exigency' to the arbitrary dictates of what those committed to 'individual self-interest' [namely, the middle class] define as 'the greater good'. This passage is as close as Howells ever comes in his fiction to a direct vocalisation of anarchist thought and it occurs within the contours of a discussion about the aesthetics of the sketch, which unlike other forms of writing does not by necessity subordinate the multiplicity of situations to a unified totality or the form of the Event. Indeed, the sketch is defined as a form by its seriality and its aesthetic of movement and relocation between spaces and circumstances in a manner that renders it an alternative to the structural consolidation and idea of coherence instantiated in the novel form.

A similar process is at play in March's decision to collect working-class ballads, which like the sketches emerge in the narrative as an ideal form of modern art. Howells notes that the songs and poems appeal to March in part because 'they trusted themselves, with syntax that yielded promptly to any exigency of rhythmic art, to the ordinary American speech . . .' (185) and that '[t]heir control . . . intimated a volatility which was not perceptible in their sentiment' (185). This is to say that what they represent to him is precisely that which Howells in his criticism would remark was essential to the modern artistic practice of realism as he understood it; a sense that at the level of form 'they cease to lie about life; let it portray men and women as they are . . . [and] show the different interests in their true proportions . . . frankly own these for what they are, in whatever figures and occasions they appear' ('Editor's Study'). Put another way, the ballads, like the sketches, may be a residual form in some respects, but also serve as a powerful marker of a modern sensibility, whereby the situation dictates the form of the artistic presentation, there is a radical trust in the work and its artist, and they do not subscribe to a singular moral or social vision of the world. This represents nothing less than an admission that March's aestheticism is not seen by Howells as necessarily an abandonment of political responsibility, but that he is envisaging an 'aesthetic regime' of power that incorporates 'working-class art' within its fold as an alternative formulation of the public sphere to the official order of representation controlled by the law of the state. The appeal of these works is that they are not wholly directed towards the expression of group life as singular or uniform, but express a volatility or excess that is not reducible wholly to the purview of the liberal state. Critical consensus generally regarding March's sketches has been to point out their inadequacy as a means of reflecting the 'real' life of the poor: seeing them as a feeble bourgeois affectation that turns the poor into a subject, too, of dilettantish aesthetic contemplation. Yet, in rendering the poor in this way (that is aesthetically) March (and by corollary Howells) also uncouples them from the forms of ethnic, racial and class-based mimesis that make them a representation of a particular locus and time alone. The classic Marxian reading of class relations turns on a critical dismissal of the aesthetic as a force for politics. But it is in contemplation of the aesthetic of everyday street life and of the ballads that March comes to a sense of the failures of liberalism and of a laissez-faire economics that justifies itself according to a social Darwinist logic of the survival of the fittest. In the ballads, March marvels at the presence of a form of art emerging from a group of people whose poverty, he had previously thought, placed them beyond the pale of art-making or the possibility of 'imagination', this is in part because, as the Eight-Hour Movement agitated for, it reveals a deployment of time that in the Platonic model the worker is supposed not to have.

Elizabeth Barnes has shown how American realism as a style often depicted acts of sacrificial or substitutionary violence, rituals that are virtualisations of the US legal system, in order to make its claims to capturing the essence of nineteenth-century American democratic society with its twinned imaginations of empathy and inclusiveness ('Bring us your huddled masses') and imperial expansion and exclusion. In *Love's Whipping Boy: Violence and Sentimentality in the American Imagination* Barnes argues that

> [E]mpathy and aggression come together in the popularly conceived and disseminated image of the substitutionary victim or scapegoat – what I term the 'whipping boy.' As an innocent stand-in for the guilty party, the whipping boy's suffering on another's behalf represents a model for the personally and socially transformative work of violence. (3)

The 'whipping boy' is, then, the aesthetic form of the state apparatus: a 'surrogate' or stand-in for whom violence against their body can serve to render transparent the disciplinary function of power. Emma Goldman would make a similar point in her 1910 essay 'Anarchism: What it Really Stands For' when she announced that 'The State is the altar of political freedom and, like the religious altar, it is maintained for the purpose of human sacrifice' (63). Importantly, in *A Hazard of New Fortunes*, Howells refuses to confront the Haymarket riot directly since to do so would be to reproduce the investigative exercises that sold newspapers and caused the arrest and murder of innocent men, but instead plays a fascinating game with the notion of the scapegoat – depicting barbarised and wounded foreigners and outsiders that serve as potential substitutionary stand-ins for the real Haymarket martyrs while never truly 'representing' them. Additionally, the final moments of the book depict the accidental death of the radical bourgeois and son of a factory owner Conrad Dryfoos, and the clubbing of Lindau (the German socialist translator and Basil March's friend) at a street-car strike. However, these deaths serve no act of redemption as such a redemption would only justify the liberal model of inclusion that incorporates both the freedom to speak as an individual and its dark inverse of sacrificial violence.

The novel fails in its task of detection, ending on an epistemological crises with everyone debating the truth or meaning of what has occurred to the characters, and so too in the most simple sense of performing a version of literary realism based in transparent rendering of representative figures who stand in for wider cultural positions. I would argue that such a 'failure' is actually a wholly deliberate exercise designed by Howells to imagine a new political space for art. The novel performs a strategic misalignment between aesthetics and the hermeneutic uncovering or revelation that in the context of the aftermath of Haymarket was enacted primarily by authorities of state power. Importantly, while the street-car strike that defines the final sections of the novel is a planned event, the main character's relation to it is defined by contingency and accident. Conrad runs to help a man being beaten by police, Lindau appears to be recovering from injuries only to die suddenly, and Basil March finds himself by happenstance on the wrong trolleycar. The novel's 'scapegoats' or 'whipping boys' – to use Barnes's phrase – are never quite ideal and in this way Howells makes a political argument about the forcing of 'representativeness' that was performed by the prosecution in the Haymarket trial; the unjust manipulation of situations into the unified, ritual form of the Event that led to the execution of men for their ideas. As I suggested earlier, the ritual of the law after Haymarket worked through the reduction of the complex temporalities of micro-events in lived experience into the form of the Event of ritual sacrifice. Yet in Howells's novel the misalignment of the scapegoat with the Event (like the slight misalignment of the magazine itself with the present moment) enacts an aesthetic process through which time is left open, multiple and conflicted – thereby resisting the choreographic force of state power. In the uncomfortable textual slippages and elisions when class meets culture that critics have seen as a crisis for the author, Howells's novel dramatises the condition faced by the jury in the trial of the Haymarket anarchists; that of representing the large-scale injustices of capitalism within the terms of an embodied individual or group. The furious speculation in the press as to the identity of the bomb-thrower points to the desire for a verifiable face of the labour struggle whose execution might serve a sacrificial role in re-establishing the status quo. Indeed, the inability of the press, police or jury to uncover the identity of the bomb-thrower expressed the irony and paradox of liberalism by demonstrating the way in which liberal iterations of identity are both the platform upon which one may base claims to liberty and a necessity of the law that makes possible the act of persecution. At the same time, discovering a verifiable face of the labour struggle was also a task implicit in the liberal project of platform, or identity, politics that the Haymarket defendants and their lawyer William Black actively opposed.

In the next chapter, I look at the international political scene of the 1890s to consider how the spectacular press that racialised subjects and reduced the multiplicities of experience into a form of police power that was galvanised after Haymarket moved its focus onto a larger political stage during the imperialist moment of the Spanish–American War. In this context, several writers – among them Charles Anderson Dana and José Martí – sought to deploy a proto-modernist literary style in their renderings of everyday life as a bulwark against the jingoism and racism of the emergent mass culture.

Notes

1. See J. Michelle Coghlan, *Sensational Internationalism*, for more on memorialisation in the American Left.
2. See Streeby; Kaplan; Hughes; Douglas E. Jones.
3. See Moten, *Black and Blur*.
4. See Morrison, *Louis Sullivan*.
5. See Stansell, *American Moderns*, and Frankel, 'Whatever Happened to "Red Emma"?' For further discussion of theatre in Emma Goldmans's work see Ferguson, 'Gender and Genre in Emma Goldman'.
6. See Couser, *Vulnerable* Subjects, and Eakin, *The Ethics of Life Writing*.
7. This is also very clearly the case in the situation of extrajudicial killing by organisations parallel to the state – such as with antiblack lynching by white mobs, the KKK, 'vigilance' groups and so forth. See Stevens, 'Absolutely Novel'; Seger, 'Deferred Lynching'; Hebard, *The Poetics of Sovereignty*; English, *Each Hour Redeem*.
8. 'Reactionary' may not be the right word here. Indeed, 'conservative' or other variants of the same evoke similar problems when thinking about politics as a dialogue about how to express 'the modern'. It might be better to think not of the 'conservative' or the 'reactionary', because a description of the past in the realm of politics is always an act in the present. Rather, it might be better to consider these things in ethical terms as different valuations of the importance of freedom. What is 'progressive' is a description of a future based on the hope of greater human freedom, dissensus, and the expression of a greater good. What is 'regressive' is its nominal inverse; a future based on reduced freedom and/or the consolidation of power.
9. See Pratt, *Archives of American Time*, and Dimock, *Through Other Continents*.

CHAPTER 2

'Pure Feelings, Noble Aspirations, and Generous Ideas': Yellow Journalism, the Cuban War of Independence and *crónica modernista*

> We learn with poignant sorrow of the death in battle of José Martí, the well-known leader of the Cuban revolutionists. We knew him long and well, and esteemed him profoundly. For a protracted period, beginning twenty odd years ago, he was employed as a contributor to THE SUN, writing on subjects and questions of the fine arts. In these things his learning was solid and extensive, and his ideas and conclusions were original and brilliant. He was a man of genius, of imagination, of hope, and of courage, one of those descendants of the Spanish race whose American birth and instincts seem to have added to the revolutionary tincture which all modern Spaniards inherit. His heart was warm and affectionate, his opinions ardent and aspiring, and he died as such a man might wish to die, battling for liberty and democracy. Of such heroes there are not too many in the world, and his warlike grave testifies that, even in a positive and material age, there are spirits that can give all for their principles without thinking of any selfish return for themselves.
>
> Honor to the memory of José Martí, and peace to his manly and generous soul.

On Thursday 23 May 1895, *The New York Sun* newspaper carried the above obituary for the journalist, modernist poet and leader of *Partido Revolucionario Cubano*, José Martí, who had been killed in the Battle of Boca de Dos Rios against Spanish imperial forces on the preceding Sunday. The obituary is interesting both for its subject and for its approach. No other major, mainstream, New York-based, English-language newspaper carried such a sentimental or laudatory account of the controversial writer in the days immediately after his death. Many referred to him solely as 'the insurgent leader', focused on the sensational manner of his death or reported the event in relation to 'the great importance to the Spanish authorities of the papers found upon his body'.[1] Martí died after ordering his men to charge a heavily fortified Spanish position in direct violation of an order from the military leader of the insurrectionists General Máximo Gómez. In fact, Martí's presence in Cuba was controversial in itself. Few of the insurrectionists felt that this scholar-poet and orator could contribute much to the war effort on the ground and would better serve the cause of independence by continuing to agitate and write in the USA. Martí had been on poor terms with Gómez since he and Antonio Maceo had visited him in New York in 1884. John Lawrence Tone has remarked, 'Gómez thought Martí made a better poet than a revolutionary. He suspected that Martí was all talk and that he feared an actual war for independence because in such a conflict he would be eclipsed by military men.' Moreover, Martí was suspicious of the motives of his fellow revolutionists, suspecting Gómez and Maceo of '*caudillismo*, that is, the desire to set themselves up as military dictators in Cuba . . . he broke with the general sending him an insulting letter that implied that Spanish rule would be preferable to a revolution in which men like Gómez held sway' (Tone 34).

The articles carried by *The Sun*'s more populist (and increasingly more popular) 'yellow paper' competitors, Joseph Pulitzer's *World* and William Randolph Hearst's *Journal*, in the years preceding the Spanish–American War of 1898 evince a clear taste for copy about the Cuban War of Independence in New York at the time, even if that was not shared necessarily by the wider nation.[2] However, they do so without *The Sun*'s clear support for Martí's revolutionary vision and often with an eye towards the potential of the conflict as the starting point for US imperialist expansion into the island nation. Indeed, the historiography of the Spanish–American War (of which the Cuban War of Independence was a major theatre) has often tied the conflict directly to competition for sales and subscribers between Pulitzer's and Hearst's news agencies, arguing that US jingoism, as well as American desire for annexation of Cuba to exploit its abundant natural resources, were partially fostered by these press magnates for the purposes of generating good copy and greater sales.[3] This argument may not hold weight since it is hard to place more blame for an invasion at the feet of the press than at the pro-invention politicians and industrialists William McKinley, John Jacob Astor and J. P. Morgan.[4] However, as David R. Spencer has suggested, 'there is considerable merit in blaming both Hearst's *New York Journal* and Pulitzer's *New York World* for playing fast and loose with the truth in their respective attempts to garner larger and larger circulation' (Spencer 124). What is clear is that in this period Cuba became a major site for testing out competing visions of US journalistic ethics. As W. Joseph Campbell has noted, reporting Cuba mobilised 'a choice between the self-activated, participatory ethos of Hearst's journalism and the detached, sober antithesis of that genre, as represented by the *New York Times* and its lofty commitment to "All the News That's Fit To Print"' (Campbell 190).

The Sun charted a course somewhere between the austerity and worthiness of *Times* reportage and the flashy, explosive capitalist imperialism of the so-called 'yellow journalism'. The paper's approach to Martí's death is not surprising once we learn that unlike other obituaries, the author of Martí's death notice was not one of the paper's numerous, largely anonymous, reporters, but the editor-in-chief of *The Sun*, the former Union soldier and Brook Farm Transcendentalist Charles Anderson Dana. Dana had drafted the notice the day before, when the Associated Press wires had carried some of the earliest confirmed reports of Martí's death in English. In choosing to print such a definitive and dignified obituary on 23 May, Dana's paper also set itself in clear opposition to Pulitzer's *World* and *Evening World*, which, for several days following his death, published a running joke claiming that Martí was alive and had been spotted at various places in Cuba and the Keys. Gossipy articles, such as 'JOSE MARTÍ IN HIDING: It Is Believed That He Is Preparing to Slip To This Country' from the 4 June edition, directly contradicted their own confirmed reports of his death, sowing confusion while driving sales. The running commentary was a clear instance of the yellow paper's strategy, deploying techniques learned from popular serial fiction and printing material from dubious sources to generate marketable copy for the newspaper.

Dana's approach was distinct from many of the other major New York newspapermen of his time, who channelled prevailing attitudes in the USA towards the insurrection in 'believ[ing] themselves to be benefactors of Cuba'; an attitude that following the War of Independence would transmute into the perception of 'Cubans as indissolubly linked to the United States by ties of gratitude and obligation' (Perez, Jr. xiii) that might seemingly justify American intervention and annexation. Instead, Dana's particular political vision did not discount the possibility of Cuban sovereignty, whose struggles were embodied in the person of Martí. Dana regrettably died just before the major engagements of the Cuban–Spanish–American War, and US journalism lost one of the few major, mainstream political voices that might have resisted the rise of imperialist jingoism in the final years of the nineteenth century. As Janet Steele has noted,

> Dana's interest in the Cuban Revolution lasted until his death in 1897. He corresponded personally with leading Cuban revolutionists, including his 'warm friend' José Martí, and met with them when they came to New York . . . In 1899 a square in Camaguey, Cuba, was renamed Charles A. Dana Plaza in tribute to his support for the New York Cuban junta.(Steele 103–4)

Before discussing the obituary in detail it is worth turning to Dana, who remains a controversial figure in American letters. Literary historians have struggled over where to place him in a dominant narrative of US media history that charts a movement from the local partisan papers of the early republic, through the antebellum era's early experimentation with a commercial press, to the era of media conglomerates and incorporated capitalist news agencies. Charles Dana has been painted frequently as a reactionary Boston Brahmin, in part because his status as an avowed member of the Northeastern intellectual elite marked him out from his main rivals – the wealthy, crass, son of an industrialist (Hearst), first- and second-generation Jewish immigrants (Pulitzer and the *Times*' Adolph Ochs), and a belligerent penny press baron (Gordon Bennett of the *Herald*). Until the eclipse of *The Sun* by Pulitzer's *World* in the late 1880s, however, the 'daily' was 'New York's most widely read newspaper', particularly among the artisan lower-middle classes, and Dana one of the most famous journalists in America (Steele 155).

We owe the relative neglect of Dana partly to the Progressive era critic Vernon Parrington, whose hugely influential 1930 work *The Beginnings of Critical Realism in America, 1860–1920*, painted a picture of the inevitable destruction of Charles Dana's intellectual project through Hearst's and Pulitzer's marriage of American corporate capitalism with aggressive muckraking journalism. For Parrington, Dana was a conservative voice in the Gilded Age, chronically out of touch with the pushy spirit of his time. By characterising him as a conservative, Parrington played into a teleological narrative of American intellectual and social development that turned the famous clashes between Pulitzer and Hearst over reporting the war with Spain into a crucible for the emergence of modern American print culture. Indeed, American media hegemony and globalisation more generally. Yet in this teleological narrative the rise of 'yellow journalism' is understood to be the emergence of a certain 'working-class' popular perspective (one that Hearst and Pulitzer were shown to have harnessed better than their competitors) into the American public sphere. Defined by low humour, bullish aggression and spectacular accounts of journalistic and personal heroism, this voice cast into shadow the more refined and educated vision of working-class production and culture put forward by *The Sun*. Moreover, this narrative of the development of American journalism towards tabloid spectacularism cast a newspaper like *The Sun*, which was actually at the heart of contemporary debates, as a residual presence on the scene, transforming the rise of Pulitzer's and Hearst's style into a historical inevitability.

Yet such an approach obscures the complex negotiations undergone by Dana's paper in navigating the contemporary newspaper scene without violating his higher journalistic principles. The year 1895, as well as Martí's death and Hearst's purchase of the *New York Journal*, also saw the release of an edition of the collected lectures of Charles Dana on the subject of press responsibility and the profession of journalism entitled *The Art of Newspaper Making*. In his lectures Dana outlined the rules of journalistic conduct in direct challenge to Hearst, Pulitzer and the new 'yellow journalists'. Dana's rules were:

1) Get the news, get all the news, and nothing but the news.
2) Copy nothing from another publication without perfect credit.
3) Never print an interview without the knowledge and consent of the party interviewed.
4) Never print a paid advertisement as news matter. Let every advertisement appear as an advertisement; no sailing under false colors.
5) Never attack the weak or the defenceless, either by argument, by invective, or by ridicule, unless there is some absolute public necessity for doing so.
6) Fight for your opinions, but do not believe that they contain the whole truth or the only truth. Support your party, if you have one. But do not think all the good men are in it and all the bad ones outside of it.
7) Above all, know and believe that humanity is advancing; that there is progress in human life and human affairs; and that as sure as God lives, the future will be greater and better than the present or the past. (Dana 19-20)

As well as being one of the founding fathers of the modern American newspaper, known for a clear, yet eloquent, prose style and insistence on fact rather than incendiary editorialising (something that was more of an aspiration and philosophy than an actual fact as is happens), he was also immersed in many of the most significant movements of antebellum and postbellum literary and intellectual culture. In a sense, Dana was something of a contradiction. He was at once a hard-edged newspaperman who advanced himself financially and socially in the capitalist Gilded Age, and a figure who in his youth had helped found a utopian, abolitionist commune at Brook Farm in West Roxbury, Massachusetts (1841-1847) committed to co-operative aims. The Brook Farm Transcendentalists had combined the spiritualism and focus on cultural uplift called for by antebellum US Romantics such as Ralph Waldo Emerson and Margaret Fuller with a rationalised model of agriculture and political organisation drawn from the writings of the revolutionary French philosopher Charles Fourier.[5] These Romantic era thinkers believed that true democracy was only possible when cultural achievements were matched with an egalitarian rationalisation of labour that dignified all work, intellectual and manual, and treated both as equal. This was a cultural politics that was also a class politics. In a speech Dana gave on 21 January 1895 at the University of Michigan he outlined the original plan for Brook Farm. Dana pointed to the twinned projects of culture and economics that would define his ethos across his life and work when he said,

> If democracy was the sublime truth which it was held up to be, it should be raised up from the sphere of politics, from the sphere of law and constitutions; it should be raised up into life and be made social. (Dana, 'Brook Farm' in Wilson 521)

Dana was the de facto editor of the West Roxbury community's in-house publication *The Harbinger*, which served as the site of his apprenticeship in journalism and an outlet for the dissemination of left-wing, transnational literature.[6] He also served as one of the primary educators of the children of Brook Farm and head of the 'work parties' or 'phalanxes' which were involved in the preparation of meals for the group. Indeed, the Brook Farm Transcendentalists were some of the earliest adopters of French radical thought, with a young Dana even writing articles published in the *New York Tribune* in 1849 in support of the idea of 'mutual banking' put forward by the anarchist Pierre-Joseph Proudhon. Rather than cultivating an intellect that functioned through intuition alone (as Emerson has often been described as doing), the Fourierist Transcendentalists advocated a regime of intellectual 'leveling up' that operated across national boundaries and highlighted the dignity of all labour as a response to the problems of class inequality in the nineteenth century. As Carl Guarneri has noted, 'cooperative living would eliminate the obstacles to spiritual growth presented by an acquisitive, unequal, compartmentalized society and would make the means of Transcendentalist self-culture available to more individuals' (Guarneri in Capper and Wright, 453). The Brook Farmers attempted to marry a distinctly Victorian attention to the edifying, improving qualities of elite literature with workers' rights and a planned economy so as to enhance the life of all citizens.

It is these values that Dana esteemed most in the obituary for his friend Martí, a figure who similarly sought to marry Romanticism in culture with radical democracy in politics. A key claim of my argument here is that both Martí and Dana represented figures that deliberately alienated themselves from what were becoming normative social, journalistic and literary practices in the late nineteenth-century Americas. In their writings, Dana and Martí sought to channel idiosyncratic literary styles into alternative visions of the political order. In effect, both Dana and Martí were examples of what Susana Rotker has called 'an intellectual elite that felt marginalized and alienated by the readjustment of social relations' in the Gilded Age, the very conditions that would some years later give birth to European modernism (Rotker 5). Yet, crucially, they did not embrace modernism fully as a set of aesthetic values, believing wholly in realism as its own form of political engagement and finding in yellow paper journalism evidence of the surrealistic excess and frivolity that was loathsome to them.

Considering Martí's work in light of Dana's intellectual project allows us to partially resolve one of the key problems that plagues Martí studies; how the Cuban exile could be at once an advocate of American romantic individualism (famously embodied in US Emersonianism) and a voice of the collective struggle (as embodied in Cuban rebellion against imperialism). Recent work on Martí such as that by Laura Lomas has considered the Cuban writer's relationship to an American Transcendentalist tradition by offering new readings of his famous essays on the US American cultural figures such as the essayist and lecturer Ralph Waldo Emerson and the democratic poet Walt Whitman. Lomas has argued that even as Martí esteemed the individualistic and egoistic wing of the Transcendentalist movement, he remained sceptical of its self-directedness and claims for ahistorical universality that could potentially serve as an apologia for the more horrifying aspects of Anglocentric imperial modernity. Lomas writes:

> In its individualism, the Emersonian subject considers adherence to a collective a compromising circumstance, whereas for Martí unity through coalition helps to ensure the anticolonial nation's futurity. Emerson's subject is sovereign, autonomous, and entirely self-engendering ... If Emerson imagines himself as homogenous and invulnerable – a standing house and not a storm-tossed ship – Martí defines subjectivity through

figures so internally heterogeneous and transitory that they threaten to split open. (Lomas 134)

Martí was attracted and repulsed by Emerson because at the time that he was writing, American traditions of individualism and self-reliance were the characteristics being called upon by figures such as Hearst and Pulitzer to justify the American annexation of Cuba. Consequently, Emerson was insufficient as a tool to describe, and mobilise, Cuban subjectivity; an identity that both depended upon and was shaped by a collective history of oppression. As a former Brook Farmer, Dana felt the same about self-culture, believing structural transformations of labour needed to precede, or happen alongside, romantic individualism in order to allow the potential of the workers as harbingers of liberty to flourish.

The obituary in *The Sun* did not only mark the passing of Martí as a man, but served as a print ritual, a performance that allowed for the emergence of Cuban–American friendship as a political alterity based in what the author describes as an earlier (though somewhat ill-defined) age of high sentimental values. According to the thinking of the time, sentimental affect was supposed to operate across borders, free from the pressures of nationalism and a 'positive and material' capitalist hegemony.[7] In this way, Dana's obituary for Martí functioned similarly to that most important of classical, republican, performative genres, the funeral oration, in being at once an account of Dana's personal loss and a moment in which the values of the democratic *polis* (embodied in the dead individual) are made manifest, re-affirmed and, often also, reorganised.[8] Dana constructed a transnational fraternity of shared republican values between Cuba and the USA by means of a print ritual that sought to challenge the fixing of national borders to particular sets of manners and behaviours in an age of rapacious American imperialism.

A problem emerges, though, in the fact that the sense of fraternity that the obituary ritualistically generates between Dana and Martí (or Martí and *The New York Sun*) was, in a sense, a politically troubled illusion. The same sense of transnational affection that Dana expresses for Martí was complicit in shaping a sense of commonality that in other instances was used to justify Cuban annexation by the USA.⁹ For this reason the Martí–Dana friendship cannot be considered free from the material realities of late nineteenth-century life, namely, the position of Cuba as a nation whose people did not confront the USA on a remotely equal footing, as citizens of brother-nations, but as potential subjects of American imperial designs. It does not go far enough to read this obituary as merely a sign of Dana's love for his Cuban friend. To do so is to ignore the audience of *The Sun* and their own particular attitudes to Cuba, which could not have been entirely free from the influence of generations of American exceptionalist rhetoric and an ongoing sense of the 'inevitability' of Cuban annexation that had predominated discussions of 'manifest destiny' in the antebellum and immediate postbellum USA.

Much of Martí's work in the years preceding The War of Independence had been devoted to addressing a North American mindset that favoured 'manifest destiny'. This was especially evident in his clashes in the press and at the Pan-American Convention (1889–1990) with the hawkish US Republican senator James Blaine, whose economic policies towards Latin America, Martí thought, were devised with the aim of destabilising sovereign nations and paving the way for heightened US intervention into the Spanish Caribbean.¹⁰ In the context of a burgeoning annexationist movement in the USA, the concept of Cuban–American friendship raised by Dana's obituary was not without its political complexities. Yet the obituary was also of value to the writer, who in speaking of Martí's employment at *The Sun* alongside idealised republican values made the Cuban writer's 'noble' qualities synonymous with those of Dana's paper.

The very values that Dana attributed to Martí: his 'warm and affectionate' nature, his value system that elevated the 'ardent and aspiring' as key 'manly' virtues, and his 'wish to die, battling for liberty and democracy', may easily have been interpreted as his qualifications (and those of the Cuban people of whom he was a paragon) for US citizenship. In other words, the hard work, passion for liberty and sentimental manhood that made him an ideal Cuban nationalist in the eyes of Dana also reflected the prevailing norms of an idealised late nineteenth-century US manhood, justifying not just a possible recourse to shared histories of revolution between

Latin America and the United States but a specifically annexationist claim to the expansion of US democracy into a nation currently engaged in a freedom struggle with imperial Spain.

Dana's obituary for Martí serves to open up a more far-reaching discussion of press and politics in the Gilded Age USA. It also helps us to resurrect *The New York Sun* as an important force in the print landscape after over a hundred years of comparative critical neglect. The death of Martí signalled not only the loss of a major Latin American thinker and activist of the Gilded Age but was also one of the last major political events in the life of Charles Dana – one of the only extant figures in US print culture who directly connected the 'new journalism' to a radical history of abolitionism and the Revolutions of 1848. To truly understand the work of obituary, it is important to explore Dana's political and commercial vision in *The Sun*. Part of this exercise may be achieved by paying closer attention to the form of the newspaper; an approach which does not consider the obituary as a single, isolated, transcendent text but as a fragment in a larger collage, considering, as well, *The Sun*'s paratexts and distribution history. By examining form more closely we can reveal the proto-modernist styles that differentiated Dana's work from that of his contemporaries.

In the age of the popular, famous, adventuring journalist (Stephen Crane, Richard Harding Davis, Nelly Bly), when newspapers competed for big-name writers who commanded high salaries for sensational feats of daring investigative journalism, Dana's paper frequently resisted the printing of by-lines on much of its copy and 'avoided using enormous headlines and splashy illustrations, which of course became normative for new journalism' (Roggenkamp 64). True to this tradition the obituary was anonymous, adopting a communal 'we' ('we learn with poignant sorrow') that tied the personality of the editor to the vision of his paper as a whole. Yet the absence of a by-line importantly does not subsume that 'we' under the aegis of Dana himself alone; this is not the 'royal we', the forced attribution of a collective to the body of an individual, but a 'we' rooted in professional values and the kinds of collective labour that Dana had cultivated as a young man at Brook Farm.

The obituary functioned more as 'literature' than as simple reportage. At a time when the New York press was gravitating towards a notion of mass culture as synonymous with the 'popular' or 'populist' aims, the politics of Dana's vision lay as much in his attention to form as in his identification with a controversial political figure such as Martí. When encountered as a print performance in the pages of the paper, the obituary strikes the reader as distinctly odd. Not only is the absence of a by-line or headline somewhat 'out of sync' with the sensationalist tenor of the contemporary 'yellow' journalism, but also it confers upon the piece a sense of what Walter Benjamin called 'aura', and which can only be defined in terms of the sacred. The obituary appeared on page 6 and was marked off from the rest of the surrounding text by thick black lines. This technique was normally reserved for 'Stop Press' late additions to the paper, but we know that Dana must have been aware of Martí's death long before the print deadline for the morning edition, since a search of the Library of Congress newspaper collections reveals that even regional papers such as *The San Francisco Call, Scranton Tribune, Salt Lake Herald* and others had reported his death as early as the morning of 22 May. Since *The Sun* was a member of the Associated Press and their offices controlled many of the telegraphic communications that came from Cuba upon which the regional papers relied for reports, there is no doubt about Dana's knowledge of his friend's death at least by the time of the evening edition of 21 May. This leads to the conclusion that the obituary was strategically deployed with a view to creating the greatest impression upon readers. Mimicking the temporality of the 'Stop Press' report produced the effect of spontaneity that could be read in terms of an outpouring of sentimental sincerity – the very ideals that the author attributed to Martí. The text, then, evokes an alternative temporality. Martí's obituary *emerges* from the page of the newspaper as an anonymous and poignant expression of feeling that is distinct from the textual objects around it by virtue of its function as a ritual object that speaks to a history of shared values and labours.

Dana's obituary stands in clear contrast to much 'new journalism' in two ways: first, by deploying the text as a material ritual object that cultivates shared feelings directed towards shared goals, and, second, through the use of an anonymous voice that renders aesthetically the sense of historical legacy. However, the text functions aesthetically not based on its status as an alienated or autonomous art object in the modernist sense but because of its relationship to the material around it, its carefully cultivated positioning as a temporal and textual anomaly. Page 6 of the paper was a space usually reserved for the reprinting of articles from regional or foreign sources not produced by in-house writers. Since this page was designed to incorporate diverse democratic publics into the narrative of *The Sun*, the positioning of the article allowed this obituary to perform its role as a sincere outpouring of the democratic public, even if it was, in reality, the product of the paper's editor-in-chief. This clever turn made the narrative he presented seem to be organic and democratic, an aspect of its aesthetic that was further enhanced by the absence of a by-line. Since the wider US public was, in reality, often quite hostile to Martí's radical image of Cuban sovereignty, this positioning and anonymity served the role of legitimating the action by means of an anonymity that made recourse to a 'public' voice.

This notion that newspapers could be sites of genuine feeling and alternative historical narratives was explored by Martí himself in an article written for Charles Dana's New York weekly *The Hour* in 1880, entitled 'Impressions of America (By a Very Fresh Spaniard)'. In this article Martí suggested that foreigners were often prone to generalisations about the USA as a vulgar nation marked by 'arrogant militarism, violation of the public will [and] corruption of the political morality' (Martí, 'Impressions of America' in Allen, 34) because they did not pay close enough attention to the American press. Martí writes, 'In the columns of a newspaper, in the page of a magazine, in the familiar chit-chat, the most pure feelings, noble aspirations, and generous ideas bravely fight for the rapid improvement of the county, in the sense of moral development' (35). For Martí, conceptualising radical democracy relied, partly, upon paying close attention to the newspapers and popular print, which often evinced ideas for progressive development that were seldom ever debated at the official state level or could not be summed up by a well-chosen, spectacular lithograph. In effect, the Cuban modernist author (like Dana himself) valued the printed word and close reading as sources of radical potentialities not possible through recourse to the photography, visual media and punchy, simple, prose styles that had come to define the new American journalistic landscape. Additionally, his narrative style highlighted its own subjectivity and artistic credibility, by permitting a lyricism that was not to be found in most 'yellow press' writing of the time. As Andrew Taylor has noted, Martí (like Ralph Waldo Emerson before him) avoided a sensationalistic and rapid-response literary technique, so as to resist a similarly platitudinous form of working-class and cultural politics, relying instead upon a treatment of American experience as messy, excessive, 'disjointed and fragmentary, composed of the collision of apparently incompatible elements' (Taylor 844) that required a sharp, educated eye to 'read'. This is a republican, working-class politics that does not give into the allure of the unified Event, but relies on the continually rejuvenating possibilities that inhere in multiplicity and literary ambiguity.

From a certain perspective, Charles Dana and José Martí's 'great works' approach to literature might be read as 'conservative'. Yet it is important to note that the aspects of Dana and Martí's work that seem 'conservative' may also be seen as the deployment of a strategic latency that cut against a dominant narrative of modernity, which attributed the sense of 'progress' to the condition of accelerated temporality. As with other thinkers of the period, among them Mark Twain, William James, Jane Addams and others, who were triggered into the foundation of the Anti-Imperial League by the late nineteenth-century collusion of imperial ambition with new media, Dana and Martí saw the Cuban–Spanish–American War as a moment requiring a renewal of American anti-imperial fervour and clear-headed, rational thinking. The yellow papers' techniques of printing unconfirmed accounts and gossip was a perfect case of their marketing as periodicals that placed speed of information and imagery before fact-checking. Dana's technique of holding back his obituary for his Cuban friend by a few days simultaneously allowed him to present the effect of sincerity and accuracy in opposition to his competitors' journalistic ethics, while also suggesting through the mimicry of the 'Stop Press' report that his paper was not being left behind. Dana and Martí's attention to high learning, cultivation and the slower speeds of text versus the more immediate effects of image, is a proto-modernist gesture that challenges the brash 'progressivism' of yellow journalism and predates the patterns of more traditional literary histories that see 'modernism' as emerging in Europe and America around the 1910s. Dana drew attention to this in his own lecture on 'The Profession of Journalism' to the students of Union College in 1893. In this lecture, Dana set his own values in opposition both to the new journalists and to his tutor in the profession, Horace Greeley. Dana wrote,

> Give the young man a first-class course of general education . . . I had rather take a fellow who knows the Ajax of Sophocles, and who has read Tacitus, and can scan every ode of Horace – I would rather take him to report a prize fight or a spelling match . . . than to take one who has never had those advantages . . . I believe in colleges; I believe in high education . . . (Dana, 'Art of Newspaper Making', 32)

Dana's insistence on the importance of high learning and 'a very beautiful and admirable [prose] style' (39) parallels Martí's own aesthetic, often referred to as the *crónica modernista*, which frequently utilised complex verbal constructions and subtle textual allusions that ran counter to the dominant narrative of the Press's accelerated speed of information and the critical language of its 'appeal' to an only partially educated working class. Indeed, as Susana Rotker has shown, Martí was not especially interested in 'the mimetic function of texts . . . the identification of reality with external phenomena'.[11] Instead, he was concerned with capturing the fragmented and discontinuous elements of experience through a complex, multivalent and largely internalised subjectivity that disrupted, rather than depicted, reality. Such an aesthetic, Martí reasoned, was better able to express utopian possibility than either a literary realism that aimed at the transparent representation of events or the new technologies of accelerated image-making frequently exploited by the New York press. What mattered most to Martí, and to Dana, was the *affect* that was rarely present in modern printed visual culture, except as a degraded, base, sensationalism.

Martí as Colleague

The Sun obituary spoke of Martí as an 'original and brilliant' colleague, collapsing the geographical and generic distances that divided Latin American *modernismo* from New York journalism, and folding him into the collective voice that was made possible within the pages of a printed artefact that frequently refused to deploy by-lines. Dana's decision to refuse by-lines reflected both the collectivist ethos of his Transcendentalist early days and a residual antebellum newspaper aesthetic that downplayed the contributions of individual authors. Partly as a marker of his esteem for Martí's work as a writer and thinker, Dana commissioned over 300 articles from him for *The Sun* and *The Hour* (the weekly sister paper to *The Sun* 'devoted to social interests') throughout the 1880s, enough for Martí to be considered a staff writer, primarily on 'subjects, and questions of the fine arts'.[12] Martí contributed articles on a variety of topics, but was known in the English-language context primarily as a roving critic, reviewing gallery openings and new book releases. His position on the staff of *The Sun* might suggest a self-censorship of his more overtly political writings (which appear to have been reserved for Latin American publications), or else a camouflaging of his radicalism behind seemingly more benign content. However, Martí's theory of art and culture in Anglophile print culture was of a piece with both his work more generally and the cultural politics of Dana's journalistic project. It would be tempting to regard Dana's decisions to have Martí contribute on the arts, rather than on politics or as a correspondent on international affairs, as a dismissal or insult, but to do so would be to overlook that in Dana's vision (as indeed in Martí's), art and culture were the proper provinces of politics, because Fourierist and Transcendentalist uplift valued the aesthetic as a political force fundamental to the project of individual and collective liberation.

Martí's complex position as critic of American imperialism, both celebrant *and* cynic towards the modernity of which the USA was an important and inevitable participant, and contributor to the project of defining journalistic practice in Anglophone New York sat quite easily within Dana's own aesthetic purview. Reading Martí's work in such a way, though, problematises traditional historical approaches to the Cuban author and leader, which have appropriated him to serve as an archetype of an uncomplicated, late twentieth-century vision of Latin American hostility to US culture. Much Latin American criticism of Martí has tended to overlook this English-language writing in an effort to depict him as a radical outsider to the American scene; a New Americanist before his time (as Andrew Taylor has noted). Even left-wing, US-based critics like Philip Foner have chosen to focus upon his exclusion and resistance to US aggression – Foner's own collection of Martí's work being provocatively called *Inside the Monster*. As Paul Giles has noted, Foner's selections were chosen to 'make Martí appear a forerunner to twentieth-century socialism', and largely excluded the cultural-critical work for which he was well known in his time.[13] More recent uses of Martí, especially by Jeffrey Belnap and Laura Lomas, have situated him as a forerunner of contemporary liberal multiculturalism or chosen to look specifically to his famous call for Pan-Latin American solidarity 'Nuestra América' as a source of a remarkably prescient, colourblind post-racialism:

> There can be no racial animosity, because there are no races . . . The soul, equal and eternal, emanates from bodies of various shapes and colors . . . anyone who promotes and disseminates opposition or hatred among races is committing a sin against humanity.[14]

Yet historicising Martí's own politics casts doubts over the legitimacy of claiming the author and thinker for twentieth-century socialist variants of radicalism. His relationship to Dana helps us to resituate Martí within the frame of late nineteenth-century republicanism, an ideology that developed more under the influence of the ideas of Jean-Jacques Rousseau, Simón Bolívar and Thomas Jefferson than Karl Marx or Pyotr Kropotkin. Indeed, Martí's work mentions Karl Marx and Marxism rarely, preferring the earlier 'pre-Marxian' variants of socialism put forward by Fourier and others. Esther Allen notes only two instances in the notebooks and one published piece in the Buenos Aires paper *La Nación*, 'A Tribute to Karl Marx, Who Had Died', from 13 May and 16 May 1883 respectively, that even mention Marx. The text lauds Marx for his reforming spirit and remarks that 'Marx studied the means of establishing the world on new bases; he awoke the sleepers' but criticises him too, noting that 'he went very fast and sometimes into darkness; he did not see that without a natural and laborious gestation, children are not born viable, from a nation in history or from a woman in the home' (*Selected Writings*, 130). Elsewhere in the article, Martí suggests that by the rage Marx inspires, workingmen become degenerated into 'beasts', remarking that 'the forced bestialization of some men for the profit of others stirs our indignation ... But that indignation must be vented in such ways that the beast ceases to be, without escaping its bonds and causing fear' (131). This sense of uplift and of preparing the ground for the organic growth of a free people by 'laborious gestation', he notes, is something Marx failed to achieve or inspire in his followers. The implication is that there is something distinctly similar in the 'forced bestialization' of the worker at the hands of capitalism and Marx's cultivation of the 'wrath of European workers' (132). This equivalence turns on a question of representation such as we also see in Rancière's criticism of the sociological position taken by many critics on the Left operating in the wake of Marx. In his writing on Marx, like Rancière, Martí speaks out against the need for an elite reader to structure thought to give meaning and shape to workers' experience, which in the process suppresses the contradictions and tensions that are evidence of a lively, autonomous working-class mind that generates its own version of the bid for freedom and equality outside of institutional practices and conventions in the service of a reductive form of solidarity. Additionally, there is much in Martí's repeated return to Marx as a force of accelerated temporality and generator of a 'kind of vortex' (*Selected Writings*, 131) that draws disparate, dissensual forces together. In the image of the vortex (as Pound and the other Vorticists of a later modernist moment would also remark) there is a conflation of the acceleration of modern life with the impulses towards the creation of a political monad that reduces difference. In the context of Martí's distrust of the emerging new journalism, this image of Marx and Marxism as a spectacular force accelerationism and aggregation has a double edge. It is at once worthy of praise for 'eagerness' (131) and also a system for degenerating the plurality of complex human life into 'beasts'. In 'Tributes to Karl Marx, Who Has Died' Martí proposes an organic socialism in opposition to the accelerationism of the modern political vortex in the form of cultural growth embodied for Martí in the figure of the working-class woman, the need for society to cultivate 'external beauty ... by continual conversation and intellectual commerce' (135) and the possibilities engendered by mass education and the university system. It is these subjects to which (with a clear sense of irony) he dedicates the majority of the article that is, at least in title, ostensibly about Marx.

In the obituary for Martí, Dana spoke of him in the highest possible terms as a 'man of genius ... imagination ... hope ... courage' that 'in a positive and material age ... [was one of those] spirit[s] that can give all for their principles without thinking of any selfish return for themselves'. Testifying to the values of Martí as both an individual and a radical willing to 'battl[e] for liberty and democracy' against the 'selfish returns' of 'a positive and material age' was a bold move for Dana in the context both of an emergent US imperialism towards Latin America (justified by the senatorial war hawk James Blaine within the 'positive and material' terms of free trade expansionism) and the rise of Pulitzer and Hearst's bullish, competitive, consumerist and jingoistic journalism. In several respects in writing of Martí in this way, Dana was attempting to draw a parallel between the values of his own paper and those of the martyred Cuban leader.

In its time *The Sun* rejected many of the central premises driving the American 'new journalism', particularly in regards to the materialism communicated by those papers' exuberant use of visuals and explosive typography, which were designed to express a new American spirit of enthusiasm, individualism and capitalist moxie. Unlike Hearst's and Pulitzer's papers, Dana's was run on subscription and resisted the drive for advertising, illustration or photography, refused to print unverified reports from dubious sources or intervene in the making of news, and also maintained a hard-fought-for independence from political parties. The effect of this was to give Dana's work the aura of the old-fashioned, a deliberately performed sense of being at odds with the *zeitgeist*. As Karen Roggenkamp has argued, where other papers struggled to marry Gilded Age culture's mania for representation of events with entertainment, Dana took a different line and endeavoured to cultivate 'an appreciation of finer styles of writing and egalitarian political ideas' among a critical and intellectually engaged working-class readership.[15]

Dana's paper presented the world as becoming increasingly monopolised by press magnates and dominated by the coercive power of corporate capitalism. In fact, Dana's concern with authority was especially evident in his distrust of the position of the Presidency, which had been growing in power and influence under successive, postbellum, Republican administrations. In his lecture on 'The Art of Newspaper Making' Dana wrote, 'There is no king, no emperor, no autocrat in the world who wields such authority, such power, as the President of the United States'.[16] Even more insidiously, Hearst and Pulitzer seemed to be using the utopian declarations of USA's providential national mission that had motivated the abolitionist movements of Dana's youth to justify the extension of free trade and US-centred mode of 'democracy' throughout the world.

In regards to Cuba, Dana's paper was also outside the main current of thought at the time. The general atmosphere in the American press surrounding the Cuban War of Independence was chauvinistic, especially after *The World* and *The Journal* began to agitate for American intervention by deploying the pseudoscientific language of racial types to explain differing cultural and political attitudes between the continental US and the Spanish Caribbean. The yellow papers frequently depicted Cubans either as feminised 'others' or as lazy and ignorant farmers to emphasise an ideological agenda that fashioned the inhabitants' as dependent upon the USA for their liberty and further the cause of those that wished to annex Cuba.[17] A history of racialised hierarchy and slavery in Cuba, which had often resulted in individuals of African slave descent remaining in predominantly agrarian professions (with light-skinned Cubans or *criollo* often taking more managerial and authoritative roles), only helped to re-enforce this ideology of dependence in the USA. In reading Cuban liberty, US citizens often projected internal racial biases against African Americans (as well as a commonly held perception that attributed the freeing of the slaves to white America and galvanised beliefs in black inferiority) onto their attitudes towards the Cuban subjects seeking independence from Spain. For example, in a dispatch for the *New York World* of 14 July 1898, Stephen Crane wrote of the 'lively contempt' felt by Americans towards the Cuban soldiers fighting alongside them against Spain, arguing that the Cubans 'manifest [...] an indifference to the cause of Cuban liberty which could not be exceeded by someone who had never heard of it'.[18] Crane's report completely misses the point, of course, since what he interprets in racially coded terms as the 'indifference' of Cuban soldiers to the ideal of *Cuba Libre* may rather have been signs of Cuban political animosity towards the American army; a display of the 'queer, racialized, and gendered modes of disaffected unfeeling that emerge [...] within dominating structures of feeling from a range of precarious positions within the axes of oppression' that Xine Yao has diagnosed in nineteenth-century culture (*Disaffected*, 6). For many Cubans, American intervention signalled less the beginnings of a period of self-rule than the opening volley of a new subjugation under the wings of the US imperial eagle. Dana, however, chose to describe Martí as 'a descendent of the Spanish race whose American birth and instincts seemed to have added to the revolutionary tincture which all modern Spaniards inherit'. In the context of anticolonial struggle, the association of modern Spaniards with 'evolutionary tincture' seems misplaced. Yet, throughout the nineteenth century Spain had undergone periods of significant liberalisation, constitutionalism and even republicanism. Ada Ferrer has noted that this very process of modernisation paved the way for the Cuban insurrection by permitting greater press freedom on the island: 'In 1886, the colonial state abolished press tribunals, which made authors subject to prison sentences and expatriation for publishing materials contrary to what officials termed Spanish "national integrity".'[19] For Dana, Martí was at once an 'American' radical (a term used to denote a pan-continental rather than purely nationalist identity) for whom an 'instinct' for liberty and democracy was natural or indigenous and a Spaniard who had absorbed the modern era's 'tincture' of free self-determination. Unlike a great many US-based authors of his day, Dana's evocation of 'American' did not mean US or even North American, but encompassed the whole Western Hemisphere. On the eve of the insurrection in Cuba, Dana printed in *The Sun* a panegyric in praise of Cuban nationalism. He wrote,

> To the brave men in arms for the independence and liberties of Cuba, to the patriots ... we send greetings ... The seventeen republics of the three

Americas desire their success ... Let foreign domination this side of the Atlantic be brought to an end forever. America for Americans![20]

Yet Dana chose his words very carefully in describing Martí in this way, since 'tincture' implied ambiguously both a low dosage and also colouration. *The Sun*'s refusal to buy in to what Shelley Streeby has called 'the late nineteenth-century expansion of the pictorial marketplace and the transformation of visual culture' posed an especially difficult problem for readers in relation to interpreting Latin American conflicts, since Gilded Age American readers often depended on the visuality of racial characteristics in shaping their perspectives on the individuals about whom articles were written.[21] Because the racial origins of individuals that seemed important to readers were often difficult to ascertain from sketches in a paper that never invested heavily in visual media, Dana's use of the term 'Spanish race' in relation to the concept of 'tincture' effectively suggested that the Cuban leader was a comparatively light-skinned European, that is, without the visual coding signifying African descent. This pandered to the commonly held racial biases of his working- and lower-middle-class New York readership, at the same time as it enfolded Martí into a tradition of US-Euro-American republicanism. By supporting Martí's project in terms that highlighted the 'American' (read 'white North American') provenance of his anti-imperial politics, while envisioning Spanish culture as a possible wellspring of future democratic movements, Dana painted an image of an autonomous Cuban subjectivity that drew its energy from Euro-American traditions of thought and culture and so circumvented a history of US imagery that associated racial 'blackness' with either feeble dependence, or threatening savagery. When the Americans finally invaded Cuba under the pretext of supporting the insurrection, imagery circulating in the yellow press painted Cubans as a racial other, a 'white man's burden' that required the support of the racially European, 'Christian' USA.[22]

The fact of Martí's racial whiteness has been extremely important to histories of the role he played as a leader for Cuban independence, as it connected his efforts with traditions of insurgency conceptualised in terms that tied Latin American sovereignty struggles with other revolutionary actions conceived as of racially European origin such as the French and American Revolutions, republican struggles in Germany and even the successes of the light-skinned Simón Bolívar.[23] As Ada Ferrer and John Lawrence Tone have both noted, one key reason for the failure of earlier insurrections against Spanish rule had been the white Cuban elite's racism towards the former black slaves that comprised a large section of the rebel army. The abolition of slavery in 1886 in Cuba left creoles concerned about the possibility of arming and supporting black soldiers from the East (*orientes*) who many felt harboured a desire for a post-revolutionary partition of the island, along the lines of Hispaniola's predominantly black Haiti and whiter Dominican Republic. Tone writes,

> One thing kept a lid on Creole discontent. When the sugar economy took off in Cuba, population [sic] grew rapidly, and the black population grew fastest of all. White Cubans thought the island was becoming 'Africanized' by the very success of the plantation economy. Racial fear . . . induced a certain docility among whites, who saw Spain as a guarantor of the slave system and of white supremacy in Cuba. (Tone 19)

The importance of Martí as a light-skinned, colonially educated creole speaking on behalf of racial harmony in 1895 (just nine years after the abolition of slavery on the island) cannot be overstated. Like Dana, who was a product of the radical wing of the abolitionist movement, Martí saw a focus on questions of class and national identity as a way of challenging pre-existing racial and cultural hierarchies. Denying the Spanish colonisers recourse to race as a tool to maintain their control became a major function of Martí's rhetoric.[24] In both the Cuban insurrectionist press and in the *New York Sun*, however, a stunning irony lay in the fact that making a claim for a 'safe' version of Cuban nationalism relied upon making a dual claim on Martí's racial whiteness. For Cuban creoles, the poet's light skin meant the possibility of people like them supporting an army made up to a large degree of black men. In the USA, it allowed Dana to tie the insurrection in Cuba to 'Western' liberatory conflicts and so differentiate it from the history of slave revolts in the Americas in the minds of his readers. As late nineteenth-century intellectuals operating in the context of essentialised definitions of racial difference, neither Martí nor Dana managed to obliterate race wholly as a socially significant construction, even as they asked for it to be 'transcended' in the service of progressive political and cultural aims. Dana had to 'use' Martí's race to make a claim about revolution, while Martí's own body gave his words potency as a means to mobilise exiled and domestic Cuban creoles. Ferrer has suggested that Martí's 'vision of a transracial Cuban essentially left intact racial categories like white and black, even as it argued for their transcendence'.[25]

Revealing Martí's link to Dana's paper helps us to describe the Cuban author's politics of race, culture and class in their Gilded Age context. As Janet Steele has shown, *The Sun*'s resistance to flashy populism and the mania for pictorial representation of events in Hearst's and Pulitzer's papers took the form of a longstanding commitment to a republican ideological stance known historically as 'producerism' that reflected the paper's origins in the artisanal economy of the 1830s Jacksonian penny press. Rather than a world divided by cultural or racial particularisms, *The Sun* depicted one divided by class, or, more properly, the relative importance of those that *created* against those that lived by the labour of others. Producerism divided society into two primary moral categories: producers and non-producers. Producers were those that created all the wealth yet owned little but their labour; non-producers were those who extracted the income of the 'industrious classes' in the form of rent, interest and the profits gained from buying labour at one price and selling it at another.[26] The ideology of producerism followed by Dana's paper was not wholly hostile to capitalism (at least in its early-market, pre-corporate iteration), and especially where small-scale free markets seemed to provide a legitimate alternative to slavery, but also allowed the paper to advocate collective action in the name of workers' rights (in the form of trade unions). Dana carried this agenda through to the production of the paper itself, which refused to use the new typesetting machines that sped up the printing process but would have led to the obsolescence of skilled printers trained in the dying art of hand-setting.

Dana's politics of producerism were not 'radical' in the sense that more modern thinkers have used the term, and *The Sun* had its blindspots politically. As he aged, Dana came to loathe anarchism, which he saw as a rejection of the fundamental basis of society in co-operation and progressive reform – a value held also by Martí. Additionally, the paper struggled to take a clear line on European expansion into Africa. The legacies of abolitionism in Dana's life and work could often be registered in his sense of 'progress', which even as it questioned corporate capitalism, saw it as a legitimate alternative to the 'greater' horrors of 'primitive' life. These tensions can be seen on the very page that carried the Martí obituary. This spread includes an article damning critics of the Belgian project in the Congo as naive in their belief that 'there is not a single square mile of the earth's surface which man, will not, some day, turn to his own advantage'. The very politics of cultivation and progress that defined producerism often forced Dana into ironic identification with those that would seek to exploit indigenous or tribal societies and the lands they occupied. Such ironies were also present in Martí's politics, which were often hostile to societies that did not accept a version of liberty rooted in some, albeit barely defined, notion of 'modernity'.[27] These similarities in their respective political visions speak to the fact that both the American and the Cuban were subject to similar cultural influences in being intellectuals attempting to find a vision for society in which a positive iteration of modernity could be compatible with both republicanism and the demands of global freedom struggles.

Dana's decision to imagine a world that was divided along economic lines, rather than the racial, national or cultural axes that were being elevated in the yellow papers, allowed Martí to find a space within the paper for his own modernist aesthetic and anti-colonial politics: what Laura Lomas has called a 'proto-Gramscian position . . . [that] advocates the cultivation of critical working-class subjects who wield the only democratic power with which to transform society . . . radical pedagogy and popular education.'[28] Readers of the paper did not see the same obsession with racialised categories or a binary between the feudal 'Old World' and the modern 'New World' that would come to justify American expansionism in the yellow papers. What they did find was an odd mixture of a broadly pro-labour stance with a writerly tone and support for the transformative value of high culture, especially the subtleties of fine prose. Articles by Martí on the aesthetics of 'Flaubert's Last Work' (6 July 1880) jostled for position on the same page of *The Sun* with pieces venerating 'The Democratic Workingmen of California' in a manner that seems to register no inherent conflict between 'high' art and working-class politics. The paper's aim was to compensate for the erosion of the citizenry's rational engagement with politics in the increased speed of information in the new media age by cultivating a social intelligence in its readers and appreciation of the free thinking that was a legacy of American transcendentalism.

In much the same way as Dana's obituary for Martí offered the possibility of an alternative politics in US–Cuban relations, to offer up *The Sun* as a legitimate counter to the dominant narrative of the era's print culture works against the grain of much Americanist criticism. In the obituary for Martí we can see the influence of a 'producerist' bias in his rendering of a man whose 'solid and extensive' learning and hard work was balanced by his instincts for the freedom of others. Yet we also see the influence of New England Transcendentalism in Dana's characterisation of the 'naturalness' of American liberty and the importance of cultivation and learning. This Transcendentalist focus on the indigeneity of American ideas of freedom is qualified by the writer's decision to highlight how the descendants of Spain might also draw upon the liberatory potential of a de-territorialised 'spirit' (or 'tincture') of modernity, understood as the rights of the labourers to the products and profits of their own individual labour. Through Dana's publications Martí found a US-based access point to a collective, international culture of modern improvement that was shared across racial and social groups, but which, importantly, did not suture ideas of 'progress' wholly to the new forms of aggressive corporate capitalism and spectacles they made. Unlike Pulitzer and Hearst who pragmatically manipulated popular taste for their own political and financial ends, Dana came to journalism with an intellectual project in mind – the extension of cultivation and learning to the lower classes and a veneration of collective labour, developed through his association with American Fourierism. During the Cuban War of Independence *The Sun* was a site of alterity within mainstream, mass-market New York print culture that charted a difficult course between the Scylla of a base populism (in the guise of the neo-imperialist yellow journalism) and the Charybdis of cultural elitism (found within the pages of competing Gilded Age literary periodicals that were much less friendly to the underclass, i.e., *Scribner's*, *Century* and *Harpers*). By bringing a Latin American *modernismo* into the orbit of US print culture, Dana's decision to adopt a middle ground in the USA reflected transnationally Martí's own unresolved modernist aesthetic in Latin American literature, described by Susana Rotker as 'the formulation of a space . . . for the paradox of disillusionment and hope . . . The literary space of the struggle' (Rotker 4). For this reason, *The New York Sun* and the Martí–Dana friendship must be accounted for in histories of both literary modernism in the Americas, and of political radicalism. Instead of seeing the paper as Parrington did, as a residue of a by-gone age of cautious, reflective journalism, I have attempted to suggest that it deployed alternative temporalities and Dana's own ill-fit with the tenor of his day in a way that was actually rather *ahead of the curve* – developing a space of unresolved tensions that would eventually speak to the emergence of global modernist aesthetics.

Dana's paper and his friendship with Martí provide a potential seedbed for the project of a shared Latin American and US radical aesthetic that was set back by the emergence of Pulitzer and Hearst as dominating forces in American cultural life. *The Sun* and *The Hour*, therefore, like Martí's chronicles for Latin American papers, may be seen as sites of deliberative liminality and self-reflexivity that are transnational by virtue of their inclusion of sub-alternated Cuban voices and their resistance to the dominant trends defining US culture in the Gilded Age. Furthermore, their friendship can be regarded as a utopian alternative to US–Cuban hostility in the twentieth century, which was interrupted by their deaths in the years immediately preceding the devastating Cuban–Spanish–American War. In bringing Martí into a discussion of North American print culture, I do not wish to 'claim' him for US American Studies so much as demonstrate how print culture and personal affection, 'pure feelings, noble aspirations, and generous ideas', however transient or illusory, can function as sites of the intersection, discussion and translation for radical individuals that might, consequently, serve as the basis for a transnational project directed against shared, global conditions of oppression. Moreover, it helps to highlight the fact that the cultural diversity of work environments – even in the often rarefied fields of literary writing – is often obscured by modes of critical reading that emphasise the incompatibility of cultural worldviews. In looking to labour we can encounter the intrinsic plurality of the everyday prior to the marshalling of multiplicity into discrete modes of *habitus*. Even in the context of conflict over the meaning of 'Cubanness' Martí was not Cuban alone, but a worker, a friend, and a contributor to a collective project of social and cultural uplift that crossed the often policed borders of race, class and culture.

José Martí's Aesthetic Politics

Due to the significant archival and translation work of Philip Foner and Elinor Randall in the 1970s and 1980s, resulting in the multi-volume Monthly Review Press editions of José Martí's works, scholars in Anglophone American Studies have been able to access a fuller body of the Cuban's writings on a variety of subjects; ranging from education and art criticism, to politics and current affairs. This has done much to contribute to the growing reputation of Martí as the pre-eminent Latin American voice in the Americas throughout the 1880s. However, in Anglophone American Studies, Martí still remains known primarily as operating in one of three modes, which present special difficulties for contemporary Martí criticism. Martí has been variously described as: a voice of radical leftist opposition and so an outsider or countercultural figure in American literature (Foner); a prescient harbinger of liberal multiculturalism who appears better fitted to the 1990s than the 1890s (Belnap); the last nineteenth-century flourishing of Pan-American Bolivarism – that is, a republican; and as an apostle of Communism in Cuba (Fidel Castro). Less well documented is Martí's position as a journalist working in New York in the 1880s, especially as a cultural critic for *The New York Sun* and the society weekly *The Hour*. Indeed, these two English-language papers represent the complex valences of Martí's literary voice – the former starting its life as a working-class paper in the penny press mould of the *New York Herald*, the latter an elite publication that covered gallery openings, new literary culture and high-society gossip. To do justice to the ease with which Martí was able to shift between registers requires analysis informed more by print culture studies than traditional labour history. Additionally, a transnational critique reveals how for practitioners and readers of Latin American *modernismo* (the group to whom Martí belonged and whose aesthetic vision he pioneered) these polarities were not in fact contradictions, appearing so only from the perspective of a US intellectual history that has consistently tracked class rather unproblematically to cultural hierarchies. Yet this project of defining class in terms of cultural values was precisely the project of the yellow journalists such as Hearst and Pulitzer who reified cultural hierarchy as a means to harness and limit the revolutionary force of working-class radicalism. For Martí those hierarchies were constantly refuted through deployment of a modernist[a] literary technique that 'uses wilfully opaque, imaginative language that refuses to hand over a positive meaning and thus calls into question the very possibility of mimetic representation' (Lomas 24). An easy conflation of class and cultural hierarchy belies the nature of his literary performances across a variety of publishing platforms and languages in the 1880s. Importantly, Martí's Cuban identity was indistinguishable in this period from the rising tide of literary bohemianism in the New York Anglophone press. That is, for most of the 1880s his political Cubanness was performed in the press as a version of Spanishness that allowed US Americans to access European culture while still clinging to the promise of democracy framed by the American Enlightenment. Moreover, in what follows I will consider more fully the formal elements of the *crónica modernista*, noting how its aesthetic rerouted 'news' through the transnational relay of translation and self-consciously 'difficult' 'art writing' imposed a delay on experience that put pressure on any easy construction of the spectacular Event undertaken by much of the popular press. In addition, then, to considering the print context of Martí's work in English, I will also attempt to outline his theory of aesthetics, which is, by corollary, also a theory of politics.

One of Martí's earliest contributions to the American Anglophone press was a series of three essays he wrote for his friend Charles Dana's society weekly *The Hour*, entitled 'Impressions of America (By a Very Fresh Spaniard)'; one of the twenty-nine he contributed to the magazine over that year. The opening of the first essay (I use this term for ease although Martí hated it), reads:

I am, at last, in a country where every one looks like his own master. One can breathe freely, freedom being here the foundation, the shield, the essence of life. One can be proud of his species here. Every one works; every one reads. Only does one feel in the same degree that they read and work? Man, as a strong creature – made to support on his shoulders the burden of misfortune, never bent, never tired, never dismaying, – is unrivalled here. Are women, those beings that we, the Southern people, like, – feeble and souple, tender and voluptuous, as perfect, in their way as men are to theirs? (32)

In *The Global Remapping of American Literature* Paul Giles considers this piece as a sincere attempt to celebrate the openness and innovation of the United States in opposition to the lazy indulgence by which he characterises European nations. What Giles attempts here is an embrace of the surface of the text, the suggestion that Martí's political commitments to redrawing the geography of modernity rendered his work in English essentially flat at a literary level, operating through a play of readable surfaces: 'Martí employed contradiction not as a method of subversion but as an engaged way of imitating how every social situation and social organization could be looked at from a different point of view' (196). Such a reading is commensurate with the liberal multiculturalist project often attributed to Martí by postmodern literary critics. However, read with an eye to Martí's wry humour, the work as self-conscious performance, the piece transforms slightly to reveal the author's aesthetic and political vision. The author, not, remember, a Latin American – and certainly not a 'Cuban' – but a 'Spaniard', is unnamed in the piece, which has no by-line, and begins by suggesting that although everyone reads in America, reading is not perhaps done in the same degree as work. This serves a dual purpose. It at once calls out the intensity of labour in the USA and self-reflexively challenges the readers of the article to bring the same intensity to the reading of this piece as they would to their money-making enterprises. Buried within platitudes celebrating the United States, then, is a call for an engaged form of close reading that would reveal the subtleties of the author's performance, a form of literary subversion. This veneration of 'work' is presented in opposition to the many consumer opportunities offered by the

United States, which threaten, he implies, to turn it into a mimic of an enfeebled European culture.

Martí's concern with the aesthetic limitations of vision in 'Impressions of America' continues throughout the three episodes. This stance responds to a print culture milieu that had begun, as Shelley Streeby has suggested, to venerate the accelerated temporality of visual spectacle and wonder over the slower, but far more valuable, finesse and subtlety of literary prose of which the poet Martí was an exponent. Episode 3 begins and repeatedly returns to the theme of 'reading' – opening with the statement 'We read in Europe' and ending with an attempt to read the crowd around the narrator as he takes his 'usual nocturne walk' around New York. Across the short piece the author entertains deviations concerning what 'we observe in the newspapers', another paragraph that begins 'What do I see?', before leaving the reader with an image of the urban poor 'seated on benches, shoeless, foodless, concealing their anguish under their dilapidated hats' (40). Yet the first of the 'impressions' begins by highlighting how 'every one looks like his own master'. The qualifier 'looks' casts doubt on the veracity of the author's visionary aesthetic. What follows is a breathless, un-demarcated discussion of plantations in Honduras and fashion on Fifth Avenue that pivots on his discussion of how Americans are prone to 'Liberty in politics, in customs, in enterprises; humble slavery in taste' (34). Real slavery is evoked in the text by references to masters and slaves – once in a discussion of the proceeds of Caribbean labour, another in reference to New Yorker's emulation of European fashions – but left materially unexplored by the essay, forcing the close reader to reflect on the disjunctions and consider how the condition of South American and Caribbean slavery contributes to US prosperity. The author notes that there is in the USA 'not a fixed mind on art, the most striking is the most loved' (34), turning ownership into an exercise of base, unworthy acquisition: 'the censurable pleasure of indiscreetly holding foreign goods bought at a high price' (34). Martí's technique, then, outwardly picks up on the detached aesthetic of European newspaper *flâneurie*, with its claims to capture fleeting impressions in a way that actually conceals a deeper political message of America's complicity with global imperial exploitation. Furthermore, by painting the speaker as a Spaniard, Martí further critiques European aesthetic and political detachment. Indeed, each of the three episodes ends with an image of the impotence of the author, who is rendered so by their aesthetic of vision. The first ends with him attempting to assist an old lady who rebuffs him, saying 'By the hands, no! Go away! Go Away', the second ends with the image of a rich man who 'has forgotten the manner of using [a plough]' (38), and the third ends with itinerant poor upon whom the author can only gaze morosely. Consequently, Martí evokes a third subjective space that lies within the gaps between hegemonic power bases.

The strength of this critique relies on the clever nature of his transnational performance as a light-hearted, 'fresh', European aesthete. The overtly dramatic nature of the piece highlights an embodied consciousness that is at odds with the detached aesthetic frequently attributed to the magazine *flâneur*. This effect is produced partly by the publication of the 'Impressions' in *The Hour*, nestled in its first printing between a news piece about the suppression of the Jesuit order in Paris and a first-hand account of the failed pursuit of Jesse James after the Northfield Bank Robbery. In that context, Martí's aesthetic of diversity and deviation, while holding to a broadly cosmopolitan and liberal vision, serves as a reflection of the author's liminal position in relation to hegemonic culture, which is also that of *The Hour* paper itself. The subtitle 'By a Very Fresh Spaniard' is a case in point, particularly the qualifier 'fresh' – a pun that connotes in several directions. First, it constitutes an image of immigration – a new Spaniard in a rapidly industrialising and diversifying USA. Immigration and the changing racial and cultural makeup of New York was a common theme in *The Hour* editorials. The final line of the first episode reinforces this. Speaking of the old lady who refuses the narrator's help, he remarks 'Was she an old Puritan?'. His puzzlement at her status reveals the changing social makeup of the United States – he implicitly questions whether she is a relic of an old America that no longer exists. The second meaning is New York slang from the nineteenth century, meaning 'impudent, presumptuous': a reference perhaps to his unwillingness to exhibit restraint in what he discusses and how he will do it. This is an embrace of an aesthetic vision. This is further reinforced by the final meaning of 'fresh', a sexual one – implying a fastness of manner associated both with the Spaniard and with the bohemian. Episode 2 of the 'Impressions' picks up on this performance of louche sexual frankness. It is a discourse on the relative intelligence and beauty of European and American women. The position the narrator adopts is complexly threatening and jovial.

I have shown above that the fact *The Hour* was edited and owned by Martí's friend Charles Anderson Dana, whose literary project represented the last true lineage of antebellum transcendentalism in the American Gilded Age, significantly impacted the nature of his literary and political project. Like Dana's daily paper *The Sun*, *The Hour* was a largely politically liberal paper that attempted to cultivate intellect in distinction to the allure of base sensationalism and untutored political passion. It was a paper in which words and arguments mattered. Where *The Hour* differed from *The Sun* (a paper for which Martí wrote hundreds of articles) was in the particular audience it catered for: a New York elite. The distinctions between *The Sun* and *The Hour* reveal the strange, and ultimately failed synthesis of liberal elite and working-class progressives that characterised Dana's vision of America (one informed, quite clearly by, radical abolitionism and transcendentalism in an earlier era). However, these unresolved tensions allowed Martí to find a space within the paper for his own modernist aesthetic. This is developed through an aesthetic of delay and questioning that opens up the world to the possibility of revolutionary disruptions as Emerson would characterise them, and creates dissensus (in the terms of Rancière). Not only does this come to the reader in the heavy reliance of the narrator on rhetorical questions, but also through Martí's own technique of multiple translation, which slowed down the perception of events and resisted the logic of the spectacle. Some of his articles were initially written in French, then translated into English by Martí himself, further distancing his chronicles from the spectacular immediacy of spectacular contemporary news. This was well-suited to the demands of his publication context. What readers found in Dana's publications was an odd mixture of cross-class sympathy, a writerly tone and support for the transformative value of high culture, especially the subtleties of fine prose, that suited Martí's demands for the importance of attentive, active reading.

The pluralism of Martí's chronicles – the shifts of topic, range of reference, and the strange temporalities of the genre – serve as an example of the form of working-class writing that Rancière suggests characterises 'modernity' and undermines the traditional pattern of politics, albeit not by means of representative spectacle, but through the material fact of the time taken in the production and consumption of the literary object; a 'free' time for aesthetics that under capitalism it is not typically the worker's right to claim. As Giuseppina Mecchia has noted in her reading of Rancière's works *The Nights of Labor* and *The Philosopher and His Poor* on earlier nineteenth-century workers' movements, a truly radical workers' writing existed outside of the institutional frameworks of ideology and in service of democracy and,

> was criticised because of its 'unseemliness': it is just not proper for a worker to write poetry at night. The very fact that the workers did indeed do so was a political act much more shocking than any labor-related demand, because it implied a deeper sharing with the privileged classes than financial privilege: the relation of language and understanding (Mecchia, 'Mute Speech: The Silence of Literature in Rancière's Aesthetic Paradigm' in Bray, 102).

The radicalism of Martí's *crónicas modernista* therefore lies in their anti-spectacular and decelerated temporality, which utilises abundance of content, changes of direction, and literary subtlety not as a marker of an elite status and knowledge that stultifies its readers as Bourdieu would read aesthetics (a value frequently attributed to later modernism proper in the hands of Eliot or Pound) but as a material reminder of the workers' right to equality; to own what they do not yet have, and claim what they have been denied. This is a radical modernism that has its roots in the specific print culture context of which Martí and Dana were a part and which would eventually be usurped by the spectacular styles of Pulitzer and Hearst's new or 'yellow' journalism in the era of the Cuban War of Independence. It represents an attempt to unify aspirations towards cultural development and education with the demands of the oppressed to equality and democracy, and serves as a reminder that revolutionary power can lie within literature beyond its capacity for spectacle, 'representation' or the structuring of the Event. The dream of modernity and democracy can therefore be embodied in the exoteric materiality of non-representational forms. The simple fact of the existence of certain styles such as that of Martí's chronicles, and the time required for their composition and consumption, points to a will to reorganise the world through the reorganisation of time, while resisting the urge to marshal diversity into a monadic unity that would close down the open plurality of potential futures. Like *The Sun*, *The Hour* was a site of alterity within mainstream, mass-market New York print culture that charted a difficult course between cultural elitism and democratic politics – drawing aesthetic pleasure from high-class gossip and obscure, literary references while clinging to the hope of progressive development.

The Hour became for Martí a space to fashion a US version of the unresolved modernist aesthetic he had pioneered in Latin American literature, described by Susana Rotker as 'the formulation of a space . . . for the paradox of disillusionment and hope . . . The literary space of the struggle' (Rotker 4). Rejecting aesthetic detachment as a politically dangerous exercise that leads to liberal impotence, Martí deployed close reading and artful literary performance as a technique with which to produce engagement and develop a subjectivity that expressed itself in the gaps between normative, hegemonic social positions – a technique that looks forward to the Harlem Renaissance and the American-in-Paris modernism of the Imagists or of the 'little magazines'.

Finally it is worth pointing out that Martí was one of New York's premier critics of European Impressionism in painting. Indeed, he was *The Hour* and the Argentinian paper *La Nación*'s primary art critic and frequently criticised Impressionism for its political neutrality and absence of rigour. In one article, 'Impressionist Painters', he remarks 'There is a great love in this country [speaking of France] for all that is Japanese and extravagant, which has unhinged the minds of the good school of open-air painters' (Martí in Allen, 169), after having dedicated much of the article to a gritty discussion of The Knights of Labor railway strike. While he regularly decried the limitations of vision in a way that might place his work on a parallel with the aesthetic project of Impressionism in the arts, what is clear from the essay is the extent to which impressionistic design, cultural attainment and a focus on aesthetics means nothing without a comparable commitment to social justice of the kind Martí advocated in his work. It is not enough to favour aesthetic impression as would the aesthete, there must also be the will to change the world. Otherwise aesthetic incompleteness indexes only inattention. The titling of 'Impressions of America' has more than a little of the in-joke about it, suggesting a negativity that is not necessarily there at the surface level of the text itself. 'Impressionism' is a trigger word for Martí, an example of flimsiness of thinking, and an embrace of speed and instantaneity that cannot serve as a meaningful critique of the worst impulses of modernity. This applies equally to New Yorkers who devour European art culture as to Europeans who produce it. Consequently, 'Impressions of America' is itself a performance of the kind of inattention against which Martí railed relentlessly, a satiric performance that calls on readers to ask for more from their art and their critics.

Martí's oeuvre blossomed in a context where racialisation and pseudo-ethnological accounts of difference were reliant upon the increasing tempo of technology and newsprint, and against the backdrop of American and Spanish imperial war. In response to this, he mobilised an aesthetic politics that rendered complexity, excess and plurality as necessary components of radical politics, countering an elite fixation on 'giving the public what they want' to control their responses and the direction of their anger. This version of proto-modernism of the political Left represents something of a road not taken for American literature, as the elite aspirations of later modernists came to bury the style's origins in a more egalitarian and progressive milieu. Like Emerson before him, Martí's Americanist literary credentials, as well as his more politically radical ones, rested on *delay* and the disruption of the spectacular Event so as to simultaneously challenge a resurgent (and potent) racism and advocate for popular education as integral to working-class liberation. In the next chapter, I will turn to the works of Stephen Crane to explore how this aesthetic politics manifested in the New York scene of the turn of the century as an attempt to marry literary experimentalism in form to radical pluralism in culture.

Notes

1. *The Evening World*, 24 May 1895, p. 5.
2. Spencer, *The Yellow Journalism*.
3. See Perez Jr., *The War of 1898*; Schoonover, *Uncle Sam's War*.
4. Ward, *Mainstreams of American Media History*.
5. See Francis, *Transcendental Utopias*.
6. This somewhat downplays the importance of *The Harbinger*, which was not only a record of life at Brook Farm but also after 1846 named 'the official organ of Associationism in the United States by the American Union of Associationists' (Delano 18). 'Associationism' was the US name for the co-operative politics described by Charles Fourier. Labour was shared out equally, as were the profits of that labour, in the hope that domestic arrangements and work might be as egalitarian and democratic as possible. For more on the history of the paper and 'Associationism' in the antebellum USA see Delano, *The Harbinger and New England Transcendentalism*.
7. As the cultural anthropologist Victor Turner famously noted, rituals often 'attempt to transcend an order based on rational principles [including an Enlightenment conflation of modernity with nationalism] by appealing to that order which rests on a tradition of co-existence among predecessors of the current community, whether these are conceived as biological ancestors or bearers of the same communal values'. Turner, *The Anthropology of Performance*, p. 91.
8. See Loraux, *The Invention of Athens*.
9. See Lowry, 'The Flower of Cuba'.
10. See Karras, 'José Martí'.
11. Rotker, p. 62.
12. González, *José Martí*, p. 12.
13. Giles, 'Parallel Worlds', p. 185.
14. Martí, 'Our America', pp. 295–6. This famous article on the politics of Latin American identity and Cuban nationalism, which has been adopted as a universal claim to multiculturalism, or even postracialism, was conceived strategically to assist Martí's project of developing a multiracial base of support for the Cuban insurgency as well as wider Latin American anti-imperialism. Jeffrey Belnap has suggested that 'Our America' was '[w]ritten in the aftermath of a set of inter-American conferences in which Martí had been instrumental in convincing Latin American representatives to reject US proposals antithetical to their interests . . . Siblings produced by the same processes of imperial miscegenation, Our America's nation-states are composed of kindred hierarchical relationships in which predominantly *criollo* ruling classes . . . rule over disenfranchised Native American, African, and mixed-race peoples' ('Headbands, Hemp Sandals, and Headresses: The Dialectics of Dress and Self-Conception in Martí's "Our America"', in Belnap and Fernández (ed.), *José Martí's 'Our America'*. See also Lomas, *Translating Empire*.
15. Roggenkamp, p. 58.
16. Dana, *The Art of Newspaper Making*, p. 23.

17. See Roggenkamp and Lowry. The Evangelina Cisneros affair, when the Hearst syndicate staged a dramatic rescue of a Cuban woman held in Havana, before using her as an example of the 'feminine' and 'dependent' Cuban people, has often been cited as a major event in the lead up to the Spanish–American War.
18. Stephen Crane in Perez Jr., p. 81.
19. Ferrer, *Insurgent Cuba*, p. 113.
20. Dana in Wilson, 497.
21. Streeby, *Radical Sensations*, p. 35.
22. Spencer, *The Yellow Journalism*.
23. See Zacaïr, 'Haiti on his Mind'.
24. See Ferrer, *Insurgent Cuba*.
25. Ferrer, *Insurgent Cuba*, p. 127.
26. Steele, pp. 4–5.
27. One can see this in Martí's initial hostility to the Haymarket anarchists. As Esther Allen has noted, 'in an article on the trial written for *La Nación* in September, 1886, Martí expressed little or no sympathy for the anarchists and no doubt at all about their guilt. He went so far as to claim that the death penalty itself was the most certain guarantor of that guilt, since the jury, allegedly threatened by anarchists still at large, imposed it at a risk to their own lives' (in Martí, *Selected Works*, p. 195). He later rethought his position, but still remained largely hostile to Anarchism and aggressive forms of Marxism, which he saw as brutish, base and, ostensibly, 'primitive'.
28. Lomas, *Translating Empire*, p. 122.

CHAPTER 3

Manacled to Identity: Fugitive Aesthetics in Stephen Crane's Pluralistic Universe

In May 1900 the American author and journalist Stephen Crane published the short story 'Manacled' in the London magazine *The Argosy*. In several senses Crane was the archetype for expatriate American authors of the later modernist era; writing, publishing and settling in England at a time when he was facing increasing hostility in the US press for the bohemian character of his work and his decadent, nonconformist lifestyle. Crane's circle of friends and associates in *fin-de-siècle* Great Britain reads like a checklist of some of the most successful and important writers of the age. Henry James and Joseph Conrad were frequent visitors to his home at Brede in East Sussex, Rudyard Kipling was approached to complete his final, unfinished novel *The O'Ruddy*, H. G. Wells wrote a glowing obituary of Crane in the August 1900 issue of *The North American Review* and Arnold Bennett and Ford Madox Ford were emphatic in their praise. Whereas his US critical notices after *The Red Badge of Courage* (1895) had been increasingly disparaging, British critics had been generally more favourable across the whole of his career. For this reason the decision to publish 'Manacled' first in the London *Argosy* rather than with the New York syndicates that had previously carried his short fiction was in keeping with the broad trajectory of Crane's career in the final years of the 1890s. Indeed, Crane did not settle in his home country and they would not readily claim him for their own, at least not until after his death. By 1895 cosmopolitan mobility became Crane's personal and artistic *raison d'être*. After leaving Asbury Park, New Jersey as a teenager

Crane lived in New York, Florida, Greece, Cuba and Britain, seldom settling for long before a new journalistic commission moved him on to pastures new.

At one time *The Argosy* had been a leading light of the Victorian periodical scene and had appealed to the middle classes through a careful pairing of the lush, Pre-Raphaelite-inspired illustrations of William Small with fictional content that shuttled between popular categories of the sensational and sentimental. By 1900, though, *The Argosy* had begun to face financial difficulties and a declining readership. In 1871 the magazine had been sold to the famous publishers Richard Bentley & Sons, whose prior successes with the publication of Charles Dickens, Edward Bulwer-Lytton, James Fenimore Cooper, Frances Trollope and other major authors in cheap 'Standard' single-volume editions seemed to suggest that the publishing house would be well-placed to help the periodical capture the rising, literate, lower-middle-class readership of late-Victorian Britain.[1] The move, though, had left the magazine awkwardly placed in a literary marketplace that was becoming increasingly bifurcated and diversified along lines of class and culture and in 1901 it folded.

In a cruel and ironic parallel with the fate of the publication in which his story appeared, by 1900 Crane was also facing severely declining health and fortunes. A month after the publication of 'Manacled' in London the twenty-eight-year-old Crane died of a lung haemorrhage at a health spa in the German town of Badenweiler. Indeed, it is tempting to read 'Manacled' biographically as both a prescient foreshadowing of his own fate and a more general allegory of authorial, artistic and critical decline. Set in the shabby 'Theatre Nouveau ... upon a street which was not of the first importance' (1291), in a transatlantic city space that is deliberately devoid of identifying features, the story describes the last moments in the life of an actor who is forced to perform a dull, artistically unambitious melodrama for a 'pitying audience' (1291) in which 'real horses drunk real water out of real buckets ... dragging a real wagon off stage' (1291). When the theatre catches fire, the unnamed actor finds that he is unable to escape because the crowd's demand for verisimilitude has led to the use of 'real handcuffs on his wrists and real anklets on his ankles' (1291). Like *The Argosy* itself, the actor is unable to balance adequately between a residual demand for sentimental melodrama and a new trend for realism that was coming to dominate late nineteenth-century transatlantic literary culture. In a neat joke Crane even transfers this problem onto the theatre itself, which is called *Nouveau* but performs material that is distinctly *passé*, even *ancien*.

In 'Manacled', Crane exaggerates the 'realness' of the fictional play so as to probe the limits of realism as an authorial practice and satirise its attempts to represent the truth of the world 'out there' through fiction. In this way, Crane's work at this point (and indeed before) undertook a kind of critical realism that questions the terms of its own composition and purpose in a way much similar to that of Howells after the Haymarket affair. By presenting the reader with a vision of dangerous effects of stasis, Crane argues that realistic fictions frequently abandoned any ethical imperatives that may have been attendant upon the writer in favour of textualising their subjects as the products of a particular temporal and spatial locus. In so doing, the author also dramatises the very process that would prompt a crisis for *The Argosy* magazine – the emergence of increasingly fixed cultural hierarchies in America and Britain organised around class position and artistic taste. Mark McGurl has argued in his Bourdieusian reading of the cultural field of late nineteenth-century American literature that as a writer operating between categories of 'popular' and 'art' fiction, Crane's work and career was shaped by an almost debilitating quest for literary prestige, to be, as it were, a Henry James of the saloon or the billiards hall.[2] The disabled protagonist of 'Manacled', bound to burn in the theatre (a very house of culture) due to the untenable demands placed upon his art, could certainly be read as a proxy for the Crane's real-life career struggles, which were many and serious. Yet, Crane's argument seems more that the search for any kind of fixed position in the culture field – either as a writing of 'working-class' fiction, as ethnographer of immigrant cultures, or as an elite high realist (positions he all held in some degree in his life) – carried its own sense of failure. His answer to this sense of failure was a body of work that sought to mobilise aesthetic dissensus for his readers as a form of literary democracy that might combat the inertia that inheres in conceptions of the literary 'cultural field'. His 'legacy' or longevity would not come to rely, then, on status in his own moment, but in a form of literature that would persist by means of works that would promote a constant kind of mental flight; a fugitive aesthetic that was not dissimilar to Crane's own cosmopolitan shuttling between distant locations and homes throughout his career.

If 'Manacled' as a title gives the impression of enslavement then it is designed to. In numerous ways, the story is a natural complement to other works of Crane that deal more directly with race and with post-emancipation identities and politics, most notably 'The Monster'. The warning is clear. The reification of identities through sociological modes of literary representation that lay claim to scientific precision is a dangerous trap, especially where they impact the precarious and neglected in the social order, because they are far from precise and often capture only the *a priori* sensibilities of those that make them. In its place Crane seeks out an alternative political purpose for art: one based on pluralism and readerly affect over and above authorial intention. Crane's setting for 'Manacled' foregrounds the importance of art and culture to his narrative, while his insistence on the status of the theatre as 'not of the first importance' flags up the relation between the story and vexed questions of taste and class. Lawrence Levine has suggested that more than any other space, by the late nineteenth century the theatre had become a clear marker of the establishment of a hierarchy of culture; a location of societal bifurcation along lines of class (Levine 88). This bifurcation of the market was also a division of the forms of culture presented, such that, for the most part, melodrama and music-hall became the province of working-class audiences, while high drama and opera were reserved for the middle and upper classes. In the terms I have outlined in this book thus far, the implication was that the literary and cultural marketplace had by this period entered into a vicious cycle of sociological and anthropological thinking that saw art as an expression of *habitus* rather than a system of values independent of cultural or class norms. With 'Manacled' Crane brings together the impulses of a high realism and the material of melodrama to highlight how both operate within troubling, fixed regimes of representation that undermine the dissensus-building and pluralistic power of literary and artistic expression.

This impulse recurred frequently in Crane's work and was shared by his benefactor William Dean Howells. An intriguing piece Crane wrote in October 1894, 'Howells Fears Realists Must Wait', dramatises this sensibility and his critique of mere mimetic verisimilitude through a fictionalised interview with Howells. The article reads like fiction. It is composed from the third-person perspective and utilises what can only be called a *de-realisation* effect to transform living people into characters in a drama or novel: a kind of proto-modernist auto- or meta-fiction. In it Crane appears as the 'other man' (*Prose and Poetry*, 615) who is interviewing Howells about his philosophy. Into Howells's mouth the author puts the following anecdote (worth quoting at length) – perhaps real, perhaps apocryphal:

> 'I have a little scene,' he at last said slowly. 'I saw a young girl out in a little Ohio town once – she was the daughter of a carpet-woman there – that is to say, her mother made rag carpets and rugs for the villagers. And this girl had the most wonderful instinct in manner and dress. Her people were of the lowest of the low and yet this girl was a lady. It used to completely amaze me – to think how this girl could grow there in that squalor. She was as chic as chic could be and yet the money spent and the education was nothing – nothing at all . . . It overturned so many of my rooted social dogmas' (615)

The quotation of 'Howells' is almost too good to be true. Indeed, the patina of fictionality that hovers over the tale through Crane's aesthetic style casts doubt upon it. Into the mouth of 'Howells', Crane puts forward the primary thesis of his novel of the year before, *Maggie: A Girl of the Streets,* in questioning the relationship between contextual squalor and personal beauty and taste in a way that suggests something of a puff or free advert for the novel – still available in bookshops. Yet beyond the powerful thesis statement of 'Howells' concerning how this individual 'overturned so many of my rooted social dogmas' about class and the relationship between context and art, which might have been drawn directly from *A Hazard of New Fortunes* or *A Modern Instance,* there is a meaningful engagement with the values of late realism, shared by Howells and Crane. What follows is a question by the 'other man' about 'The Story of a Play' (Howells's real work in progress) as to whether the author should 'raise [his] voice towards reforming the abuses that are popularly supposed to hide in the manager's office' (615). 'Howells' replies 'I do not', before continuing to note that 'it does no good to go at things hammer and tongs in this obvious way ... A man should mean something when he writes' (616). The statement seems confused, and it would be tempting to suggest that Crane is criticising Howells for vagueness and political neutrality (a criticism that could hardly be levelled seriously after his public position on Haymarket), but the claim that a 'man should mean something when he writes' (616) is not so much hypocritical as it is a defence of literature as an aesthetic regime of power that exists somewhat apart from the moralising pieties of reform writing. Reform novels, Howells seems to suggest, risk a violence to their subjects by having 'their noses ... [too] tight against life' (616) and disrupting the 'important matter' (at least for fiction) 'proportion' (616). In much the same way as Crane, 'Howells' here sees a lack of 'perspective made for the benefit of people who have no true use of their eyes' (616) – that is, American readers – in reform writing and characterisations of the working class that render surprising or alien the moments when class does not match context (as in the moment with the girl from Ohio), when, in fact, 'daily life in the most exact terms' (616) is full of such instances. Having one's 'nose' too 'tight against life' is to produce a flat image devoid of hope or futurity. The title of the piece, 'Howells Fears Realists Must Wait', does two things. It is a headline that captures the concerns voiced by the 'other man' (Crane) about the fate of realism: 'Last winter ... it seemed that realism was almost about to capture things, but then recently I have thought that I saw coming a sort of a counter-wave – a flood of the other' (617) (namely, a sentimentalism that overly adorns life or a hard naturalism that reduces it to scientific systems), to which 'Howells' replies sagely, 'we shall have to wait' (618) . It is also an aesthetic claim that realism exists to slow down the accelerated tempo of moral judgement and the erosion of 'perspective' that comes with it when writers too quickly turn literature to the ends of ideological propaganda. Realists will have to wait and see what follows, but realists should also be willing to make their readers wait and withhold their judgements, a technique that relies upon the ambiguities of literary language.

To call out the peculiar spatio-temporal imaginary of cultural determinism, the sense that it is both too quick to judge and situates its characters in a deep time of little relevance to the present moment, in 'Manacled', Crane cleverly couches cultural hierarchies in the language of geology in order to reflect his own creative moment, when the demand for verisimilitude in representation and what George Stocking, Mark Pittenger and others have diagnosed as the dominant Lamarckian and Darwinian theories of evolution and heredity in Gilded Age thought, were attaching increasing importance to the role of environment in the shaping of social manners and behaviours. George Stocking has argued that more than Darwinism by some way the most dominant theory of evolution, heredity and adaptation in the transatlantic *fin-de-siècle* was a version derived from the work of the French naturalist Jean-Baptiste Lamarck. Rather than locating evolutionary change and development within the remarkably *longue durée* of geographical 'deep time', in which is nigh on impossible to know precisely what organisms or groups will thrive ultimately under present conditions, Lamarckianism stressed how more immediate social and environmental factors could be registered by the organism and passed on within the space of a single generation. Stocking argues that

> The Lamarckianism of the *fin-de-siècle* American social science also had sources within the tradition of nineteenth century social thought itself. A number of its major figures – among them Auguste Comte, Lewis Henry Morgan, and Herbert Spencer – were either implicitly or avowedly believers in the hereditability of acquired characteristics. (Stocking 1982: 240)

In Crane's own moment the dominance in social scientific and literary circles of Herbert Spencer (a scion of ideas of Lamarckian heredity) ensured the continued presence of Lamarckianism in the late nineteenth-century scene long after the academic acceptance of Darwinian evolution. The implication of this Lamarckianism was the absolute dominance of one milieu on the shape of one's character, a sort of rigid cultural determinism that nineteenth-century aestheticism sought to combat through its sense that the world was artistic and the future could be effected by creative will.

As the fire rips through the theatre, Crane notes how

> the building hummed and shook; it was like a glade which holds some bellowing cataract of the mountains. Most of the people killed on the stairs clutched their play-bills in their hands as if they had resolved to save them at all costs. (1291)

Not only can the actor not move because the manacles demanded by the audience's taste for realism physically inhibit him from doing so, but the playgoers die fixed in attitudes precipitated by their cultural choices, which, since the Lamarckian bent of popular discussions of behaviour described one's cultural choices and values as a product wholly of one's environment, trap the individual in an inexorable feedback loop. Importantly, 'the people killed on the stairs' clutch neither at each other for comfort nor at the railings or doors for safety, but at 'their play-bills', as if identifying and preserving their cultural status and position was more significant than preserving their own lives. In this passage Crane generates connections between processes of artistic consumption, geographical deep time, death and the will to 'resolve' or 'save' in a way that seems to render the actions of the individuals historical in a manner that is reminiscent of anthropological and geological practices of observation and classification.

Crane's use of the term 'resolve' is particularly interesting in this context. The word exhibits a peculiar ambivalence; simultaneously connoting an individual's will (their resolve) and in an age of the photographic image, both the process by which a picture emerges on a plate (to resolve) and the 'resolution' i.e. the quality of the visual rendering of that object. The word 'resolve' therefore does a considerable amount of cultural work in Crane's story by suggesting that techniques of representation – perhaps here the 'resolving' photographic plate – condition the expectations of the subject of that representation – their will. There is a peculiar temporality at play that suggests that the people on the stairs are 'resolved' in their cultural attitudes prior to their capture in the fire, which acts as a kind of fixative agent. This is a photographic and sociological imaginary that shapes the subjectivity of the subject through a kind of ambient preconditioning. The audience know how they will react and what values they hold prior to the writer's rendering of that event. What the ambivalence of 'resolve' in both its meanings as the ongoing process of condensing disparate elements into one, and as an act of will, does in Crane's story is remove from the image of the people fleeing a burning theatre the element of shock or contingency – even in a moment of actual crisis. The word highlights the collapse of temporality into a flat plane devoid of hope that occurs when culture and class positions are relativised into discrete Others. The Event of the fire, therefore, is predictable. Fixed cultural positions, when made synonymous with class and taste (that is, when made *habitus* in the sense Pierre Bourdieu would use the term), are a form of social death. Moreover, there is a kind of feedback loop between the reality effects of the mechanical photograph and the creation of *habitus*, while the poetics of Crane's prose mobilise both possibility and critique. The more accurate and 'realistic' the 'resolution' of the rendering of the Event, the more it promotes 'resolve' in the subject, leading to a kind of reality trap or feedback loop. Sociological accuracy conditions the subject towards seeing themselves through the eyes of the oppressive regimes that empowered that representation and by no other means. Aesthetic complexity, by contrast, opens the subject up to the possibility of other worlds. The temporal ambiguity generated through literary word choice – 'resolve' as both the precondition for action and the process of the appearance of the rendering of an event – liberates the literary reader in a way mere accuracy cannot.

Natalie Cecire has noted in her comparison of Crane's poetic technique to the expositional epistemology of flash photography that 'In its instantaneity, flash offers brevity. Yet this in not a brevity of sparseness or withholding. Rather, flash's brevity is one of sufficiency, even plentitude, suggesting condensation or contraction' (*Experimental*, 57). Yet Crane's aesthetic, the often short sentences, intense visuality and so forth that we see in works like 'Manacled' is a literary technique that more than reflecting flash photography's speed, parodies or travesties it, since 'while flash always rests its authority on a sense of instantaneity, that sense may be produced by the condensation of information gathered slowly, laboriously, and tediously into a single coup d'œil, rather than the scene of instantaneous production on which, for instance, the flash photograph relies' (57). Importantly, Crane's aestheticism is based on the reader taking time with words. It is a form of manipulated or overworked realism that transforms the spectacular Event into a complex pattern of less coherent or easily digested linguistic microevents that inflect the verisimilitude of late nineteenth-century image-making with ambiguity and potentiality by liberating the spectator to trust their own aesthetic interests.

Crane's poetics in 'Manacled' recall the criticisms of photography and mechanical image-making undertaken by his contemporary, the art photographer Alfred Stieglitz. In an 1892 essay 'A Plea for Art Photography in America', Stieglitz undertook something of a heresy against the photographic purists when he argued that the 'art photography' based in photomanipulation and interference with the print such as he would come to undertake with the Photo Secession and his editorship at *Camera Work* magazine from 1902 was necessary for real life to be given a spirituality and luminosity that could challenge the utilitarianism of capitalist America and the tool-like use of photography by ethnographers and sociologists. Moreover, by means of photographic manipulation photography could be an artform in the service of freedom and social change. In the essay Stieglitz sought to champion a photographic practice that fashioned neither 'far-fetched and unnatural'[3] scenes as an easy path to 'originality', nor adopted 'conventionality' by depicting 'the same types of country roads, of wood interiors, the everlasting waterfall, village scenes; we see the same groups at doorsteps'. Instead he favoured the production of 'tone' within everyday scenes to cultivate an 'atmosphere' and feeling of possibility. He wrote

> Atmosphere is the medium through which we see all things. In order, therefore, to see them in their true value on a photograph, as we do in Nature, atmosphere must be there. Atmosphere softens all lines; it graduates the transition from light to shade; it is essential to the reproduction of the sense of distance. That dimness of outline which is characteristic for distant objects is due to atmosphere. Now, what atmosphere is to Nature, tone is to a picture. (Stieglitz, 'A Plea for Art Photography in America')

What Stieglitz meant by 'atmosphere', as it pertained to Nature, was that in the 'softening' of 'all lines' (in the de-resolution of the image) a sense of movement and fluid temporality could be generated. Transitions between shades become 'gradual', rather than stark, and a 'sense of distance' (which is also a sense of future time) is cultivated. As Stieglitz goes on to note in a statement that is at once aesthetic and political: 'The sharp outlines which we Americans are so proud of as being proof of great perfection in our art are untrue to Nature, and hence an abomination to the artist.' Stieglitz's pro-immigrant pluralism and socialism therefore found their aesthetic compliment in the complex tonalities of photogravure printing, which resisted the documentary demands of a merely scientific photography while not abandoning its focus on the real world of everyday life. The energy of an image such as Stieglitz's 1902 photogravure 'The Hand of Man' (Figure 3.1) depends upon this sense of atmosphere and tonal ambiguity, which transform a frequently loathed quotidian object, the steam train, into a carriage of modern possibility and social hope. The same impulse is at play

Figure 3.1 Alfred Stieglitz, 'The Hand of Man' (1902, printed 1910).

in his most famous photograph, 'The Steerage', where in transforming another frequently loathed micro-event, the arrival of immigrants into the USA, into a source of aesthetic contemplation and wonder, he reworks the regimes of power that undergird the political transformation of people into 'types'. Stieglitz's photograph is of a piece with Howells and Crane's realism in its suggestion that to capture everyday life art must be more, not less, 'aesthetic', precisely because the precarity of the everyday in the modern world is felt by its subjects as an experience of endless change, such that in viewing a photograph that itself appears to shift we are brought onto a plane of democratic empathy with its subject. With an image such as 'The Hand of Man', as with the poetic vibrancy of Crane's prose style, the urge for representation (a kind of stock-taking of Gilded Age and Progressive Era materiality) gives way to an experience of encounter with the art object. The aesthetic regime of the image or story intervenes in the process of 'resolution'; of the mapping of an image onto a set of predefined behaviours and attributes. This new feeling is what Rancière has referred to as art's capacity to affect a 'redistribution of the sensible', whose impacts are political since they mobilise a critique of common-sense/normative understandings of the relationship between an image and its referent. In reckoning with the aesthetics of literary and artistic works in the late nineteenth century, therefore, we cannot fall into the habit of assuming that works of art fit easily and comfortably within established patterns of social organisation such as is implied by Pierre Bourdieu's sociology, since in describing art this way the critic too becomes a cog in that machine of unfreedom, not truly engaged with the process of critique, which is an exercise not only of description but of imagining other worlds and opportunities. As Rancière remarks in *Aesthetics and Its Discontents*,

> Sociology in Bourdieu's time had doubtless left behind its original dreams of social organization. For the good of science, however, it has continued to desire what the representative order desired, for the good of social and poetic distinctions: that separate classes have distinct senses. (13)

The aestheticism of Crane or Stieglitz, then, is not designed to exclude, but to open up the possibility that a truly potent art is also a democratic one, available to all who choose to engage with it, regardless of the position from which they start.

Returning to Crane, the word 'resolve' therefore self-consciously 'naturalises' the individual within a cultural and environmental context, collapsing the distinction between individual subjectivity and the act of viewing: the first and third person. This is picked up in the story through a repeated technique of deliberately confusing the human and the non-human and the living and non-living. As the conflagration grows, the narrator remarks how 'the thunder of the fire-lions made the theatre have a palsy' (1293). The elemental 'fire' is transformed into 'lions' and the material space of the theatre seems to have the distinctly nervous, organic response of 'a palsy'. The narrative of the story consistently jumps between third-person descriptions of events and images and the internal, subjective thoughts of the protagonist in a way that embeds character within context, implying that forces seemingly beyond their control have begun to overwhelm the individual. As the actor succumbs to the effects of the fire, he is described as feeling 'very cool, delightfully cool' (1293). Like the figures on the stairs, he perversely seems to freeze to death as if he were in the heart of a glacier when he is, rather, in the heart of a raging fire: the subject of an irredeemable geographical and mental inertia. The lexical and tonal similarity between the protagonist's feeling and the image of the crowd draws the reader into a third space of representation that is neither subjective, nor objective. Patrick Dooley has remarked that Crane's aesthetics, shaped by the influence of American pragmatism, allowed him to develop a style in which 'neither the spectator's nor the participant's view deserves pre-eminence or authority . . . [because] the point of view of every participant is selective and limited' (Dooley, *The Pluralistic Philosophy of Stephen Crane*, 29). Instead, a third view is made possible that exists only at the level of literary language and aesthetics, which suspends the pull towards the first or third person, the foreground and the background, context and subject, naive individualism or incapacitating collectivism.

Following the American Civil War, and the challenges it posed to the older perceived certainties of antebellum nationalism, writers sought new sources of authority in which to locate and ground narratives of contemporary experience. Brad Evans has noted that this new search for authority produced a boom of interest in 'ethnographic enquiries' (Evans 2005: 83) into folklore and 'local color' that allowed the scientific classification and survey work of groups such as the American Geological Survey and the Bureau of American Ethnology to find popular readerships. This ethnographical survey work began at precisely the moment that the broadly sentimental narrative of national unity began to decline in the face of a developing modernity. In effect, a version of nationalism organised around collective feeling and sympathy could not survive the rise of corporate capitalism and the fracturing of the nation, what William Dean Howells called (borrowing from Shakespeare) 'A Hazard of New Fortunes'. Instead of national unity, American social scientists began to cultivate an image of American national experience organised around diversity. Such an agenda became all the more complex when class came to be seen in the same terms. The contemporary trend for slum writing, reform journalism and urban exposés, best exemplified by Jacob Riis's bestselling phototext *How the Other Half Lives: Studies Among the Tenements of New York* (1890) and Charles Loring Brace's infamous *The Dangerous Classes of New York* (1872), contributed to a sense that class position resembled the forms of cultural and racial difference studied by the ethnologists. The sense that there were distinctive, transparent differences between the classes was apparent in the title of Riis's work, which otherised the behaviours and lifestyles of the urban poor to render them acceptable subjects for the exercise of reform. As Mark Pittenger has claimed, the pursuit of difference in Gilded Age and Progressive Era writing led to the 'belief that workers and the poor were somehow fundamentally different – a strange breed in classless America' (Pittenger 1997: 28). While the romantic and transcendentalist mind of the antebellum era had largely imagined authority over culture as lying in the hands of 'representative men' (to borrow Emerson's phrase) with unique aesthetic and visionary capacities to capture the 'universal' patterns of historical development and shape experience according to their own will, the turn of attention towards environmental factors in science and art had turned culture into a mere adaptation to context and placed new limits upon human flourishing. Culture became less something to be acquired in the pursuit of a better life for the individual and more a reflection of the situation of that individual in relation to place. One did not accumulate culture as one had in previous times. Instead, as with Louis Althusser's diagnosis of ideology, it was something *always already* present in the life and actions of individuals and groups.

Keith Gandal notes in *The Virtues of the Vicious* (1997) that the increasing attention paid to environment and 'culture' in realist and naturalist art radically affected the capacity of narratives of class to represent the possibility of upward social mobility. 'The traditional novel of the poor was centred around a moral struggle and transformation . . .', writes Gandal, and 'usually involved a battle to resist the bad influences of the slums and the pressures of physical misery . . . slum characters are often mercifully saved from participating in their surroundings' (Gandal 1997: 45). Whereas the preferred character of sentimental and romantic art had been the lower-middle-class mechanic – a figure of potential whose skills and wits afforded them the capacity to 'overcome' the physical constraints of their environment and generate sympathy across lines of class and status – by the time of works like Crane's *Maggie* (1893) or Frank Norris's *McTeague* (1899), environment seemed to be everything. These figures now seldom triumphed over their world, but were, instead, products of it that attempted to survive and learn to adapt to the expectations of their culture.

The struggles of Crane's characters to be treated and understood in terms that were not wholly contained by their origins, and not to read their life and words through the overdetermined lens of their milieu, reflected a personal as well as intellectual need for Crane. By the 1880s, many authors and readers had begun to define authorial skill in social-scientific and bio-evolutionary terms through one's capacity to realistically render the particularities of group-based differences and their adaptation to environment (Elliott 2002 and Barrish 2001). For this practice to operate, realists had to be sufficiently versed in the particularities of dialect and behaviour specific to regions and locales. In Crane's case this frequently resulted in critics associating him with the people he represented in his fiction. Within a climate that profiled people according to the environments they inhabited and the classes to which they seemed outwardly to belong, Crane was often the subject of a remarkable double standard. At once lauded for his attention to specific details and hauled before the courts for 'slumming it' among the drunks and prostitutes of New York's notorious Tenderloin District, Crane could not find an easy home in Gilded Age USA. At the same time, though, Crane's New York bohemianism became one of the main draws for readers of his fiction. For the cosmopolitan Crane thought simple correspondences between environment and behaviour were dangerous and depreciated the value of the author as a transmitter and mobiliser of culture across the wider Atlantic world. By removing identifying features and the revealing specificities from his description of the theatre fire, such as its precise location or the specific names or 'races' of the individuals involved, Crane in 'Manacled' destabilises the presumably fixed correspondences between locales and cultural or classed regimes of behaviour demanded by both reformist slum literature and ethnographical surveys. Furthermore, by publishing the tale (like most of his other more overtly 'American' works) first in England, Crane deploys the reach of transatlantic print to put culture into dynamic circulation, cultivating a sense of Anglo-American similarity organised around universal, transatlantic class inequalities that disrupts the political project of objectification along lines of 'culture', 'race', 'national identity' and geography. 'Manacled' therefore reveals a cosmopolitan sensibility in Crane's work that I would argue has been inadequately captured by critical practices that have the nation as their central focal point. This is not to imply that Crane wholly abandoned particulars in favour of blandly universal forms of narrative but rather that Crane's forms of regionalism, realism and specification were always filtered through a print culture that was implicitly, even intentionally, transatlantic.

In Crane's own moment this cosmopolitanism was finding its outlets in the transnational Aesthetic Arts Movement, whose publishing and artistic centres in New York, Paris and London deployed their localities less to highlight the particular exceptionalism of their cities and more in order to cultivate a particularly bohemian international form of urban *chic*. In 'Manacled', Crane, the ultimate bohemian author, very deliberately engaged with this movement and its international style by centring the action of his own story around the distinctly Parisian-sounding 'Theatre Nouveau'.

When the narrator talks of the near musical 'hum of the flames' (1292), or offers heavily alliterative, near-purple descriptions of how 'smoke, filled with sparks sweeping on spiral courses, rolled thickly' (1292), Crane courted an abstraction that was reminiscent of the decadent, cosmopolitan style of artists like James McNeill Whistler, Walter Sickert or Charles Baudelaire. Brad Evans has noted how *Maggie* (1893), 'while ostensibly about the ghetto, seems even more to be about blowing apart the contrived staging of reform journalism . . . with an exercise in pure aestheticism – "the girl, Maggie, blossomed in a mud pile"' (Evans 2005: 141). What makes Crane's work translatable across national borders, therefore, was its refusal to attach to culture the qualities of an especially unique or distinctive character. The confusion of simulacra generated by a sentimental melodrama being played in a French-named theatre in an unknown city space produces the effect of aesthetic dissonance. Or rather, at the very moment that he risks objectifying a culture through textualisation, Crane places that text in circulation by adopting a distinctly transatlantic aesthetic posture. In this way, Crane's art object (his stories) deliberately abandoned their status as representative of a particular locale in order to become something more like the collective inherence of a wider Atlantic civilisation. In his time, Crane was criticised for his refusal to, as an article called 'Mr Crane's Sketches' in the 27 April 1898 edition of *Westminster Gazette* put it, 'give [. . .] us the complete novel which some day or other we all expect of him' (in Monteiro 2009: 169). However, I would argue that in adopting the sketch form as a model in his novels and short stories, Crane was deliberately generating a version of literary realism that was more easily diffusible internationally and deploying a fleeting lightness of touch that served as an antidote to the thickly descriptive tendencies of ethnographic literature.

Rather than being a simple meditation on decline, therefore, 'Manacled' speaks more generally to Crane's literary project of challenging the sense of stasis evoked by the turn towards environmental and cultural determinism in literature and social science through a cosmopolitan, transnational narrative that highlights how individuals and cultures are seldom fixed by context but can diffuse and translate across borders. More particularly, the story is the final example of Crane's career-long meditation upon the complex interrelationships between realism as an authorial practice that 'valorized the firsthand observation and textual representation of group-based difference' (Elliott 2002: xiii), class, identity, and competing, nascent understandings of the meaning of 'culture' in the transatlantic world that he had begun in his early New York sketches and *Maggie*. Recently, scholars such as Michael Elliott and others have begun to investigate how

> the conflict between different concepts of culture – one that relies upon ideas of static irreducible difference and another that offers the possibility of universal cultural development – was central to the debate surrounding the nature of literature in the age of realism, as well as to the products of literature. (Elliott 2002: 48)

Adding to this growing body of scholarship, I suggest here that Crane's work is engaged in an important discussion about the various meanings and values attached to the term 'culture' that was the subject of renewed attention in European and American intellectual discourse in this period. For this purpose it is beneficial to situate Crane alongside two other key intellectuals of the late nineteenth-century transatlantic world, Matthew Arnold and Franz Boas, whose radically distinct, but I would argue, equally cosmopolitan notions of 'culture' were directed to the same implicit goal of freeing individuals from the tyranny of class and cultural stasis implied by the turn towards environmental dominance in understandings of human behaviour.

In late nineteenth-century cosmopolitan cities like Crane's New York or London the ideas of the British poet and sage Matthew Arnold had considerable purchase. In his important collection of essays *Culture and Anarchy* from 1869, and later during his 1884 lecturing tour of the USA, Arnold had defined 'culture' as a universal, progressive and acquirable ideal directed towards 'the pursuit of perfection'(Arnold 2006; 52) that was, at least partly, synonymous with the values of a social order he called 'civilization'. For Arnold, 'culture' was the struggle of beauty and truth against the harsh, 'Philistine' world of laissez-faire capitalism and utilitarian governmentalism, a continual process of 'growing and becoming' (36) that developed from within the individual and extended outward to shape the wider social world. More significantly though, 'culture' was for Arnold decidedly not an 'engine of social distinction' and did not 'separate[e] its holder, like a badge or title, from other people' (33). What characterised Arnoldian 'culture' was a certain form of romantic discontentment with the 'machinery' of the status quo, including its class and social distinctions; 'a dissatisfaction which is of the highest possible value in stemming the common tide of men's thoughts in a wealthy and industrial community, and which saves the future . . . from being vulgarized' (39). Rather than cultivating a state of rather passive conditioning by environment such as Lamarckian adaptationists like the American Geological Survey and Bureau of American Ethnology had argued in relation to tribal societies, Arnoldian 'civilization' was intently acquisitive, attentive, dynamic, omnivorous and forward-looking. For Arnold, culture was the opposite of bland utilitarianism and might even serve as the basis for a new politics of inclusion.

From our contemporary perspective, Arnold's vision of cultural perfectionism and use of the terms 'civilization' and 'Philistinism' appear at best snobbish and at worst a possible vehicle for Anglo-Saxon supremacism. However, Arnoldian culture also offered the late nineteenth century a useful language for critiquing one's own national or local scene by liberating thought systems from their immediate context and situating them in a new order of meaning. Arnold's romantic vision of the possibility of a universal, collective inheritance of 'high culture' does not necessarily conflict with another conceptualisation that is often presented as its inverse: the pluralistic, relativistic and ethnographic 'culture concept' developed in the late work of the American-German-Jewish émigré anthropologist Franz Boas. Indeed, lauding late Boas for his relativism and denigrating Arnold for a racist particularism and chauvinism that he vehemently rejected has become a mark of faith among the liberal-left in American literary studies. This is because, while the Arnoldian definition drew from the Anglo-American traditions of John Stuart Mill and Ralph Waldo Emerson to argue that 'culture' was synonymous with the progressive values of social and personal 'cultivation', Boas's education in the German anti-Enlightenment thought of figures such as Herder and von Humboldt led to his stressing the particularities and pluralities of group behaviours in a manner that speaks more directly to our contemporary interest in questions of 'identity' and 'diversity'. However, this division between Arnoldian 'civilization' and Boasian 'culture' ignores the extent to which Boas's work drew a distinction between the 'esoteric doctrine' (the control and delimitation of the province of culture by an elite in-group) and the 'exoteric doctrine', which was more open, fluid and belonged to the 'common people', as I argued in the introduction. In contradistinction to pre-existing narratives of human behaviour put forward by the American Geological Survey and Bureau of American Ethnology – who had used regressive Lamarckian evolutionary hierarchies to argue that cultural development occurred solely *within* separate racialised and particularised groups (a principle known as 'independent invention') – Boas argued that humanity was essentially dynamic and shaped its cultures through processes of constant borrowing that emphasised the incorporation of objects from other cultural groups which served specific needs, the best that had been thought and said, but not always in the ways the originators intended. This was a pragmatic sense of aesthetic value that measured objects based on their use-value within a relativist framework, rather than in universal terms (which were really a mask of Anglo-Saxon or Anglo-Celtic supremacism). In fact, George Stocking has suggested of Boas: 'for Boas, man was essentially rather uninventive, but his creativity was expressed in his imaginative manipulation and reinterpretation of elements given to him by his cultural tradition, or borrowed from other cultural traditions' (Stocking 1982: 226). In one of his most famous pieces of fieldwork among a variety of tribes on either side of the Bering Strait, The Jesup North Pacific Expedition of 1897, Boas sought to test out existing theories of the autonomy of cultural groups against his vision of culture as shaped by processes of exchange. In the introduction to the report Boas wrote

> The peculiar interest that attaches to this region is founded on the fact that here the Old World and the New come into close contact. The geographical conditions favor migration along the coast-line, and exchange of culture. Have such migrations, has such exchange of culture, taken

place? This question is of great interest theoretically ... it is necessary to investigate with thoroughness all possible lines and areas of contact ... (Boas in Stocking, 1982: 108–9)

By foregrounding the importance of 'contact' rather than the coherence of cultural traditions within autonomous tribal groups, the young Boas forced anthropology to consider the role played by global currents of political and social history over and above a romantic fixation on the defining 'genius' or character of a people. By the 1920s, however, and the ascendancy of his students 'The Boasians' as part of a moment of 'modernism proper', this cosmopolitan character would give way to a more rigid sense of cultural determinism.

Reading Crane in light of these late nineteenth-century cosmopolitan discourses allows us to interpret the horrifying image of stasis in 'Manacled' as indicative of the author's concern that the realist practice with which he had become associated in fiction frequently fixed class within a liberal, identitarian framework that we have come to call 'cultural relativism', contributing to a conception of the immutability of differences generated by wealth disparity that ironically served to reinforce a political conservatism that he avowedly opposed. Indeed, Crane's observation concerning people's desire to cling to their culture unto death in 'Manacled' has distinct resonances in our own era of American literary studies. Walter Benn Michaels has argued that the very concept of 'cultural relativism' has re-emerged in American Studies through our collective 'commit[ment] to [a] principle of [an] identity essentialism' (Michaels 1995: 140). Yet, I would note that such a vision of essentialism is actually distinctly un-Boasian. Specifically, in valorising 'culture' as a pluralistic category that helps cultivate 'diversity' of thought and action within a representative democracy, without paying sufficient attention to the question of diffusion, transmission and change that occupied Boas, Crane and Arnold, we have replaced one version of essentialism (the biological or racial determinism of Lamarckian pseudo-science) with another (cultural or identitarian determinism). Michaels has suggested that embedded within contemporary theories of multiculturalism is the potentially dangerous assumption that one's systems of thought and action are both conditioned by, and representative of, one's culture alone, leaving little to no space for the individual. In this way, we have come to live out the legacy not of Boas but of the Lamarckian Bureau of American Ethnology in our attempts to locate within texts representative values that might allow us an access point to the beliefs and behaviours of particular diversified groups that emerged historically within certain local areas. While this is important for the preservation of difference and for the representation of difference within the existing political order, it serves us little in developing a sound critique of that order, which is based on inequality and which we would do well to abolish. Possessing a sense of self-esteem within a distinct 'working-class' culture or as a person from a racialised minority is, after all, scant compensation for the reduction of potential that comes with lack of availability of resources. In drawing attention to the awkward conflation of social class and culture with *habitus* then, Crane can be seen to critique an exceptionalist American narrative, such as that which characterised the twentieth-century vogue for 'national character studies', that frequently elevates the notion of one's irrefutable right to a 'culture', while obfuscating the presence of genuine, longstanding, transnational inequalities in shifting focus from unfair economic practices to ethnographical questions of taste and behaviour.

Michaels's observation that class as a category has always existed in uneasy relation with the contemporary valorisation of cultural diversity organised around the traditional triumvirate of post-modern representation (race, gender and sexuality) is particularly pertinent for approaching Gilded Age realism. Amy Kaplan's *The Social Construction of American Realism* (1988) typifies the critical approach taken by much American literary scholarship to reading realism that I have described above. In this work Kaplan adopted a Foucauldian perspective to argue:

> [C]lass differences struck the realists less as a problem of social justice than as a problem of representation. They were less concerned with the accuracy of portraying 'the other half' than with the problem of representing an interdependent society composed of competing and seemingly mutually exclusive realities. (11)

Yet, the critical realism of figures like Crane and Howells drew no clear distinction between aesthetics and politics. In highlighting how the realists falsified coherence through discourse in order to combat the 'mutually exclusive' nature of realities in the late nineteenth century and foregrounding postmodern questions of representation, Kaplan's work has contributed to an understanding of realism that aims to trace a clear genealogy from nineteenth-century writing to twentieth-century multiculturalism. Brad Evans has recently noted that while the idea of 'culture' is treated with considerable suspicion in contemporary anthropology, 'cultural theorists working in the humanities, and particularly Americanists, have not been . . . eager to engage in a similar critique' (Evans 2005: 17). I would argue, then, that the commitment to a liberal version of multiculturalism has frequently resulted in a reduction of the capacity of pre-existing American Studies methodologies to accurately account for economic inequalities that are the products of distinctly transnational processes of exchange and trade. As Charles Briggs has noted, 'rethinking multiculturalism can help us unmask how the liberal claim that everyone is equally entitled to their own culture is being used to disguise the creation of inequalities within and between nations' (Briggs 2005: 78). Reading Crane's work about the lower classes as harbingers of twentieth-century multicultural purviews rooted in what Charles Briggs has described as a nationalistic, 'liberal program for confronting racism that celebrates autonomous cultural worlds' (76) therefore foreshortens its capacity to speak more generally for Atlantic modernity. Crane's fiction often benefits from an approach that more accurately reflects its moment, in which an emergent Boasian and pragmatic pluralism existed alongside the Arnoldian, humanist conception of 'culture'. This can be seen in an earlier work of Crane's, *George's Mother*, in which Arnoldian perfectionism is presented as a more appropriate model for the treatment of class in fiction, because unlike a relativised understanding of social behaviours that highlighted the plurality of 'autonomous cultural worlds', Arnold's vision opened up the possibility of social mobility. In other words, Crane's novel critiques the liberal search for 'identity' as a politically conservative process that seeks out a static conception of selfhood rooted in one's affiliation with the behaviours of a particular, autonomous, relativised group that raises the continual spectre of race. He does this by reading the American fixation on 'self-esteem' and the making of a case for the value of one's discrete, pluralised 'culture' as a kind of self-destructive addiction.

George's Mother and the Culture Habit

George's Mother dramatises the effects of conflating class with a theory of culture grounded in the specifics of place as a conflict between a boy and his mother over the former's incipient alcoholism. When it was first published, the novel was read as a classic temperance tale of the kind that was common to late nineteenth-century audiences where a 'fundamentalist morality' was juxtaposed with 'the cynical, braggart amorality of the street' (Murphy 1981: 88). Reviewers of the novel often read it in this light as a didactic tale of the importance of avoiding the daemon drink. One reviewer from the *Philadelphia Evening Bulletin* even went as far as to suggest that the story was for children and 'should receive a place on the fat shelves of our Sunday-school libraries' (Monteiro 2009: 71). Readings in our own era have tended to follow the lead of Maxwell Geismar in offering liberal, psychoanalytic interpretations of the novel as a 'tragic-comic oedipal love relationship' (Geismar 1953: 94) that is centred around George's search for individual and group identity that might separate him from the control of his overbearing mother. Such readings focus upon George's essential difference from his mother and his flawed quest for self-identity and a 'culture' of his own among the hard-drinking 'roughs' of New York's Lower East Side.

As George Kelcey becomes more and more dependent upon alcohol he comes to more accurately reflect what are shown to be the demands and 'secrets' of his 'culture': 'He understood that drink was essential to joy, to the coveted position of a man of the world and of the streets. The saloons contained the mystery of the street for him' (Crane 1984: 258). Kelcey's alcoholism is presented as a form of ritualised initiation into the secrets and patterns of behaviour undertaken by an esoteric sub-culture of the Lower East Side. These produce in him feelings of 'self-esteem' that temporarily compensate for his rejection by his 'dream-woman' (237)

Maggie Johnson. Kelcey's gradual development of 'brotherly feeling' towards his fellow drinkers is expressed by Crane in distinctly scornful ethnographic terms. As the young men drink they recite stories and sing repetitious songs, while Crane's rendering of the effects of alcohol upon the pronunciation of their already idiosyncratic street dialect produces a radical effect of alienation on the part of the reader, as if trying to interpret another language: 'G'l'm'n, I lovsh girl! I ain' drunker'n yeh all are!' (247). When another uninitiated individual enters the private drinking room at the pub where they are stationed, Crane writes 'The men sprang instantly to their feet. They were ready to throttle any invader of their island' (228). In their efforts to locate for themselves a sense of attachment to a culture or set of localised behaviours, the drinkers have abandoned the Boasian dream of circulation and exchange for a dynamic of in-group and out-group. In this sense, *George's Mother* dramatises the process by which the 'esoteric' aspect of a culture, as Boas described it, extracts by violence and secrecy a position of authority from the 'exoteric' 'common people'. Crucially, this process effects a kind of backsliding away from modernity. Rather than being products of a cosmopolitan city space, then, Crane ironically renders the street gangs as oddly and self-consciously separated from modernity, behaving in a way that situates them outside of their Gilded Age moment and within the circumscribed space of a 'primitive' tribal other described by contemporary ethnographic and reform literature.

Readers who have sought to differentiate George from his mother have often missed Crane's suggestions in the text of how ultimately similar the two characters come to be. This is because what really motivates Crane in the novel is exploring the danger of fixed identities as an index of the abandonment of hope among the *fin-de-siècle* working class. Consequently, the novel can be read as a symbolic enactment of how new definitions of culture in the nineteenth century that highlighted the significance of environment and context in shaping experience ultimately limited and reduced the worldviews of individuals. Crane approaches this topic by means of a discussion of the idea of 'habit'. The author charts the course of George's alcohol addiction alongside that of his mother, whose increasingly fervent religiosity becomes habitual. Indeed, the words 'habit' or 'habitual' appear frequently through the novel. Chapter VI opens thus,

> The little old woman habitually discouraged all outbursts of youthful vanity upon the part of her son. She feared that he would think too much of himself, and she knew that nothing could do more harm. Great self-esteem was always passive, she thought, and if he grew to regard his qualities of mind as forming a dazzling constellation, he would tranquilly sit still and not do those wonders she expected of him. (234)

In this passage, Crane introduces several key themes of the novel: 'habit', the passivity of 'self-esteem' and the desire of human flourishing. In the novel, the establishment of a sense of identity in George produces a staggering passivity. When confronted by his mother about losing his job after frequently failing to turn up, George responds with hostility: 'Ah, whatter yeh givin us? Is this all I git when I come home f'm, being fired? Anybody 'ud think it was my fault. I couldn't help it' (266). In locating an identity for himself among the alcoholics of the Lower East Side, George has begun to passively enact the expectations of the esoteric sub-culture he has joined and whose rituals and behaviours he comes to police. Unlike her son, George's mother is defined not by her emotional connection to the fellow denizens of the tenement, but by her continued struggle towards transcendence and the cultivation of an aesthetic and moral beauty that is distinctly Arnoldian. When Crane first introduces 'the little old woman' she is in the 'flurry of battle . . . through the cloud of dust or steam one could see the thin figure dealing mighty blows. Always her way seemed best. Her broom was continually poised, lance-wise, at dust demons' (219). The narrator's tone here is richly ironic, even sarcastic. Yet, the nature of the struggle is clear and provides a counterpoint to the 'passive' indoctrination into a group identity and 'self-esteem' undergone by George. For Matthew Arnold, as for Ralph Waldo Emerson and, eventually, William James, 'cultivation' or the pursuit of cultural achievement was an ongoing, strenuous effort of will characterised by disenchantment and disaffection rather than positive feelings of attachment. What ultimately scuppers this process in *George's Mother*, though, is that the actions she associates with the improvement of her life and environment become habitual and mechanical – the very opposite of Arnold's vision of progressive development. Crane captures this aesthetically by repeating the same scene, in which Mrs Kelcey enters George's room and attempts to rouse him to action, several times.

George's Mother appeared at a moment when the role of habit and habituation in the shaping of cultural behaviours was a hotly-debated topic in popular and social scientific journals. The pragmatist philosopher Charles Sanders Peirce had first introduced this idea in an essay entitled 'How to Make Our Ideas Clear' in the January 1878 edition of *Popular Science Monthly*. In this essay, and an earlier piece entitled 'The Fixation of Belief', Peirce argued that one's perception of what constitutes truth or value is largely conditioned by the relation of a new idea or sense impression to a pre-existing conception. 'The essence of belief', wrote Peirce in 'How to Make Our Ideas Clear', 'is the establishment of a habit; and different beliefs are distinguished by the different modes of action to which they give rise'.[4] For Peirce, one's ideas are fixed by their pre-existing modes of action, which are designed to appease doubts and uncertainties: 'If beliefs do not differ in this respect, if they appease the same doubt by producing the same rule of action, then no mere differences in the manner of consciousness of them can make them different beliefs . . .'.[5] If Peircean pragmatism turned all concepts into the search for habits or fixed modes of being that allowed us to 'appease the irritation of doubt' it did so in a way that sought to emphasise more fully the potency of individual will and action to reshape realities than the Lamarckian theory of culture's emphasis on the conditioning role of environment alone. That is to say, pragmatism (especially as it developed in the hands of William James), rather than being of a piece with the Lamarckian impulses of reform and sociological literature in the period, frequently partook of an Arnoldian or Emersonian counter-impulse of self-making. If Lamarckian science made habit inevitable, rendering a retrospective temporality and deep time the key influence on the present, pragmatism offered a future-led alternative in the argument that the fixation of beliefs through training also offered an alternative in the possibility of multiple, future worlds. As James would say in his attempt to marry Peircean philosophical pragmatism (or pragmaticism as Pierce labelled it) to the emergent discipline of psychology, 'Man is born with a tendency to do more things than he has ready-made arrangements for in his nerve centres' (*Principles*, 113). Consequently, different choices might generate different habits that occasion different forms of the future. For George, though, such an 'appeasement of doubt' and the positive feelings of inclusion signal the potential triumph of one's milieu over their individual will. In its place, the author advocates a more dynamic, fluid and aesthetic approach to life that abandons the search for a fixed identity in order to pursue a cosmopolitan sensibility motivated by a desire for cultural improvement. *George's Mother* is a novel set against the adolescent search for identity that Crane associated with the American intellectual impulse towards the ownership and possession of a discrete 'culture' within the multiplicity of American immigrant lives.

Crane's democratic aestheticism – his simultaneous belief in both democracy as a social value and the redemptive quality of aesthetic contemplation and complexity – has an important descendent in the work of Gertrude Stein, thereby linking late realism to a more established modernist canon and doxa. Stein's training as a pragmatist through her undergraduate work in psychology and philosophy with William James while at Radcliffe permitted her to marry a resounding faith in the potential of demotic language with a cultural aspiration towards modernist complexity. As Isabelle Parkinson has noted of Stein's short-story collection *Three Lives* (1905/06),

> As author, Stein includes her 'low-life' subjects in order to broaden representation, and her experimental realism is an attempt to make her representation more 'true', but by the same token they are the subjects of a literary experimentation that seeks to probe, explicate, contain and account for them. (45)

Like Crane, Stein was a critic of a dull realism that removed the enchantment from everyday life, and had a vision for a renewal of the democratic politics of writing that moved away from the regressive politics of simple, anthropological racial typology, and turned, at least in her early work, on an engagement with the concept of 'habit'. In works such as 'The Good Anna' Stein bound herself to a limited vocabulary to capture the limited worldview of the protagonist (who never experiences much beyond a work of toil), but also to explore the Jamesian preposition that education was a form of habit and 'the enormous fly-wheel of society, its most precious conservative agent' (121), keeping one class from mixing with another. Taken at face value this would imply a Bourdieusian position on education and training (or habit) as being prohibitions against class fluidity and movement. Yet, Stein's aesthetically conscious, repetitious use of language also exhibited a freeing potential that evokes the Boasian principle of cultural diffusion within the 'exoteric doctrine'. By making language aesthetically mobile through the deployment of literary techniques of irony and grammatical play, Stein suggested that even within the limited framework of *habitus* and training (captured by the limited vocabulary of the story's working-class subject), words can be made to mean different things under different contexts. Consequently, there was no 'primitive' language and/or 'elite' language; at least in terms of class. The very relativism of subject positions – what Boas would consider to be the fact that different peoples used different objects for different means depending on their culture – became a means for Stein to envision a democratic potential in everyday speech that did not reduce language to base hierarchies of value. Language, as a tool, was not used in a universal manner, but operated within the relativised framework of culture. Also, at the level of the readerly encounter with the text, the opening up of language to uncertainty creates the effect of a slowing of our encounter with it, disrupting the process by which history intrudes instantaneously on the present so as to create a stereotype. What we have rather than representation is delay. Even distinctly moralised values, such as the 'Good' in the title of 'The Good Anna' and 'The Good Lena' from Stein's short-story collection, might carry different meanings dependent on context or by effect of repetition. The shifting landscape of words within the Steinian cultural-democratic aesthetic schema therefore dramatised both the Jamesian pragmatic focus on choice (we can choose how we read and therefore what habits we choose to acquire) and the Boasian focus on cultural relativism as it related to the use-value of inherited objects. Thus, even within the framework of a literary 'realism' whereby Stein's vocabulary and setting never gave into surrealism, fantasy, or the speculative and clung therefore to the Howellsian mantra of 'show[ing] the different interests in their true proportions', Stein's aesthetic self-consciousness cleaved to a democratic impulse in suggesting that other worlds of meaning existed and were equally worthy of respect within the twinned frameworks of social class and culture. Moreover, for the reader, this democratic impulse relied upon an ethics of encounter in the moment of the text's consumption as while habit might have suggested that literature is always approached within a totally absorbing context of prior experience, Stein's pragmatically inspired realism (like Crane's) also suggested that reading was an experience in itself that reshaped existing relations to language and meaning by virtue of an encounter with an ever-evolving text world.

Returning to Crane, it follows, then, that only from the standpoint of a late twentieth-century Bourdieusian impulse towards the description of literary works as directed only to discrete positions of class and training would his cosmopolitan radicalism be understood to be of a strange breed. Within its moment of the turn of the century, to be at once 'conservative' in one's insistence upon the importance of cultural development and human flourishing, and 'progressive' in one's refusal of ethno-racial and socio-economic particularities was no contradiction. Neither, indeed, was to be 'cosmopolitan' and 'working-class', as the Haymarket anarchists had shown. Consequently, with the anarchists (and later with the 'modernists') Crane brings a strong vein of internationalism and class critique to American literature that serves as a warning within our present American scene that so often seems to possess an ideological blindness to the dangers of the liberal search for 'identity'. In order to challenge the ethics of working-class representation, Crane suggested that resisting cultural and environmental determinism demanded that the poor be rendered more, not less, 'aesthetic' and beauty, by whatever means it was brought into the world, was a right for all as fundamental as democratic representation at the level of the law. Through this resistance to mimetic representation – confusingly still undertaken in the name of 'realism' – Crane destabilised the fixed correspondences demanded by theories of biological and cultural heredity that foregrounded the role of environment in the shaping of behaviour. Just as Alfred Stieglitz would imagine a new aesthetico-political Americanism that countered the impulse towards 'sharp outlines' he saw as pre-eminent in culture and politics through an embrace of the destabilising potential of 'tone' and 'atmosphere', and Stein would destabilise language to develop new frameworks for democratic participation, what characterises Crane's ethos was not, therefore, his protagonist's now-clichéd search for identity or a culture of their own but the dangers implicit in the fact that they might actually find it. The playgoers in 'Manacled' worship their cultural possessions as George's alcoholism gives him a sense of completeness and inclusion, but both ultimately lead to further, greater suffering. Crane's fictions can therefore be seen to provide an antidote to a version of Americanist literary canon-formation centred around identitarian notions of 'culture' and 'diversity' and are an important locus for the development of a more transnational, less nationally specific, literary criticism. In what follows I will consider how Crane's aestheticised realism represents something of a road not taken for depictions of class and race in America, as the 'culture concept' first proposed by Boas as the system for the diffusion and interpenetration of cultural materials across the world *hardened* in the twentieth century into a fixation on identity as the primary cause and need of the political Left.

Capturing the 'Working-Class' Voice in the Twentieth Century: 'Lifelets', 'Proletarian Art' and FSA Oral History

In American literary studies the slave narrative's printing of letters of endorsement and verification by white abolitionists in the early republic and antebellum era offer some of the most famous examples of how working-class life writing has operated historically in relation to a normative, white, liberal power. However, it was with the development of industrial modernity in the postbellum era that there was the greatest expansion of the genres of working-class life writing. In the Progressive Era the collection and publication of working-class life texts took on a new intensity. It was these works, alongside the more familiar genres of slum and reform literature, that Crane was most interested in rebuking. One important instance of this emerging genre was the publication between 1902 and 1906 of a series of seventy-five short 'autobiographies of undistinguished American men and women', called 'lifelets', by Hamilton Holt of the New York *Independent*. These short life stories can be seen as an important motivation for later documentary projects in the genre.

Following the initial success of the 'lifelets' in *The Independent* Hamilton Holt published a selection of sixteen of the works in book format as *The Life Stories of Undistinguished Americans as Told By Themselves*. In the book version, Holt and his protégé Edwin E. Slosson provided introductory framing materials that reflected on the intentions of the initial project. According to his 'Note', Holt believed that the 'lifelets' would 'typify the life of the average worker in some particular vocation ... make each story the genuine experience of a real person' and also 'represent the five great races of mankind' (xi). Consequently, the selection of subjects for publication was made based upon an assessment of 'sociological importance' and 'human interest' rather than from any 'literary point of view' (xi). This urge to categorise according to indexes of race and social type extended to the names of the works themselves, which consistently drew attention to the birthplace of the writer, many of whom were actually naturalised American citizens at the time their life stories were composed. Titles such as 'The Life Story of A Swedish Farmer', 'The Life Story of a Lithuanian', 'The Life Story of a Chinaman', etc. revealed an attempt to preserve historical markers of national or racial identity in an era characterised by state-sanctioned processes of 'Americanization'. Like many other progressives of his time (Randolph Bourne, Willa Cather, Franz Boas and Horace Kallen among them), Holt regarded 'Americanization' as a set of policies that were framed according to Anglo-Saxon middle-class norms and so sought to elevate cultural pluralism as an alternative national formulation. Ironically, most of the titles that did not refer to an individual's place of origin were reserved for the stories of people deemed already to be sufficiently 'Americanized', two, three or more generations from emigrants. 'The Experiences of a Chorus Girl', 'The Autobiography of a Football Player', 'The Story of Two Moonshiners' and a number of other texts in the collection are not described in terms of ethnicity, calling on ideological assumptions about normative whiteness.

Holt's insistence on rendering the particularities of ethnicities and cultural practices was implicit in the process of collecting the stories. According to Werner Sollors, Holt's team:

> [L]ooked for 'average' and representative people in order to get answers to such questions as, where do you come from? if you were not born here, then why, when, and how did you come to America? are you better off or worse than you were in the past? what is your job? how much money do you make? what house do you live in? how do you spend your day? what are your pastime activities? and, are you happy? (viii)

Consequently, the texts were written either by their author according to careful generic guidelines, and directed to certain 'pertinent' questions, or else constructed from interviews by one of Holt's several fieldworkers.

The lifelets enact a strangely contradictory process of inclusion *and* disavowal of working-class life stories. Taken individually, the lifelets offer powerful personal accounts of their writer's lives and relationships to work, and capture a fact too often overlooked in America; that its working class is and always has been multicultural. So obvious and essential a fact is this that to speak at all of a 'white working class' as a distinct, coherent and unified group is an exercise of remarkable and wilful naivete that risks overlooking history and contemporary fact both. Yet the process of collecting these life stories in the form of a book imposes a framework on those works that affects their meaning. Taken collectively, the 'lifelets' serve as a snapshot of an American national culture that Holt wished to present as an alternative to the homogeneity favoured by 'assimilationists'. Ironically, however, the book performs a process of Americanisation all its own, as the desire to 'typify the life of the average worker' gives way to a multicultural, ethnographic urge to represent ethnic and racial heterogeneity and particularity. Not only does the 'short story' formulation frame out continuous processes of development and change, when encountered in the form of the book, it transforms a discrete object interacting in complex ways with the paratextual material of the newspaper and current events into a historical mosaic, a composite photograph, and so a temporally static sociological text. In this formulation social class becomes merely another aspect of identity contained in an American multitude that is nonetheless not pluriversal.

The distinction between the multitude (or the multicultural mosaic) and the pluriverse is crucial, and rests upon the question of time. A 'multitude' is temporally 'locked' in the sense that it frames time and holds a group to ethnographic markers of difference in a perpetual past; one's culture, race or class marks one in a certain way for all time. It also operates in relation to a sense of contemporary time and in relation to extant social relations, which are expected to exist in perpetuity. The term 'multiculturalism' as it operates as a facet of neoliberal capitalism and globalisation is a case in point. As such the multitude can be synonymous with the impulses of American exceptionalism in rendering US society as in some sense outside the current of history. Or, rather, only within a current of history whose ultimate teleology points to an increasing acceptance of 'diversity' but leaves social class largely untouched as a concept. As Martin Savransky describes this, it is a mode of epistemology in 'modern alliance with monism' (19) and Enlightenment science. As such it can make peace with the closing down of future possibility in the service of present representational concerns within the frame of a single, ultimately-knowable, and predictable, world. When it is assumed that there is only one world and one future, the task of politics is representational alone within that modern monistic system. By contrast, a pluriversal mode of reasoning presumes a 'partial, fragile, ongoing, and unfinished weaving of a tremorous form' (21) that includes time in the equation and also suggests that there is no 'one ontology . . . there are, of course, "multiple ontologies"' (43). In an age of rising American hegemony such as the Progressive Era was, sociological reasoning mobilised epistemology and questions of representation to serve the project of American unity, which was also understood to be the marker of a global security for all time, thereby closing down the multiple futures and multiple worlds implicit in a sense of the future as uncertain and ontologies as plural. This, in turn, is a question of form, since this uncertain sense of futurity is a necessary feature of a newspaper, but is somewhat impeded by the form of the book.

The refashioned literary framework of the lifelets in codex form, then, reveals an essentially liberal American exceptionalist ideological agenda in which class is reified in the process of its identification as an aspect of cultural identity. The effect of this is that class remains an unchallenged assumption in the book. The paratexts of the work do not seek to highlight the mutability of class, its complex oscillations in a nexus of upward and downward mobility, and certainly do not make a Marxian claim for its eventual obliteration by revolution. As with ethnic identity, the titles of these texts fixed individuals according to certain claims about the work that they did, even if this did not reflect the life story itself. A case in point is 'The Life Story of A Greek Peddler', which by the time of writing is not, in fact, the story of a peddler but a one-time peddler, solider, and naturalised American greengrocer. The artificial frame of the book imposes a historical temporality that arrests processes of development and change in order to render the life-writer representative of the group identity sought out by the fieldworker or journalist. Most of the stories actually describe a process of education and development that the authors are proud of and keen to place centrally in their life texts. Yet Holt and his team mark their historical conditions as the key argument for their inclusion in the book.

Edwin E. Slosson's 'Introduction' is potentially more revealing than Holt's own 'Notes', though. In addition to serving as a collector and transcriber for Holt's newspaper, Slosson was known as a populariser of science and the scientific method, and was by training a chemist. His 'Introduction' speaks of the lifelets as 'representative of each of the races which go to make up our composite nationality' (4) and at several points establishes his authority by recourse to scientific or mathematical terminology, describing the book as 'a mosaic picture composed of living tesserae' (4) and the genre of the lifelet according to the mathematical formula: 'Lifelet : autobiography :: short story : novel' (4). The double colon here indicates equivalent ratios, implying that the lifelet is to autobiography as the short story is to novel. Recognising the historical problems of slum and reform writing in suppressing the voice of the 'common people' in the exercise of work nominally conducted on their behalf, in Slosson's conception the book was 'intended not merely to satisfy our common curiosity as to "how the other half lives," but to have both a present and a future value as a study in sociology' (5). For Slosson, the archetypal Progressive Era thinker, the collection of working-class life stories had to be conducted by means of a scientific model because their value was primarily understood to be descriptive and sociological, even if he tried to recognise life in the dynamic form of 'living tesserae'. In this way, the 'lifelets' were part and parcel of a changing intellectual and literary culture at the turn of the century. A key figure in this new landscape was Franz Boas, who took up the chair in anthropology at Columbia in 1899 and with whom Holt and Slosson both corresponded. The scientific processes of data collection that Boas helped to develop became central to the work of progressive reform, of which Slosson considered himself an exponent. Yet in the process of this institutionalisation they lost their radical empiricist edge. The 'Introduction' to the lifelets made claims on the short narratives as the ideal form for the analysis of class as 'culture' because their brevity, 'crudity and indefiniteness of aim'(4), their lack of stylistic finesse, allowed them to perform as if they were 'oral narratives' of the kind Boas and other anthropologists were collecting from tribal and native peoples. Slosson wrote: 'the short story is older than the art of writing' (4), suggesting that the authority of the texts included in the collection was drawn from their relationship to 'premodern' forms. He thereby sought to authenticate the printing of working-class life writing in the terms of historical preservation and assessed its value solely as a culturally representative form.

This practice of working-class life writing taking on forms synonymous with the institutionalisation of 'the culture concept' in the early twentieth century was not the result of the interventions of liberal, middle-class reformers like Slosson and Holt alone. Indeed, it was not always a process of 'top-down' institutionalisation of the working-class voice. Proletarian activists frequently deployed the frame of 'culture' themselves to serve certain ideological aims. In 1921, Mike Gold (still known at this point as Irwin Granich) published an article entitled 'Towards Proletarian Art' in the February issue of *The Liberator*. Many scholars of working-class writing see Gold's article as an important turning point for the field in America.[6] What Gold inaugurated was the study of 'proletarian culture' as a discrete entity modelled on the definition of the Russian *Prolet-Kult*; a formal approach to writing in which any expression of the voice of the working classes was *always already* directed towards state-socialist revolutionary aims. Gold's model was radically at odds with Marxism-Leninism, which was vanguardist and sought to raise the working classes up through education (an inheritance from nineteenth-century European traditions of *bildung*), rather than adopting a 'bottom-up' approach that acknowledged the legitimacy of existing proletarian cultural forms. Speaking of how this literature was to be collected and disseminated, Gold wrote, 'the method of erecting this proletarian culture must be the revolutionary method – from the deepest depths upward' (70), implying that Communist Party literary collection practices fully represented the intentions of all working-class writers and thinkers for all time. Gold's insistence that 'proletarian culture' had to be 'erected', made a further claim on the importance of discursive practices such as literary criticism and ethnography as forces that imbued reality effects into forms of literature he claimed were already *out there* in the world. The irony lies in the assumption that if 'proletarian culture' already existed de facto it would not require a frame to be 'erected' to give it meaning. Additionally, Gold's vision of proletarian culture was inflected with a popular modernist primitivism redolent of the very bourgeois little magazines (*Seven Arts, Little Review*, etc.) upon which he regularly levelled virulent critique. He argued that the approach taken to the study of working-class culture should be as respectful and scientific as a modern ethnographer might wish to be towards a primitive religion, while the work of its writers should be sacred and devotional: 'The Revolution, in its secular manifestation of strike, boycott, mass-meeting, imprisonment, sacrifice, agitation, martyrdom, organization is thereby worthy of the religious devotion of the artist' (67). For Gold, 'proletarian art' corresponded with the approach to culture taken by later Boasians (but not necessarily by Boas himself) and would come to be more fully defined later in the century in a separatist version of multiculturalism. Gold slipped between a Marxian tradition that saw social class as a condition of historical oppression and an ethnographic one in which it is just one culture among many, an autonomous *thing* that could be studied in the same way as ritual, religion or behaviour. This position was remarkably inconsistent given his professed Marxian commitments to the dialectical force of history.

Indeed, Gold mined turn-of-the-century anthropology for a language to speak of the working class, writing of deep time, 'historic Man', the 'spiritual cement' of culture, 'ancient heroism' and 'the religion' of work (69). In building a resistant force to capitalism he mobilised an essentialism that could run in one of only two directions: towards vanguardist anti-democracy, or a pessimistic garrison mentality that accepts the permanence of capitalism and so closes the gates to historical uncertainty and change.

For critics of working-class life writing, it is the 1930s that have exerted the greatest archival influence on the discipline. The New Deal galvanised early twentieth-century Progressivism's view of culture into institutionalised, state-funded forms of data collection and publication. The era saw a boom in literary works attempting to capture the speech, writing and behaviours of working-class subjects.[7] Works such as *Unwritten History* and *Lay My Burden Down* (oral histories of slavery), *The Disinherited Speak* (a collection of sharecroppers' letters from the Southern Tenant Farmers' Union), *These Are Our Lives* (an oral history of Native peoples), the American Guides Series, and even the far more complex *Let Us Now Praise Famous Men* by James Agee and Walker Evans (derived from articles commissioned for *Fortune* magazine on sharecroppers in the US South) were the products of large-scale state, political and corporate investment in the collection of various forms of working-class and minority life writing and culture. Among the most significant moments in which the American culture concept came to directly shape government policy was with the appointment of John Collier in 1933 as FDR's Commissioner on Indian Affairs charged with enacting the 'Indian New Deal'. Collier was trained in Boas's programme in Anthropology at Columbia in the 1910s and was informed intellectually by the Boasian sense of the discrete nature of cultural groups. Boas's student Zora Neale Hurston was responsible for the FSA American Guide to Florida, and *Anthropology* (1923), a textbook by another of Boas's PhD students, Alfred Kroeber, was required reading for all students at Columbia, and was on the curriculum of most humanities courses at most universities in the USA until the end of the 1940s. In essence, university-educated young people coming into government fieldwork in the New Deal would have assimilated the underlying assumptions of the 'Boasian' culture concept, at least in the form it came to them through the more prescriptive and professionalised Kroeber. Either conducted under the auspices of the government-organised Federal Writers' Project, Works Progress Administration, or through the efforts of 'scores of other ethnographers, documentarians, and journalists [who] sought to preserve oral perspectives they perceived as rapidly vanishing' (Staub 1), writing at this time solidified a US intellectual tendency to describe the working classes in the emerging ethnographical terms of 'cultural determinism' that Crane's work of the 1890s and 1900s had warned so vociferously against.[8] Techniques and practices drawn from turn-of-the-century salvage ethnography and sociology, including methodologies such as participant observation and informant interviewing, began to reify the dominant forms of what would later come to be called 'working-class life writing'. Many of the earliest attempts to capture the life of the working class in their own words are therefore marked by a generic determinism engendered by a formalisation of practices of data collection and a commitment to the logic of cultural 'conservation' that has left the indelible mark of institutions on two dominant genres of working-class literature in particular: oral history and personal narrative.

The views obtained by these projects were diverse, but, as with the 'lifelets' before them, the frame of 'culture' served to impose extra-textual limits on the expressive range of the oral and literary texts. Much of this ethnographical work ultimately confirmed the mythology of American Exceptionalism in two ways. First, by seeing working-class culture as an authentic expression of a larger 'American culture' as I suggested was the aim of the 'lifelets' in the 1900s.[9] Second, by rendering it as a vanishing or historical entity, which only served to reinforce the popular capitalist imaginary about the modern absence of a recognisable working class in the USA. Both of these tendencies imposed limits on the radical and oppositional potential of texts by working-class individuals by co-opting them under the umbrella of American liberalism. The second of these exceptionalist tendencies can be seen to be a repeated concern of James Agee's narrative in *Let Us Now Praise Famous Men*, which is deeply critical of the ethics of various New Deal 'alphabet' relief agencies, including the FSA and WPA, but whose ethical form of aestheticism is sadly, largely outside of the purview of this book. Writing of this era James Miller notes,

> A stunning amount of this era's cultural work was imbued with what might be called an indexical-excavatory enthusiasm: the desire to limn the nation's derelict spaces for vestiges of its most vividly ruined (material and human) antecedents. Focusing its attention on those places and people feared to be most immediately threatened by industrial-commercial development (e.g., 'traditional' Pennsylvania Amish communities, impoverished Mississippi Delta sharecroppers, dispossessed dust bowl farmers, the denizens of the breadlines in virtually every city), such work strove to fashion the social and economic fringes into receptacles for . . . the remains of its beleaguered, 'vanishing' past. (375)

The work of New Deal reform emerged out of what had become a common strand in American intellectual practice by the 1930s, affording a people suffering under economic or social deprivation the meagre compensation of being seen as an autonomous and vital 'culture'. The irony is that this kind of work only confirmed the status of the group under the lens as 'vanishing'; a deathly and artificial sense of vitality. This sense of cultural 'vitality' was part and parcel of the contradictory status attributed to other groups such as various Native American tribes, who were defined at once as 'noble savages' and imbued with the mythology of the 'vanishing Indian'; a process of simultaneous valorisation and disavowal that helped to shape US government policy historically.

As I have suggested in this chapter, and as Stephen Crane first noted, cultural pluralism (even cultural determinism) in America became something of a 'habit' in the twentieth century, so dominant a 'distribution of the sensible' that it became harder and harder to perceive alternative modes of being and thinking about economic and social behaviours. This has undoubtedly laid the ground for the hegemony of New Historicist and Bourdieusian methods of reading that either see all cultural objects as expressions of class-bound norms, or imagine that understanding a given group demands the uncovering of an esoteric archival or anecdotal 'key' whose master-code could unlock what a text means within the society that produced it. Yet this impulse is counter to the more aesthetic tendencies of much major late nineteenth- and early twentieth-century art and literature. The question of literature as a medium with genuine democratic credentials, one whose speech should be theoretically available to all in the modern world and that disturbs existing political regimes of power and control through its imagination of multiple futures, is taken up in the following chapter, albeit from a strange angle. It might not seem obvious to take Edith Wharton – the embodiment perhaps more than any other writer of the American canon of privilege and lineage – as a source through which to consider questions of diversity. Yet her work prior to the 1920s is engaged in complex ways with the intersections of class and the culture concept as they relate to the power of fictions of the everyday as sources for the contemplation of alternative futurities and ontologies.

Notes

1. Richard Bentley also had a history of publishing US writers. The first English publication of Edgar Allan Poe's 'Fall of the House of Usher' was in *Bentley's Miscellany*.
2. McGurl, *The Novel Art*.
3. 'A Plea for Art Photography in America' (1892). <https://photocriticism.com/members/archivetexts/photocriticism/stieglitz/pf/stieglitzpleapf.html> (accessed 15 July 2022).
4. Peirce, 'How to Make Our Ideas Clear'.
5. Peirce, 'How to Make Our Ideas Clear'.
6. See Bloom, *Left Letters*; Homberger, 'Proletarian Literature'; Foley, *Radical Representations*.
7. A complete list of the WPA Writers' Program publications is available in the *WPA Writers Program Publications Catalogue: The American Guide Series* (Washington, DC: Government Printing Office, 1941).
8. For more on this see Feintuch (ed.), *The Conservation of Culture*.
9. This was the professed aim of a work such as Constance Rourke's *American Humor: A Study of the National Character*.

CHAPTER 4

Getting Some of the Way with Undine Spragg: Cosmopolitanism, Ethnography and War Work in the Novels of Edith Wharton

> 'To know any one thing one must not only know something of a great many others, but also ... a great deal more of one's immediate subject than any partial presentation of it visibly includes.'
> Edith Wharton, *The Writing of Fiction* (11)

> 'Is there no place left, then, for the intellectual who cannot yet crystallize, who does not dread suspense, and is not yet drugged with fatigue?'
> Randolph Bourne, 'The War and the Intellectuals' (13)

In her 1925 collection of essays on craft, *The Writing of Fiction*, Edith Wharton reflected on the basis of her literary technique and her belief in the formal weaknesses of an emergent literary modernism. Coming towards the end of what scholars frequently recognise as her greatest period of production in fiction, beginning with *The House of Mirth* (1905) and topped off by *The Age of Innocence* (1920), Wharton used her literary fame and the platform it gave her in *The Writing of Fiction* to question what she saw as an emerging cult of 'originality' whose values were drawn from a neo-romantic fixation on 'inspiration' and vanguardism, and a desire that new psychological fiction (Woolf, Joyce and Proust are particularly referenced) capture all that was subject to the senses in a given moment. For Wharton, this modernistic adoration of totality and aesthetic completeness was a hubris of sorts that found its style in the deployment of the uninterrupted, unimpeded Jamesian (William) 'stream of consciousness' that she loathed.

Excluding materials from appearance in art, for Wharton, was not a withholding of one's right to see and feel all things, but was, rather, a generous and humble exercise that not only made art 'better' in her view, but also opened it up to other potentialities. These potentialities were experienced by the reader as a democratising sense of wonder as to how things might be different through the deployment of a different form or focus of attention. Rather than relying on the energy of the creative writer to capture all things at all times, Wharton's theory of art created drama through a certain exercise of modesty that could provoke the reader's contemplation as to other possible outcomes, forms and ways of being. The irony is that for all the attention that has been paid to Wharton's sociological precision, seen by many as a mark of her sense of literary realism as a static and descriptive force whose purpose is to reify and render objective the often opaque operations of class, her aesthetic theories emphasised a certain democratic 'openness' to the reader that was only possible when one rejected the artist as a force of clarifying, visionary inspiration, and accepted art as a self-consciously partial and relativistic lens on life. As Paul Ohler has noted, in *The Writing of Fiction* Wharton objects to the 'meaningless precision' of 'the stream of consciousness method [. . . whose] very unsorted abundance constitutes in itself the author's subject' (Paul Ohler 'Forms of Ambivalence to 'Tabloid Culture' in Edith Wharton's *The Custom of the Country,* 56), redirecting the value of the novel from what it might reveal about life to the author's own skill alone. If the younger modernists had taken from William James's metaphor of the operations of the mind as 'stream of consciousness' a desire to render all things at once, Wharton had taken from him (or, rather, come simultaneously with him to the realisation of) the far less ambitious, but more democratic, proposition that 'Reality, life, experience, concreteness, immediacy, use what word you will, exceeds our logic, overflows and surrounds it.'[1] In Wharton's philosophy no aesthetic form or artist is wholly original and no art is total. In short, the woman Henry James called 'The Angel of Devastation' took a surprisingly merciful and generous view of art.

In the terms Jacques Rancière has deployed, Whartonian realism (as opposed to the high modernism that scholarship has often venerated as a high point of literary achievement in the West in this period) would be understood as creating a radical potential for 'dissensus' – the breaking and remaking of worlds – that was obscured or undermined by the younger modernists in whose obsession with unassailable artistic potency and 'inspiration' Wharton saw a march towards authoritarianism. Moreover, Wharton's understanding of the evolution of fiction in *The Writing of Fiction* – from the novel of manners, through the high point of French, Russian and Anglo-American 'realism', to the 'modernist novel' of Joyce, Woolf, etc. – was a theory of readerly time and engagement. The 'realist' novel for Wharton was superior to the new modernist aesthetic in part because the 'inspirational theory is seductive' to those who advocate for a 'general "speeding up"' of the world (*The Writing of Fiction*, 12). That is to say that unlike an earlier realism whose achievements lay in the creation of uncertainty and space for thought, there was something inherently fascistic, Taylorite or totalitarian in the emergent modernist doxa's conflation of artistic value with intellectual speed; a belief that the artist had all the answers the reader needed and was greater than the layman because they came to them quickly and without visible effort. Put another way, if Whartonian realism cultivated 'intelligence' in its readers by inspiring a spirit of enquiry or growth that developed the values of mid-century transcendental self-culture, 'high' modernism operated, as Mark McGurl has also noted, within the new twentieth-century realm of 'IQ'.[2] It favoured speed, efficiency and individual control. Wharton writes,

> Many people assume that the artist receives, at the outset of his career, the mysterious sealed orders known as 'Inspiration,' and has only to let that sovereign impulse carry him where it will. Inspiration does indeed come at the outset of every creator, but it comes most often as an infant, helpless, stumbling, inarticulate, to be taught, and guided; and the beginner, during his time of training his gift, is as likely to misuse it as a young parent to make mistakes in teaching his first child. (11–12)

Two things in particular are notable in this passage. The first is, as I have suggested above, Wharton's distinctly un-romantic distrust of pure 'inspiration' as too often a cover for the making of bad art. The second is that in the use of the word 'sovereign' we can see Wharton's sense of the new modernist aesthetic's political unconscious. Crucially, this sensibility is both patriarchal ('carry *him* where it will') and oddly neglectful and cruel. The child of art is given none of the male artist's time to grow and develop and, as such, remains 'helpless, stumbling, inarticulate' (11). That is, the 'child' in the hands of much modernist literature becomes an ideal dumb subject of control and not a reasoning citizen capable of their own meaningful thought and action. Both abusive in its neglect, and authoritarian in its self-regard, the modernist novel's cult of inspiration was a danger to the flourishing of a democracy. Wharton understood 'inspiration' to be an elite discourse that was notable for its privatising function, and whose power derived from the elitist, furtive and conspiratorial place of the 'sealed order' whom none but the eyes of the artist might perceive. Like the seer-philosopher of Thomas Carlyle, the modernist artist dressed themselves in the habiliments of the law-bringer so as to wrest power from the common reader with their democratising force of dissensus and reify their own intellect and esteem. In the terms Franz Boas has laid out, modernism is the aesthetic style of the 'esoteric doctrine', while realism (so often seen by Theory as the more aesthetically 'rigid' form) becomes the style of the 'exoteric'; the style, as Boas saw it, of the radical, destabilising and racially and culturally 'impure' 'common people'.

At the beginning of this book, I spoke of the aesthetic dimension that has often been overlooked in Franz Boas's understanding of the culture concept. I suggested that the sheer abundance of materials that might pertain to a particular 'culture' required the trained aesthetic vision of the curator-anthropologist to render them meaningful. Yet even as it seemed to imply the controlling power of the anthropologist over 'primitive' cultures that replayed in microcosm the hierarchy of colonial power, this early Boasian mode of reasoning also assumed the partiality of the anthropologist's reason, suggesting, radically, that no individual or group could have the full facts of a culture's operations at their hands enough that they might describe it wholly and for all time. This facet of Boas's work caused him to draw ire from fellow anthropologists for his lack of systemisation, or unwillingness to plot materials on a clear teleological hierarchy of value from 'primitive' to 'civilized', so that the later Boasians deemed it necessary to remedy it through their embrace of 'national character studies'. Moreover, if Boas was uncertain about the power of the outsider (the anthropologist or the artist) to render a complete and longstanding picture of a discrete culture, Boas's 'exoteric doctrine' also resisted the pull towards rendering 'culture' as essentialist and pure from *within* by members of the tribal group. Boas saw the idea of 'purity' in any given culture as the work of an elite class whose 'sovereign' vision abolished the truly cosmopolitan matter of life and disrupted the productive interpenetration of groups and historical forces. 'Cultures', in the Boasian system, were not 'original' or pure works of inspiration that were long lasting, but fragile exercises of temporary formal arrangement. Still more, the study of 'culture' was always implicitly a study of class, and vice versa. To be a good anthropologist was to be a modest one, as uncertain about the longevity of their work as history itself is about the capacity of one form of group life to sustain itself undiminished or unaffected across time.

It is not a common enterprise to place the aesthetic theories of the patrician, frequently anti-democratic Wharton alongside the pluralism of an anti-imperialist, anti-racist American-German-Jewish Boas, but in this final main chapter, I will seek to show that both Boas and Wharton were similarly concerned about the pull of theories of culture towards totalities that cut out multiplicity and change from the equation in favour of the elite control of the artist or the economically powerful. When read alongside Boasian anthropology (something it is very unclear whether Wharton was consciously and directly aware of), Wharton and Boas's aesthetic theories display similar concerns and point to a specific mode of Progressive Era thought that I have described in this book as 'the aesthetic of everyday life' that would be supplanted by later twentieth-century-modernism's 'cult of originality' in the decades after the First World War.

Wharton's critique of the cult of originality that surrounded modernism turned on her belief that the artist was not a font of inspiration who existed in some prophetic and accelerated space of the intellect able to perceive all and to explain it for all time, but was a 'creative imagination' whose 'experience' could 'make a little go a long way, provided ... it remain[ed] long enough in the mind and is sufficiently brooded upon' (12). In the place of the immediacy of the modernist's oracular vision, the realist artist was a more lumbering beast, ruminating and brooding on experience; a metaphor that Wharton held too for the realist novel as a form able to provoke contemplation and not give over its meaning too readily and speedily to its reader. In her disagreement with 'originality', which she did not see as a prime mover or purpose of art and culture, Wharton's philosophy has much in common with the famous critique of 'independent invention' made by Boas (as discussed in the introduction). Boas argued against the idea that civilisations existed in a natural teleology and moved through spectacular, evental 'stages' that permitted the invention of objects and tools (a succession of epiphanic great leaps forward). Instead of visionaries propelling culture forward through lineal, hierarchical time, Boas argued for a more gentle 'creative intelligence' within groups that incorporated materials from other cultures and used them in new ways; a pragmatic, collectivist version of tool use theory. Like Wharton's aesthetic critique of modernism, then, Boas's critique of 'independent invention' underplayed the role of 'originality' and foregrounded use-value, plurality and diversity. Additionally, the Boasian theory of tool use worked against linear time. This created an imaginary based in a speculative anthropology awakened to the possibility of alternative propositions and ontologies. An object might be used one way in one moment and another in another moment, rather than being marked by the 'unity of mankind', which was monadic, monumental and given to the establishment of racial and cultural hierarchies.

In what follows I will bring together Wharton's aesthetic theories with cultural anthropology through a reading of the work that engages most closely with American materials and social science, *The Custom of the Country*. Following this I will turn to Wharton's post-First-World-War work, *A Son at the Front*, to think through that novel's treatment of cultural diffusion and flow in the context of military conflict – something that was hotly debated in the public sphere by contemporary (or near contemporary) cultural theorists like Randolph Bourne. In my reading of *The Custom of the Country*, I build on Jennie A. Kassanoff and Nancy Bentley's work on Wharton and ethnographic science, but also deviate from them in key ways. Kassanoff has argued for a straight reading of racial meaning in the anthropological lexicon Wharton deploys in the novel that takes biographical facts of Wharton's life (her known occasional, personal antisemitism and class bigotry) and applies these to her novels, arguing that one cannot be separated from the other and that art has a direct, mimetic, relation to real life. She sees in Wharton's description of 'invaders' and the Old New York upper crust as a doomed race of natives a racial subconscious that situates the book as a response of Wharton's own fears about Gilded Age immigration overwhelming the 'white' Eastern population. Contrarily, I see this work as a dramatisation of Wharton's thinking on the role of the artist as a 'creative intelligence' that is disrupted by the elite influence of money, capital and the Progressive Era culture of acceleration and efficiency. That is, I take the novel more seriously as a politically radical work, which, despite the origins and status position of its author, argues that under conditions of equality and in the presence of the right kind of intellectual and aesthetic training, democratic participation and social hope are possibilities in the future. I suggest she does this by means of her attention to a figure who *might* have become such a disruptive, radical force, but under the influence of elite capitalism ends up doing the very opposite: the irrepressible Undine Spragg. Moreover, while Nancy Bentley reads the novel through a Bourdieusian lens to show how 'culture' confirms status positions and undermines progress, I see the novel as deliberative, caustic and full of deliberate inconsistencies and spaces of subjunctive reflection: moments when time might go one way or might go another. The very fact of the seeming contradiction that Edith Wharton the person (an anti-democratic individual) could make novels that contained critique of existing capitalist social relations and imagined new forms of sociality dramatises perfectly her aspiration for the value of the novel as a form that can come uncoupled (divorced) from the relationship between status/habitus in real life. In Wharton's theory of the novel, as I suggested above in relation to *The Writing of Fiction*, we can find democratic potential even if its author does not outwardly profess it. The novel can hold positions we do not and imagine opportunities we cannot foresee.

Divorce Has Its Uses

The year 1913 was an important, transitional one for Edith Wharton. The period was punctuated by some of the major events of her long and productive life: her divorce from Teddy after twenty-eight years of marriage, her surprisingly exuberant participation in modernist upheavals as an audience member for the Ballet Russe's infamously riotous performance of Stravinsky's *Rite of Spring*, and the inauguration of what Henry James referred to as her years of 'whirligig' existence travelling with various friends around Europe and Africa. The period also saw the serial publication in *Scribner's Magazine* of *The Custom of the Country*, Wharton's most acerbic, comic and ruthless long work, which she had been working on through all the years of her separation from her husband. *The Custom of the Country* is a story of how a newly wealthy Midwesterner from the fictional Apex City, the loveable-loathsome anti-heroine Undine Spragg, becomes one of the richest women of her age through a series of strategic marriages to, or rather divorces from, members of the Gilded Age cosmopolitan elite. Crucial to the plot are Undine's negotiations over the ownership of a set of apparently priceless medieval wallhangings after the termination of her marriage to the French aristocrat Raymond De Chelles. The novel, then, is a story of vulgar capitalists and their penchant for plundering the Old World, as critics have often noted. But the novel goes beyond a rewriting of Thorstein Veblen's intellectual satire of the 'conspicuous consumption' among the new American rich, *The Theory of the Leisure Class*. When considered in light of its publication context, the novel becomes a more intellectually engaged piece – embedded within contemporary debates about what Michael Elliott has called the 'conflict between different concepts of culture – one that relies upon ideas of static, irreducible differences and another that offers the possibility of universal cultural development' (Elliott, *The Culture Concept*, 48). Indeed, the novel emerged at a moment when American social science was undergoing a revolution equal to the effects of Darwin on biology. With the 1911 publication of Boas's *The Mind of Primitive Man*, American intellectuals were forced to confront the possibility that nineteenth-century race hierarchies mattered little in human development when set against the effects of imperialism and/or cultural diffusion of other kinds, driving a significant turn towards artifact collection and a paradigm shift in understandings of human creativity and intelligence. For Boas, 'creativity was expressed in the imaginative manipulation and reinterpretation of elements given ... by cultural tradition, or borrowed from other cultural traditions' (Stocking, *Race, Culture, Evolution*, 223). Boas argued that mythologies and cultural patterns operate by the 'accretion of foreign material', but that this foreign material is not taken on unchanged. Instead, it always undergoes an adaptation according to the culture that inherited or acquired it.

Since her youth Wharton had been a reader and contributor to Charles Scribner's Sons various publications – including the sister periodicals *Scribner's Magazine* under Edward Burlingame and *The Century Illustrated* under Richard Watson Gilder – and was an avid consumer of these magazines' peculiar, and barely demarcated, mixture of European high art criticism, literary realism, anthropological field reports, and adventurous narratives of exploration and travel. This mixture was particularly suited to Wharton's own aesthetic vision, which never settled easily into disciplinary categories. As Mark Noonan has noted of the elite periodicals of age, *The Century* and *Scribner's* especially may be seen as a Gilded Age 'touchstone' for the development of a distinctively American version of modernism that participated in the developments of the European avant-garde but yet also remained productively at odds with its associated formal and sexual revolutions; holding fast to the US character of what Wharton's friend George Santayana usefully called the 'genteel tradition': a moderately Puritanical and somewhat bloodless understanding of progress. Noonan writes that 'the magazine tried to corral dispute and far-flung geographic regions and cultural topics into a coherent publication, performing 'America' with every issue – each performance an effort to define and control the meaning of the term' (2010: x). That performance of 'America' was, quite obviously, a performance of growing American power as Scribner's Sons' focus on plurality of content made claims for the USA as the newly crowned torchbearer for a version of 'civilization' after the 1880s that married imperialism to an emergent cultural pluralism.[3] Among the performances of a paradoxically American version of cosmopolitanism that Scribner's publications were especially invested in was charting the changing landscape of anthropological research culture in the USA from the late 1870s and the founding of the Bureau of American Ethnology, under the directorship of the *Scribner's* contributor John Wesley Powell, to the late 1910s and the birth of a fully-fledged pluralistic 'culture concept' in the work of Franz Boas and his students Zora Neale Hurston, Margaret Mead, Ruth Benedict and Edward Sapir. The pattern of American ethnography differed significantly from the European social scientific model through its emphasis on first-hand observation, deductive particulars before inductive systemisations, self-reflexivity concerning data collection, and increasing resistance to bio-evolutionary explanations of human behaviour. As I suggested in the introduction, all of this contributed to an attention to the effects of cultural exchange between semi-autonomous tribal groups, rather than what the anthropologist Leslie White called the 'beautiful simple order' of evolutionary ethnology. Yet, for Wharton this form of what would later be called 'American multi-culturalism' was made possible by the perverted forces of American global capitalism as the USA arrived in the late nineteenth century, chequebook in hand, on the world stage. Indeed, if Stravinsky's *Rite of Spring* interbred James Frazer's narrative of human cultural origins in substitutionary violence with Freud's attention to sexual desire, and so birthed a form of modernist primitivism, then *The Custom of the Country* is its moderately Puritanical, depthless, but no less ruthless, American cousin – a story that partially rejects primitive essence in favour of the flat plane and spatio-temporal compression of something like plurality and cultural diffusion, yet shows how this form of exchange and appropriation is seldom an antidote to modern capitalism, but rather its corollary. While Wharton focused on sexuality most clearly in other works such as *The House of Mirth, Summer, The Age of Innocence*, etc., as Gloria Erlich argued in *The Sexual Education of Edith Wharton*, even turning her hand to pornography in her personal notebooks, critics have puzzled over the essential sexlessness of Undine Spragg. As Arielle Zibrak recently noted, 'despite all the effort and attention that Undine devotes to looking sexy, Undine hates sex'. (6) What she does enjoy, though, is uncoupling.

I would argue that Wharton's metaphor of divorce in *The Custom of the Country* serves as a means to reflect on three developments in American social science that she would have encountered in Charles Scribner's Sons journals and her other wider reading in contemporary American literature: first, the development of participant observation as ethnographic practice; second, the sense of culture as plural and not bound to an implicit hierarchy that begins with articles in *Scribner's* on the Zuni pueblos by Frank Hamilton Cushing and was raised, too, by archaeological discoveries that undermined the temporal arrangements of evolutionary ethnology; and third, how the growth of American capitalist power in the period undermined the radical potential of these new cultural theories.

As Jennie A. Kassanoff and Brad Evans have both shown, among Charles Scribner's Sons' most notable and oft-discussed articles in the years when Wharton began contributing to the magazines were Frank Hamilton Cushing's 'My Adventures Among the Zuni' – three sketches published between 1882 and 1883. As Evans has remarked,

> Cushing has been remembered historically as not only the colorful figure who helped invent the ethnographic practice of participant-observation but also as one of the few American anthropologists, perhaps the only one, to have predated Franz Boas in using the term 'culture' in its plural, relativized form'. (Evans, 25)

Cushing's then 'eccentric' approach to observing the pueblo involved the ethnographer becoming adopted into the Zuni system of tribal kinship. In this way, Cushing implicated the 'private' matters of sexual and domestic union directly within the 'public' operation of social science. The reality, of course, is that this relationship was already well established within the colonial rape culture of imperial conquest ethnography, but seldom before had marriage been so outwardly defined and thought through as a scientific method, something that must have fascinated a twenty-one-year-old Edith Wharton. Indeed, in his sketches for *The Century* Cushing highlighted how such adoption or marriage into another culture was necessary if one was to gain comprehensive knowledge about it. Furthermore, Cushing noticed that 'the most powerful and most perfectly organized of all native associations, in some respects resembling the Masonic order' (Cushing, 28) were the 'Priests of the Bow' who were the 'only truly esoteric of all [native] bodies'. 'Early learning this', writes Cushing, 'I strove for nearly two years to gain membership in it, which would secure at once standing with the tribe and entrance to all sacred meetings . . . I succeeded' (29).

What made Cushing's articles revolutionary was their effective abandonment of the racial demarcations that often shaped Gilded Age treatments of the tribal other. In *The Custom of the Country*, the account of Undine Spragg's adventures begins with a similar move from observation to participation within a sect that is described by Wharton in similar terms to Cushing's account of the Zuni – as a society which in being viewed by outside forces becomes subject to the threat of annihilation. Wharton writes that Undine's first husband, the well-connected, old-moneyed Ralph Marvell of New York, 'sometimes called his mother and grandfather the Aborigines, and likened them to those vanishing denizens of the American continent doomed to rapid extinction with the advance of the invading race. He was fond of describing Washington Square as the 'Reservation', and of prophesying that before long its inhabitants would be exhibited at ethnological shows, pathetically engaged in the exercise of their primitive industries' (*Custom*, 297). Indeed, Undine's early attempts to acquire a box at the opera by emotionally blackmailing her father (a Masonic banker no less) artfully combines the act of viewing the social world around her with a desire for social inclusion that mirrors the shaping tensions of American ethnographic practice in Cushing's essays. Wharton writes

> she had looked down at them, enviously, from the balcony – she had looked up at them, reverentially, from the stalls; but now at last she was on a line with them, among them, she was part of the sacred semicircle whose privilege it is, between the acts, to make the mere public forget that the curtain has fallen. (*Custom*, 290)

By describing Undine's entrée into New York society thus, Wharton brings together a number of important themes of the novel as a whole. Among these are the spatial dimensions of power,

New York society's interest in the movement of culture more than an aesthetic appreciation of its objects (a theme she would return to again in *The Age of Innocence*), and the feminist claims of the novel concerning the power wielded by women in the new marriage market, which, while not the 'equal' of male financial capital, Wharton argues repeatedly puts female influence and intelligence 'on a line' with patriarchy. But still more, the author here captures the driving force of the novel's satire and its radical potential – that an outsider can learn the ways of an existing elite, mimic them, and also destabilise them. Undine is not just an invader buoyed along by and cresting the waves of changing market forces beyond and outsider her, she is an active 'Agent' of disruption in deep cover, playing all sides and utilising her creative intelligence to advance the agenda of herself and her family. It is this facet of her character that makes her so compelling and allows the reader to follow her for four hundred or so pages without exhaustion. As Paul Ohler has remarked, Undine represents a potent hybridising force that counteracts the closed cultural world of Old New York and whose 'expansion into a boundary zone of mixing forms during a period of a dissolving cultural stratification present both the vanishing world of Ralph Marvell and the ascendancy of the conditions that shape Edith Wharton's reform-minded, Progressive-era fiction' (Ohler, 59). Implicit in Wharton's aesthetic is a sense of potentiality. We read Undine's *bildung* in full dramatic awareness of the sense that Undine might use her powers for good. The possibility is always there. Perhaps. Wharton's novel shows that the world she disrupts *needs* disrupting and Undine *might* be the agent of our radical demos. She also might not. Yet what comes between this radical potentiality and its conservative actuality is money and nationalism. It is in this aspect that the novel gains its power as a satirical masterpiece. Outside of agit-prop, *The Custom of the County* is among the era's most ardently anti-capitalist novels, deploying a dialectical vision that is almost Marxian in its dual recognition of the necessity of democratic accountability and the sense that capital's power of disruption might yet be harnessed for progressive aims. In order for this sensibility of future potentiality – the sense of the might, but not-yet (as Ernst Bloch would categorise the 'utopian' impulse) – to be effective, the novel must constantly hold categories in suspension, committing neither to its own implicit radicalism nor deploying an aesthetic that would close down potentiality in a morass of thick description.

It is in this aesthetic sense that the novel cannot be read as a full and unadulterated exercise in thinking with race, as Kassanoff has suggested. The novel is far too pragmatic in its deployment of unstable linguistic registers and meanings to hold fast to a singular racial imaginary. Undine is both an American 'barbarian' from the Mid-West (a categorisation that would have resonated in a society reeling from the effects of the recent Ghost Dance War against the Sioux of South Dakota) that sacks the traditional centres of civilisation *and* an anthropologist, blurring hierarchical distinctions as does the participant-observer. Wharton and Cushing's shared observation that sacredness lies 'on a line' with both knowledge and inclusion reflects their joint participation in the Scribner syndicate's complex aesthetic and political project. Yet both writers also shared a sense of the dangers implicit in such attempts at cultural mixing; Wharton because of her conservatism, and Cushing because of his conflicted position as both loyal 'Priest of the Bow' and Western salvage ethnographer. In *The Custom of the Country* Wharton cleverly presents moments in which Undine undergoes a sort of culturally-assimilative overreach to maintain this aesthetic of questioning concerning what is and what is not acceptable. These are moments when as readers we are forced to cringe at what to modern audiences would be seen plainly as cultural appropriation. The American ex-pats of Paris, for example, perform their 'Americanness' through the acquisition and expression of forms to which they have no rightful claim. Wharton's novel dramatises, in a typically dry and ironic way, how the performance of 'Americanness' conducted by Undine Spragg is both hopefully cosmopolitan *and* regressively nationalist-imperialist. Remarking on the French fetish for Americans that Undine begins in Paris, Wharton writes:

> Madame de Trezac had lately discovered that the proper attitude for the American married abroad was that of a militant patriotism; and she flaunted Undine Marvell in the face of the Fauborg like a particularly showy specimen of her national banner. The success of the experiment emboldened her to throw off the most sacred observances of her

> past ... she resuscitated Creole dishes, she patronized negro melodies, she abandoned her weekly teas for impromptu afternoon dances, and the prim drawing-room in which dowagers had droned echoed with a cosmopolitan hubbub (*Custom*, 502).

The grim spectacle of Undine and Madame de Trezac 'patroniz[ing] negro melodies' (in which we read both meanings of 'patronise' as endorse and also undermine) evokes, of course, blackface minstrelsy as a notable example of misguided, and culturally-appropriative overreach. What causes this moment of hesitation in the reader concerning the right of Undine and Trezac to ownership of certain forms of cultural material is the question of time, as the present and the future of culture collide and interpenetrate. Undine's vision of a world where all objects and cultural forms are fungible can only exist in a utopian space outside of a present 'representative regime' that is built on, and maintains, racial and social inequality. As Gabriel Rockhill has noted in his gloss on Rancière's work on the politics of the modern novel, *Mute Speech*, what is deemed to be 'appropriate' and 'efficacious' is determined by a 'poetics of representation' by which certain genres of performance or types of object are defined as the realm of only certain types of people. These ethnographically locked cultural forms rely on 'fables' (blackness cannot be whiteness, Frenchness cannot be Americanness, working class cannot become upper class) that contain within them a prescriptive political vision that closes down the potentiality of full expressivity. He writes,

> In the poetics of representation, fables, understood as arrangements of action in fictional space-time, belong to genres, which are defined by the subject represented and are organised around the appropriate nature of action and discourse within the real field of efficacious speech. (13)

What Rockhill is pointing to in Rancière's work here is the acknowledgement that under current social arrangements certain genres have specific political affordances and can be deployed only by certain organisations of group life. Contrarily, Undine operates within a different timeline, in a kind of utopian, cosmopolitan free-market space where all things are available and where the flow of actions, images, forms is not bound to regimes of 'appropriateness'. This is her privilege. The privilege to be out of time with the world as it is. The nightmare of Undine's performances lies precisely in the clash between this future cosmopolitan regime of expressivity (which she believes exists in her present) and an extant regime of representation where forms have their 'appropriate' addressee. It nonetheless contains within it the seed of a utopian proposition of a radical dissensus and remaking of the world in which objects exist without implicit hierarchy or cultural impediment upon their free flow. It is not, after all, unimaginable that race, culture and class might be differently conceptualised in the future, such that to shift from one to another is a real and accepted possibility. Indeed, left progressivism relies on the social hope that they might. For Wharton, almost as if she were a Marxian historian, what impedes this move from a pure regime of representation to a pure space of expressivity is the fact of capitalist exploitation – the sense that Undine is 'privatising' and expropriating or extracting from one cultural tradition ('negro melodies', say) to enrich another without compensation – which as readers we are made affectively to respond to through her aesthetic of the cringe. In the terms Boas lays out in his work on 'esoteric doctrines', Undine and Trezac use their status to extract an 'esoteric' cultural force from the common pool of 'exoteric' potentialities. This 'esoteric' force is capitalistic and, also, crucially, nationalistic and 'white'. Wharton's argument here is perhaps surprising to us in the ethical and political understanding of the problems of exploitation and nationalism it shows. Yet it also aligns with her understanding of 'good' art in *The Writing of Fiction* as a work that is selective about what it includes and excludes in its form. Taken at face value Wharton's call for selectivity appears to mean refinement, or a Bourdieusian sense of exquisite 'taste' that serves as a cover for racial hierarchy, but when seen alongside the arguments about cultural appropriation made in *The Custom of the Country* it contains an ethical force too; a sense that there is something deeply immoral and dubious about an art that believes it can have all things in it in a world still riven with racial, cultural and economic injustice.

Undine's performances are not the only reference made in the text to nations or cultures being especially rich material for stagey demonstration. Indeed, the truly tragic figure in the novel, her first husband Ralph Marvell, considers his own family in roughly equivalent terms. As I quoted earlier:

> Ralph sometimes called his mother and grandfather the Aborigines, and likened them to those vanishing denizens of the American continent doomed to rapid extinction with the advance of the invading race. He was fond of describing Washington Square as the 'Reservation,' and of prophesying that before long its inhabitants would be exhibited at ethnological shows, pathetically engaged in the exercise of their primitive industries (297)

As anyone who has taught the novel and had to contend with student horror at this passage will know, the dominant affect here is not tragedy alone, but ambivalence. Like Undine performing 'negro melodies', what right does Ralph have to place his historic Dutch-American wealth 'on a line' with the genocide of many nations of people? Perhaps the answer is none. But Wharton's blankly satirical realism poses the question and, as such, the audience are made to participate in an ongoing, temporally extended construction of meaning.

In describing anthropological displays and culturally insensitive performances in the novel, it is highly possible that Wharton is making reference to the most famous of these exhibitions – the ethnological exhibits at the 1893 Chicago World's Fair, which Boas himself organised as first assistant to Frederick Ward Putnam (who had been Director of Ethnology and Archaeology for the Fair). This exhibition included a troupe of fourteen Kwakiutl people who were made to reside in a mock village designed by Boas and perform their daily activities as a show for tourists. The reference in Ralph's account, then, runs deeper than being simply a humorous description of the decline of Washington Square. They are, in addition, a self-conscious account of the performative 'doubling' at the heart of Wharton's realism. The author's account of Ralph's conception of Washington Square life does not extend sympathy to Ralph alone by aligning with him and his hierarchical vision of evolution in seeing imperialism and the destruction of a 'primitive' culture by a more 'civilized' one as inevitable. Rather, it also shows how residual forms of ethnographic display in the Gilded Age constructed this sense of hierarchy by mapping certain peoples onto forms of 'industry'. These shows did not engage in a display of all everyday life of a people, but captured them at forms of manual labour so as to create a conflation of social class with a position on the hierarchy of evolutionary advancement that had white collar work by white people at its height. Much as in Plato's Republic, forms of labour were therefore shown to overlay onto a sliding scale of politically legitimate speech. Not only are the people in 'ethnological shows' not supposed to speak as political subjects, they are also made racially other by their display as figures bound wholly to forms of labour and never given the right to the multiplicity of potentialities in time that defines everyday life under modernity. That is, in her reference to ethnological shows, Wharton demonstrates how hierarchies of value attributed to labour helped to define a group's position on a hierarchy of social progress, thereby undertaking a fascinatingly far-sighted analysis of the relationship between spectacle and the reification of class and race categories. Rather than being merely a direct, realist account of experience, Wharton's technique is engaged, therefore, in an exercise of critique that fights on all fronts; questioning Ralph's white naivete in the same moment as she undertakes an analysis of the stultifying effects of contemporary scientific spectacles. As such, she acknowledges the temporalities of older forms of ethnographic description, accounted for in Johannes Fabian's famous critique of anthropology *Time and the Other*, as a practice that inadvertently condemns to historical fixity – therefore social death – the subjects of its analysis.

Being a wealthy woman of the upper crust, we would perhaps not expect such a critique of the relationship between power, cosmopolitanism and race/class differences from Wharton. Indeed, we might assume that Wharton believed in and wholly endorsed the hierarchy of value attached to objects that are mapped simply onto a teleological trajectory of primitive to civilised that has British, American and French culture at its apotheosis. Certainly, in her most propagandistic writings on behalf of France, such as *French Ways and Their Meanings* written during the war and in support of American intervention, as well as in her personal letters, we see her cleaving to this civilisational discourse. Yet this overlooks that novels do not operate as carriages of an artist's personal views alone. The aesthetics of her novels, and the affective valences they mobilise at the level of form and style, propose a different hypothesis. Indeed, there is more than a little of the anarchist in Wharton's aesthetic politics. We are driven to social hope in Undine's powerful career of destruction of the *ancien régime*, while also made to respond to the open question of how far is too far as it pertains to imperialistic cultural appropriation and acquisition. This question is inspired, consciously, by the novel's critique of capitalism. It forces us to imagine alternative ontologies and trajectories in the present, while also recognising the problems of contemporary conditions and institutional imperatives that variously impede them. The force of much of Wharton's critique lies in her engagement in the book with the problems that occur when the utopian aspirations of 'exoteric', ethnographic circulation meet the privatising impulses of 'esoteric' capitalist control. Like the anarchists of the Haymarket, Wharton suggests that we can only have aestheticism – an idealised life lived in the pursuit of beauty alone – if we first abolish private property and resist the appeal of the spectacle. Undine is an anthropologist of sorts, a disruptive force against tired old regimes of power, but she is also a spy – embedding herself in another culture and advancing the aims of American capital as she does so. In this way, *The Custom of the Country* reflects directly, too, the Communist Boas's fears about the institutionalisation of anthropology in the period. Boas, following the First World War, would come to outwardly denounce the use of his science for the advancement of imperial and capitalist aims, writing to *The Nation* magazine in 1919 that

> [A] businessman whose aim is personal profit within the limits allowed by a lenient law—such may be excused if they set patriotic deception above common everyday decency and perform services as spies . . . Not so the scientist. The very essence of his life is the service of truth . . . A person . . . who uses science as a cover for political spying, who demeans himself to pose before a foreign government as an investigator and asks for assistance in his alleged researches in order to carry on, under this cloak, his political machinations, prostitutes science in an unpardonable way and forfeits the right to be classed as a scientist. (Boas, 'Letter to the Editor', *The Nation*, 20 December 1919)

Under the guidance of Madame de Trezac, like Scribner's magazines to which Wharton's career was wedded, it is nationalism, or the performance of it, that becomes in *The Custom of the Country* something that allows Undine to circulate. Yet she also functions as a kind of agent of US imperialism who operates behind French lines, and Wharton never allows us to abandon the sense of ambivalence we have about her mission. Undine's power as a figure of satire lies in part in how she functions as a node in a wider cultural debate concerning the direction, meaning and rights of the nation. Undine's 'performance' and circulation has much in common with both the circulation of native artefacts and the growth of magazines like *Scribner*'s and *Century*, which presented their Americanness not as backwardness but as a path to a form of cosmopolitan, capitalist prestige. In this way, the 'Culture Concept' and the capitalist 'Culture Industry' (both under formation in this period) are drawn together in the novel through a shared interest in attention, performance and circulation as the path to the creation of meaning and value. What I am arguing here is that Wharton analysed an attitude in the American mind that found little contradiction between 'cultural pluralism', of sorts, and capitalism; that praised diversity and liberated desire, and only denounced the capitalist vision of the world when it interrupted the operation of choice. This is what makes the title of the novel so remarkably subtle and prescient in its self-reflexive analysis of the ethnographic impulses of social fiction. The 'Custom of the Country' means, of course, to fit in with acceptable modes of being, something like 'When in Rome', so evokes a capacity of infiltration or dissembling such as might be undertaken by an anthropological informant. It also engages in a pun similar to Hawthorne's in 'The Custom House', in meaning both capitalism *and* tradition. Yet, the 'Custom of the Country' has a moral component too. The phrase was drawn from a play by John Fletcher that referred to *droit de seigneur* in medieval France – the right of a lord to sexual relations with peasant women. This was, of course, an act of sexual violation that was reliant upon the inequality of power relations. The title connotes, therefore, an exploration of exploitation, desire and power in the context of new American wealth. Consequently, it draws together something like 'culture' with exchange, trade and power, prophesying an admixture of cultural pluralism with capitalism that was an especially American proposition and would come define the country's foreign relations in the twentieth century.

Like Undine, whose simple acquisition of a theatre box permits her to enter New York society and triggers a sequence of events that eventually leads to her bankrupting Ralph Marvell and running off to Europe with his best friend, Cushing's act of inclusion into the famously secretive and private Zuni tribe assisted with the imperial projects of American modernity. 'During his stay at Zuni', Evans writes, 'Cushing helped Smithsonian collecting expeditions acquire over 12,600 Zuni artefacts, a shocking number when considering the pueblo's population numbered less than 2,000 residents' (Evans, 33). It is here that we see how Wharton's idea of divorce operates in the novel. At a moment when the author herself was witnessing the creative freedom that came with the release from her marriage to Teddy, her heroine Undine experiences divorce both as a means to allow the flow of objects and currency around the world and precipitate her own form of creative-cultural development.

In the novel Wharton renders divorce as an aesthetic practice that disrupts the patterns of traditional kinship, allows the acquisition of cultural knowledge, and serves as a droll reflection on the US forms of ethnographic culture concept pioneered by Boas and Cushing. As James Clifford and George Marcus famously noted in *Writing Culture* (1986), American ethnographic practice is caught in a double bind, since it must, at once, participate within a culture and yet eventually gain sufficient distance to critique and describe it. In other words, a border must be breached in order to be made; we must participate within a culture to know that it really is something distinct and separate, which writing then reifies and makes 'real' at a geographical or psychical remove. Such a two-step move is implicit in anthropological fieldwork that Boas in America, and Wharton's friend Bronislaw Malinowski in Britain, came to make central to the professionalisation of the field. In the context of the elaborate systems of tribal kinship that mark traditional societies (such as the Zuni or the characterisation of Old New York in Wharton's novel), this required an inclusion into kinship then a subsequent extraction from it: a marriage and then a divorce.

The conflation between emergent cultural pluralism, imperialism and the rage for American collecting can be seen in popular accounts of Franz Boas's and Frederic Putnam's work at the American Museum of Natural History in New York. A *Sunday Illustrated* supplement in the *New York Tribune* from 28 October 1900 proudly announced that the effect of the collecting conducted on one of Franz Boas's largest expeditions, The Jesup North Pacific Expedition of 1897–1902, was to permit the expansion of the museum into a new large hall. The paper writes:

> A unique feature of the Museum work for the last three or four years is the Investigation, through the munificence of Mr Jesup, of the relations between the aborigines of America and the Asiatic races. This inquiry has been conducted along the North Pacific Coast of this continent, and has extended

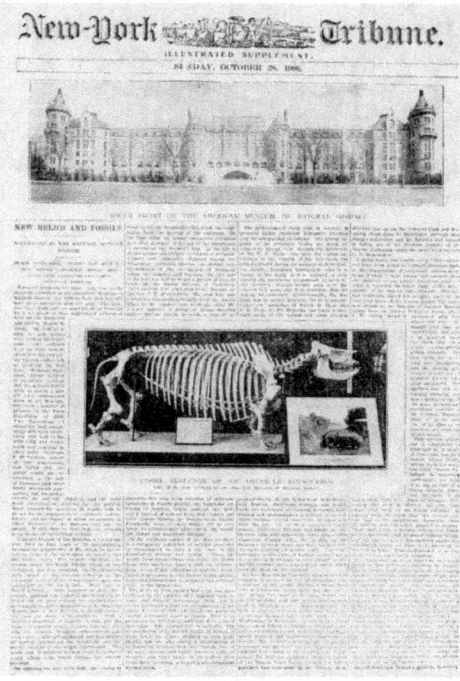

Figure 4.1 Cover, *New York Tribune Illustrated Supplement* (Sunday 28 October 1900), 'New Relics and Fossils'.

into Northeastern Asia. Much of the material collected by the numerous parties of the Jesup expedition is now assembled in the north hall.

Because the Boasian culture concept, pre-empted in some ways by Cushing's fetish for Zuni art, forced anthropology to confront the infinite variety of material and expressive forms that were the product of intercultural exchange and human intellectual diversity, it was far from anathema to a cynical, imperial-capitalist American framework. Even if Boas demanded generosity and humility in the exercise of anthropology, his method, if unchecked, stood to be a collector's paradise. Multiplicity was favoured before the uniformity or consistency across time implied by an evolutionary focus on the stages of man. The New York mind of the Gilded Age and Progressive Era may have baulked at the racial implications of the Boasian turn and its challenge to a biologically deterministic narrative of human development, but it leapt at the expansion of multiplicity, the justification it gave American anthropology for an almost limitless potential collection. Nothing now was old, or conformed to a consistent, universal pattern of development, so nothing now was boring.

At least in theory. Because *The Custom of the Country* is a work that is fascinated with the question of boredom and its relation to capitalist acquisition. Why would a generation given more than any before it and infinitely able to experience forms of diversity and difference in a transnational, cosmopolitan space of exchange be given over so often, as Undine Spragg is, to fits of depressive, stultifying boredom? It is through this theme that *The Custom of the Country* develops its critique of the shifting meaning of 'culture', from 'civilisation' to diffusion and pluralism. And it does so by thinking through, as Wharton would do again in *The Writing of Fiction*, the question of intelligence. Namely, what measure and what character must intelligence take to render meaningful the sheer multitudinous proposition of the cosmopolitan abundance of the era intellectually and socially?

The novel ruminates on the subject of Undine's 'intelligence', which is taken eventually to mean something other than either an IQ measure or the acquisition of actual knowledge. Ralph Marvell notes that:

> Her mind was as destitute of beauty and mystery as the prairie schoolhouse in which she had been educated; and her ideals seemed to Ralph as pathetic as the ornaments made of corks and cigarbands with which her infant hands had been taught to adorn it. (355)

For all its 'destitu[ion] of beauty and mystery', Wharton imbues Undine's mind with an almost superhuman capacity to acquire resources and put them into circulation. Indeed, Undine's capacity is not for invention in the slightest, but for manipulation of available resources, including other people, so as to claim what she desires. This version of human intelligence as a capacity for reworking rather than for originality was central to the development of the American culture concept as Boas first understood it and played an important role in his first challenge to evolutionist ideas in the public debate of the 1880s with Otis Mason over 'independent invention' (the question of how and why human societies developed similar kinds of tools at different times and at large geographic distances). George Stocking has described this thus:

> the evolutionists, cultural creativity was expressed in independent invention. For Boas, man was essentially rather uninventive, but his creativity was expressed in the imaginative manipulation and reinterpretation of elements given to him by his cultural tradition, or borrowed from other cultural traditions. (226)

For Mason, 'independent invention' was a sign of deep, encoded evolutionary patterns of development. Even as it relied on a very strong hierarchal sense of racial and cultural value, it was essentially optimistic and spectacular, defined as it was by the idea that every culture, separated from every other, underwent sudden moments of radical epiphany. Moreover, independent invention implies a unity of mankind in the assumption that every society could undergo the same process of progressive evolution from savagery to civilisation. This would mean that technologies which appeared in one area of the world at one moment might suddenly appear in another civilisation at a later date. In effect, the world was subjected to multiple timelines simultaneously. By contrast, what characterised the difference between one culture and another in the Boasian method was a form of desire to acquire and to utilise an object that already existed in a different way in the shaping of one group's world. This was not, as with Lewis Henry Morgan's or Otis Warren's vision, a standardised and inevitable process of cultural evolution from simple to complex forms. Intellectually, then, the 'culture concept' under development liberated desire, transforming it into a means for objects to move in space. Boas challenged the dominance of race by emphasising the historical dominance of imperialism and trade to the making of the modern world. In her novel, Wharton excavates the feminist implications of this new anthropological theory of culture. Various critics, including Arielle Zibrak, have read *The Custom of the Country* as a feminist novel, by arguing that 'through the negative portrayal of Undine and the positive portrayal of characters like Lilli Estradina, Wharton argues for a sophisticated female sexuality informed by women's own desires' (11). I do not disagree. Yet, the argument extends beyond sexuality to find in female acquisitive desire the apotheosis of the potentiality for cultural change and advancement that Boas's hypothesis established. For Wharton, Undine's relentless desire for new things (and her capacity to rework them to the best effect) is a female-centred version of Boas's ideas concerning the radical potential of desire to make objects move through space and across the otherwise-reified borders of cultural tradition. Undine is a figure of female wanting, and female wanting, for Wharton, if exercised with intelligence, disrupts stultifying convention.

Undine is entirely uninventive. She has, according to the narrator, little to no originality. She 'makes' nothing. What she has is an almost limitless desire to adorn her world with objects. 'With her quick perceptions and adaptabilities', Wharton writes, 'she would soon learn to care more about the quality of the reflecting surface; and meanwhile no criticism ... should mar her pleasure' (340). Just as when a child she adorned the prairie schoolhouse with 'ornaments made of cork and cigarbands', so in her adult social mobility does she begin to adorn her life with other things, little considering their deep meaning or traditional value. Her qualities are depthlessness, assimilation, speed and a capacity for pleasure – but crucially, not of a sexual kind, since in Undine's world in which women do not have a clear and unequivocal right to choose whether that sexuality results in children, sex always runs the risk of relocating one from a flat space of potentiality into a rigid world of historical, biological time. Consequently, Undine is the Boasian character of human intelligence *in extremis*. She is no deep scholar, yet she manipulates cultural forms with consummate skill, playing fast and loose with longstanding traditions of heredity and kinship.

Yet Wharton also shows how the flipside of radical desire is boredom, a trait that also defines Undine's relationship to material things. At various moments in the novel, her restlessness is impeded by circumstance and she falls quickly into the doldrums of debilitating indifference. Following her marriage to Raymond De Chelles in the second half of the book, the narrator remarks that

> Her constitutional restlessness lapsed into apathy ... and the least demand on her activity irritated her. She was beset by endless annoyances: bickerings with discontented maids, the difficulty of finding a tutor for Paul, and the problem of keeping him amused and occupied without having him too much on her hands. (520)

Reflecting the transitional moment of the novel's composition, in it Undine's mind represents a radical potential for disruption that is nonetheless not moderated by an equivalent capacity to maintain interest, to ruminate, or to accept limitations; all features that Wharton saw in her critical writings as essential to the production of good art. What indicates the failures of Undine's mind as a carriage of progressive radicalism is that she feels boredom. She cannot be the utopian force we hope her to be because she baulks at the difference presented before her, even as she desires it, and her mind becomes barren in the presence of possibility. She cannot work out what to do with the forces of change she generates because she never thinks beyond herself and her own needs to the wider world riven with inequality. This is the opposite of the ideal reader-citizen-subject Wharton wants, that is, someone who is disruptive but also motivated by social concerns. In this way, Undine represents the problems of the modernist mind. As Wharton argues in *The Writing of Fiction*, the modernist mind makes for ultimately dull art because it is prone to boredom, frustration and solipsism in the face of multiplicity. It ultimately abandons the radical potential of the everyday it mobilises through its reliance on an aesthetic of 'stream of consciousness' that favours a self-centred celebration of the achievements of the individual artist over the production of ontological uncertainty. Moreover, the modernist mind as Wharton characterised it was an impatient one which, much like Undine at Saint Désert, cannot exist with any contentment in a state of suspension or deliberation. It crams in everything and then becomes impatient for immediate answers. For Wharton, modernism's aesthetic of 'stream of consciousness' is evidence of a boredom with the world that pulls the reader away from the social world by taking the multiplicities of modernity and reducing them to the monadic Event of a fiction itself that can be judged by the category of artistic 'originality' alone and not according to ethical or social values. As Sianne Ngai has remarked, boredom is an aesthetic response to moments of capitalist acquisition when the hyperabundance of material objects available in the world produces a lag in language, 'a kind of linguistic overlapping or simultaneity'[4] as the pattern-ordering processes of the human mind become unequal to the challenge of pure mass. Within the cosmopolitan spaces Undine occupies, and within the intellectual remit of the acquisitive rather than deliberative Boasian culture concept, this boredom becomes a particular problem. Yet crucially, as Ngai suggests, this is a problem of time as much as of space, since it is the simultaneity of objects that obliterates Undine's capacity for understanding. At Saint Désert Undine exists in a desert of abundance, not of lack. Her boredom is a response to all the things her mind and her capitalist milieu demand that she acquire, and with which, lacking a social conscience or awareness of inequality, she has no idea what to do. The problem, it seems, is hereditary. Mr Spragg, too, is unable to comprehend modern abundance in part because he lacks the radical imagination to comprehend the value it might hold as a means to remedy social inequality. Considering the hotels of Europe, he is only 'haunted by a statistical curiosity as to their size, their number, their cost and their capacity for housing and feeding the incalculable hordes of his countrymen' (*Custom*, 450). The reference to 'housing and feeding' is really the nub of his incomprehension. Faced with multitude, it is the gesture of hospitality or grace that is well beyond the Spraggs' understanding since it violates the capitalist ideological imperative concerning the private value of accumulation.

In contrast to this modern mental constipation (whose roots lie in deep solipsism and narcissism), the Whartonian intelligence as presented in *The Writing of Fiction* is social and ethical. It resolves the problem of the abundance of everyday life by emphasising the capacity of the ideal artist to be able to present multiplicity while leaving open the question of the future to deliberation by the reader. Concerned less with private style and with the esteem it confers than with a social impetus to present an abundant world containing choice, the Whartonian variant of modernism captures the spatial dimension of capitalist acquisition, but rejects stream of consciousness's temporal reduction of multiplicity to the monadic form of the literary Event. This can be seen in the ambivalent, satirical tone of her work that resists modernism by resisting the urge to have, simply, too much dominating style. Crucially, it is also in the moments of her deepest boredom that Undine becomes tyrannical, 'bickering [. . .]' with her class underlings, being short or aggressive with her family or her son. Reading forward into Wharton's observations about literary form in *The Writing of Fiction*, we can see the modernist mind under development in Undine's impatient frustrations. This is a mind that is given to the fascistic acquisition of all experiences under one umbrella (her own), and not one whose release of multiplicity causes a radical democratic *dissensus* such as Wharton (and later Jacques Rancière) would find in the high realist novels of Tolstoy or Flaubert. If the modernist stream of consciousness emphasises the urge *to have and to hold* as the aesthetic form of a fascistic desire for control, high realism of Wharton's kind often emphasises the ethical inverse; an aesthetic of divorce: *To have and to let go.* In this way the novel asks an old question anew: Can Beauty make us ethical? Yes. But only if with Beauty comes knowledge of the ethical limits of its forms and its potential inclusions. Otherwise the search for Beauty is indistinguishable from imperialism. This is why, for Wharton, the aesthetic-politics of expression is to be favoured over the politics of representation. It opens up the world to the knowledge of a true difference, which is a difference in time and not merely of shape or colour alone.

Undine Among the Anasazi

Returning to the context of anthropology with which Wharton engages in the novel, it is worth taking some time to note also how the concept of plural temporalities (or multiple, conflicting visions of the past and the future) was a hotly-debated topic in the period. And not only within the confines of American pragmatist or Bergsonian metaphysics. The discovery and colonial acquisition of various historical, tribal civilisations disrupted the simple time-line of evolutionary ethnology. This simultaneous acquisition and disruption that can be seen in the period's anthropological work is reflected not only in *The Custom of the Country*'s own aesthetic of radical ambivalence but is a microcosm of the dialectical forces within capitalism and nationalism themselves that, if we take our lead from Marx, contain the seeds of their own destruction. Much of this anthropological work was done in the Mid- and South-West, giving Undine's birthplace a particular resonance in the context of disruptive challenges to existing thought and cultural systems of meaning-making. As the nominal heartland of American continental dominance in the post-Civil War era, the Mid-West is both the apotheosis of American providential destiny, and the site, at least for Wharton, that most stands to undermine established intellectual mores. In a sense, the moment of the late nineteenth century was defined intellectually (as it was personally for Wharton) by its disruption, as experiences and events became effectively 'divorced' from longstanding narratives of development and consistency. Scholars including Nancy Bentley, Julie Olin-Ammentorp, and Jennie Kassanoff have suggested that for Wharton, Progressive Era anthropology and archaeology offered solace through its frequent confirmations of her long-held racial biases. However, this does not fully capture how the colonisation of the West, and the uncovering of ancient artefacts there, was a profoundly disturbing process that overturned numerous assumptions about race and evolution. Additionally, this disturbance of hierarchy led to questions about how to deal with multiplicity that came to turn, as Wharton's novel does, on the question of 'intelligence' and its role in cultural development. In his popular 1892 account of a journey through the Mesa Verde region of Western Colorado, the

American businessman, mountaineer and amateur archaeologist Frederick H. Chapin, baffled by how to account for his experiences in the cliffside settlements of a group of 'Ancient' Puebloans dubbed the Cliff Dwellers or Anasazi in Navajo, tried his hand at a new, burgeoning late nineteenth-century fad: Speculative Fiction, or as H. G. Wells called it, 'Scientific Romance'. The book is a travel narrative that popularised Colorado and surrounding regions and also an attempt at a synthetic anthropology and archaeology of the Anasazi. Writing of his ride through the upper canyon plateaus of the Mesa Verde, Chapin slips into an almost Wellsian mode of travel in time and relative dimension in space, leaping first into the past and thence to the moon, before, as the book ends, being propelled finally into a distant future itself haunted by the spectre of the past. Chapin writes:

> Beyond the southern Rockies, where Utah, Arizona, and New Mexico border upon Colorado's frontier lines, is a strange land, inhabited by strange people, and containing monuments and relics of yet stranger tribes of an unknown antiquity ... [A] sandstone plateau ... a network of canons that gives to the landscape an appearance resembling the face of the moon. Among some of these deep cuts and weird valleys dwell remnants of wild tribes which once hunted among the mountains to the north and east. (11–12)

Later, he notes:

> It has been inferred by some writers that there must formerly have been a greater annual rainfall, in order that such a population could have been supported by agricultural employment; but judging from so much evidence that we found in the way of tanks and fragments of large water-jars, it would appear that the country was lacking in water even when occupied by the Cliff-Dwellers. And thus the hypothesis of a change of climate therefore becomes unnecessary ...' (181)

Chapin's account, with its references to the 'strangeness' of the Cliff Dweller settlements, the sci-fi 'weirdness' of their lifeways, and the presumed inevitability of their romantic destruction, picks up a number of popular tropes about the Mesa Verde that had emerged in the years since the earliest explorations of the region documented by Westerners, first by the famous photographer William Henry Jackson in the 1870s and then by the Wetherill family in the 1880s. These tropes came to a head in the 1893 Chicago World's Fair, where the Cliff Dweller display constituted one of the most spectacular and visited of the scientific and ethnological shows, housed in an artificial reconstruction of a Colorado cliff and funded by private interests. As Michael Tavel Clarke has shown in his article 'Lessons from the Past: The Cliff Dweller and New Historicism', this spectacular frenzy resulted in a popularisation of the region and its culture that led Theodore Roosevelt to establish Mesa Verde as one of the first US National Parks in 1906 – dedicated to preserving 'the historical works of man' against a booming, private relic-hunting industry. Yet it was not evidence of consistency and the confirmation of racial hierarchies that Roosevelt was preserving so much as a productive uncertainty. Clarke writes,

> Between roughly 1875, when knowledge of the ruins became widespread, and 1930, the cliff dwellings and the stories that circulated around them provoked considerable interest and fascination, inspiring or influencing an impressive range of cultural artefacts. Among them were no fewer than six novels: Henry B Fuller's *The Cliff Dwellers* (1893), Willa Cather's *The Professor's House* (1925) and *The Song of the Lark* (1915), Zane Grey's *Riders of the Purple Sage* (1912), George Allan England's *The Afterglow* (1913) from his Darkness and Dawn series, and Charles Abbott's *The Cliff Dwellers Daughter* (1899) (396).

What attracted so many to the Anasazi was their precarious, but nonetheless ingenious, mode of life and the extraordinary architectural achievements of their civilisation that struck many with a resemblance to the skyscraper-dwelling precariat of the Gilded Age.

What the Cliff Dweller craze served as a test case for, ultimately, were new forms of incorporation that were early instances of epochal shifts towards the Progressive consensus: The US State through the National Parks and preservation efforts of Roosevelt and Jesse Fewkes (a Bureau of American Ethnology anthropologist who documented Mesa Verde settlements), the professionalisation of anthropology, and the emergence of professional art practices understood as avant-garde. What emerges in the texts associated with the Cliff Dwellers is a 'weirdness', a disturbance of the dominant sensorium that may yet be reworked into a new political order but which primarily exists as a kind of suspension; an unsettled assemblage of data that does not quite fit; as precarious as a mountaineering pick stuck in the edifice of nineteenth-century science and culture. The form and the content marry here, because the Cliff Dwellers, too, were conceived of by many as a kind of evolutionary state of exception that never saw out its potential in its own time.

What is perhaps most compelling about Chapin's account of the Cliff Dwellers is the way in which a sense of respect and even tenderness towards the Anasazi (as he imagines them from the fragments of their culture left after their evacuation of the settlements) gives way so rapidly to a defence of manifest destiny and a denial of man's weakness before nature. What first appears as an awareness of the fragility of life itself within nature, modally shifts across the book towards an exercise in grandly melodramatic social Darwinian conceptions of human struggle and survival. Chapin is very much more willing to accept the inevitability of human destruction by war than he is to accept migration, hybridisation and cultural diffusion. He idolises the Cliff Dwellers for their romantic spirit, and cannot decide whether to call them out as a race of intellectual weaklings – hardly able to bear up to the cruel realities of a world of constant war and making too many beautiful pots and not enough arrowheads to fight back 'savage foe' – or celebrate their stoic resilience. In essence, his aesthetic imagination of the Anasazi disrupts the moral force his nineteenth-century mind came to associate with certain sets of behaviour. As Michael Tavel Clarke has remarked, 'The fate of the Cliff Dwellers contradicted American faith in the foreordained victory of civilization over savagery and thus challenged American faith in its new program of overseas imperialism' (400). Such thoughts play through Chapin's imagination as a kind of panic about white genocide – a wish to praise the Cliff Dwellers, while also fearing the conclusions they seem to expose and so disavowing them. In Rancière's terms, the plot (which always maps forms onto a moral logic within the context of a certain historical 'representative regime') breaks down for Chapin in what is a kind of negative epiphany – a moment of 'dissensus' – a new 'distribution of the sensible'. In his struggle with deep time we see a similar tendency to dramatise (render as plot) the experience of historical incident, undergirded by his post-Darwinian culture's kneejerk response to see history as a melodramatic 'survival of the fittest', only then to splutter and falter emotionally as the terms of that drama no longer seem to hold.

What was fascinating about the Cliff Dweller settlements is that in 1892 'dissensus' was their greatest contribution to science. Instead of unanimity, what there was were a series of speculations from diverse subject positions that brought fields into interdisciplinary collaboration. In several ways, what is revealed in the affective shifts undergone by Chapin's text (from compassion to aggression, pride to envy, sense of kinship to sense of exclusion), as well as the generic uncertainty it displays, is the uncomfortable intellectual terrain on which models of temporality and evolution found themselves in the latter decades of the nineteenth century and into the twenty-first. Since neo-Lamarckists tended to give strong sway to the immediate effects of environment, as their notion of the heritability of acquired characteristics made Man malleable in the face of environmental factors, this raised the question of human agency and will. James Mark Baldwin, the influential early Princeton psychologist, called this problem in models of historical evolution the problem of 'intelligence' – why was it that certain organisms adapted and others died out, was there something instinctive in certain civilisations or organisms that rendered them better able to suffer the slings and arrows of outrageous fortune? To answer this question, Baldwin offered an important definition of intelligence in his period that synthesised different conceptions of the trait, calling it in *Darwin and the Humanities* (1909) 'conscious adjustment'. In other words, Baldwin considered the role of human will as a force in change and progress – especially in the context of societies that protected humanity in various degrees from operating within the fold of what was conceived as the Hobbesian 'state of nature'. If intelligence and will could drive evolution – and the Anasazi settlements showed incredible creativity, will and 'intelligence' in their people to be constructed – why then did they disappear so suddenly and not simply die out over time?

If the sentimental and romantic traditions of the nineteenth century implored, as Harriet Beecher Stowe had demanded, that people 'feel right', Chapin in considering the history of the American continent is left feeling 'strange'. Caught in what Rancière calls a moment of 'warped conjunction' where one order of the world meets another, Chapin is completely incapable of understanding how the Cliff Dwellers were able to build such settlements and exist in such a complex state of civilisation at such an early moment in historical time. The fact that they seemed agriculturally settled, with a system of social organisation not seen elsewhere, disrupted his understanding of the terms of civilisation, in which the organisation of time required to produce such advanced architecture and art must – for him and many in his period informed by Lewis Henry Morgan's cultural evolutionism – rely on there being an imperialist enterprise and the organised overproduction of food.

In his 1895 analysis of pots and baskets taken from the Cliff Dweller settlements and included in the famed Hazzard Collection, which he first encountered at the World's Fair expo, Frank Hamilton Cushing made similar observations to Chapin about the lack of water in the region, but came to different conclusions to Chapin as to the meaning of the objects. Less inclined towards a presentation of the Anasazi as an alien other, or vestigial evolutionary offshoot, Cushing concluded that the long distances required to travel for water – indicated by the size and utilitarian functionality of the baskets and pots (including double handles and other features) – potentially indicated that the Anasazi were a trading people. Cushing wrote:

> Owing to this long period of its development, the basketry art of the cliff dwellers was, although still comparatively plain and utilitarian – the finest and most highly perfected of the western hemisphere, and in it occurs examples of every kind of type of basket work devised by the natives of America, North or South. (Cushing in Hinsley and Wilcox, 303–4)

Additionally, he suggested that their knowledge of Boracic alum dyes in their art pointed to 'a knowledge known in no other portion of America at the time of the discovery save in Old Mexico and Peru' (368).

The Anasazi raised a few problems. Cushing's analysis pointed in a number of different theoretical directions that were rooted in how one chose to view their 'culture': either as an aesthetic 'object in space', coherent and holistic; as a vestigial Darwinian offshoot; or as a system of inclusion of foreign material and influences. Cushing's reading might to us now suggest that the Anasazi were not a discrete 'culture' or *Volk*, but a 'multiculture' or 'interculture'. Without the language to express this eventuality precisely (except in terms of imperial conquest and/or assimilation), this is raised as an undeveloped horizon of thought that emerges through contemplation of aesthetic questions. The design of the pot – its dyes, design, and form of its beauty – points to the insufficiency of extant modes of reason. Alternatively, and this is the more common interpretation in the period, the Anasazi were seen as a founder culture: a genius node that gave shape to all subsequent native cultures north and south in the Americas. They were either an origin point, or a waypoint; a base camp, or a highway.

The Cliff Dwellers troubled nineteenth- and early twentieth-century ethnography because they fit easily neither within the terms of earlier Bureau of American Ethnology cultural evolutionism (savage, barbarian, civilised) nor within those of the emerging American culture concept (holism, particularism). However, their isolated position required the co-ordination of the various sub-disciplines of anthropology to excavate and analyse. The famed 'four-field' approach to anthropology (ethnology, archaeology, linguistics/folklore, and physical anthropology), which was united by Boas and other progenitors of the American culture concept, had an early test in the Cliff Dweller excavations, which also relied on a peculiarly American collusion between private and state interests and funding structures. This combined effort can be seen in the organisation that was required for the presentation of the private Hazzard collection of Anasazi artefacts at the Chicago World's Fair, where the display was a blockbuster. As James Snead has noted,

> The most dramatic installation of southwestern artifacts was set up to the south of the Anthropology Building, where H. Jay Smith exhibited the Hazzard collection in a lath-and-plaster replica of a Colorado butte, complete with artificial vegetation, climbing trails, burros, and

sheep. The interior featured scale models of the cliff palace and balcony house, made by exhibition artist Alex Fournier, along with artifacts and a female 'mummy' named 'She' after the H. Rider Haggard character. (Snead in Hinsley and Wilcox, 290–1)

Wharton's understanding of the complex temporalities and multiplicities that existed within understandings of culture put her on a line with many artists who became interested in how realist literary technique might reflect the multiplicity and temporal instability of the period, rather than just serve as a reification of difference and historical stasis. Among these was George Bellows, whose painting *The Cliff Dwellers* (1913) was displayed for the first time in the same year as the publication of *The Custom of the Country*. The canvas captures the drama of the everyday, which the title pushes into the context of the same drama of evolution and history as does Chapin's account of the Anasazi. This might suggest an urge to ennoble the poor, given Bellows's socialist affiliations and the common understanding of the nobility of the Anasazi, yet it also raises the possibility of annihilation and precariousness. The struggles of everyday life might be seen as the crucible of a stronger, grander civilisation, but they also might lead nowhere (to a historical dead end). The painting serves aesthetically to promote a deliberative exercise and sense of potentiality within realist art, which raises the possibility of the political – nurturing hope and apocalypse at once.

Bellows's sense of contemporary history in the wake of anthropological revolutions such as the Boasian culture concept and the discovery of Mesa Verde is captured in the canvas aesthetically in the form of the two-way street that runs through the direct centre of the painting. In the image a tram goes left, while a horse and cart goes right. Modernity one way, history the other. This is signalled also by placing the children and the black man – in a state of deliberation himself – to the left of the canvas, highlighting images (in Bellows's left-wing mind at least) of future possibility. Yet, that is not the whole of it. Time is at a weird temporal disjunction. The canvas as a whole has a zigzagging geometry. Looking from top to bottom the eye is tugged left and then right by the interplay of line and light, with left and right having been coded to the viewer as

Figure 4.2 George Bellows, *The Cliff Dwellers* (1913).

temporal by the two-way street in the centre. Furthermore, the form of the painting has depth, but Bellows obscures the vanishing point, inviting us to consider what goes on beyond or around the corner. Bellows was well-aware of cubism – where simultaneity of perspectives on a flat plain stood in spatially for the temporal – having helped organise the Armory Show in the same year that 'The Cliff Dwellers' was painted and displayed. But what is occurring here is a resistance to the flat plain of cubism and geometric abstraction – an urge to cling to the aesthetic techniques of an earlier realism, while still (as John Fagg and others have remarked) blurring the faces and focusing on intensity of colour in ways that consciously reference such abstraction.[5] That flat plain, and attempt to capture all of time simultaneously in works by Braque, Duchamp and others, is the fine-art version of the modernist desire for totality that Wharton criticised so vehemently in the 'stream of consciousness' aesthetics deployed by younger writers in *The Writing of Fiction*. Bellows's painting, by contrast to modernist totality, is a measure of weird time, a redistribution of the sensible that throws its lot behind neither modernism nor realism, but leaves both in a state of suspension, dissensus and potentiality. In this way, Bellows reflects debates that raged in his time about the Cliff Dwellers in terms of older and newer definitions of culture. His canvas does not seek the holistic spatiality of modernism, yet nor does it accept the complicity of a mimesis undergirded by the evolutionary plot of nineteenth-century post-Darwinian science. Instead, he leaves much up for grabs – yet to be reassembled in terms of the political order – reflecting the productive and deliberative uncertainty that Wharton captures in *The Custom of the Country* and the Cliff Dweller settlements mobilised in the minds of the period's social scientists.

Wharton and Bourne: Culture as War Work

> We must save Beauty for the world; before it is too late we must save it out of this awful wreck and ruin. It sounds ridiculously presumptuous, doesn't it, to say 'we' in talking of a great genius like you and a poor speck of dust like me? But after all there is the same instinct in us, the same craving, the same desire to realize Beauty, through you do it magnificently and objectively, and I . . . I do it only by a ribbon in my hair, a flower in a vase, a way of looping a curtain . . . But I oughtn't to be ashamed of my limitations . . . Surely everyone ought to be helping to save Beauty; every one is needed, even the humblest and most ignorant of us, or else the world will be all death and ugliness. (Wharton, *A Son at the Front*, 120)

If the period of the 1880s to the start of the 1910s was characterised by moments of significant intellectual ferment when attempts to marry cosmopolitanism to radical politics turned on questions of literary form with which Wharton was actively engaged, then it would follow that the period of the First World War and its immediate aftermath would be seen as the moment when these debates went into overdrive. Yet, as with Undine Spragg's mind baulking before the multiplicity of abundance she encountered in the world, and unable to develop a social vision that matched the cosmopolitan facts of the world, it is notable that many intellectuals saw the birth of modernism proper as a moment of surprising intellectual torpor and retrenchment. Indeed, this was precisely the thesis of the left-wing, bohemian, intellectual Randolph Bourne who was concerned that the war only confirmed longstanding American impulses against radical thought. For Bourne, rather than bringing energy and ferment to thought, the period was defined by a slowness of mind that was a consequence of a kind of intellectual boredom with the uncertainty that had shaped the late nineteenth century and which manifested in a desire for easy, quicker, answers; the will to efficiency married to an exhaustion with the ongoing nature of ethical debate and the growing complexity of everyday life. In 'The War and the Intellectuals', written in 1917 as America entered the war on the side of the Anglo-French Alliance, Bourne remarked that:

> The American intellectual class, having failed to make the higher synthesis, regresses to ideas that can issue in quick, simplified action. Thought becomes any easy rationalization of what is actually going on or what is to happen inevitably tomorrow ... Their mental conflicts have been resolved much more simply. War in the interests of democracy! This was the sum of their philosophy. The primitive idea to which they regressed became almost insensibly translated into a craving for action. War was seen as the crowning achievement of their indecision At last action, irresponsibility, the end of anxious and torturing attempts to reconcile peace-ideals with the drag of the world towards Hell. An end to the pain of trying to adjust the facts to what they ought to be! Let us consecrate the facts as ideal! Let us join the greased slide towards war! ... Hesitations, ironies, consciences, considerations, – all were drowned in the elemental blare of doing something aggressive, colossal. (11)

For Bourne (who had a complex and uneasy relationship with pragmatism generally but here echoed William James in many respects) the pull to immediate and decisive action was a consequence of the allure of the 'ideal', which was not noble but, rather, a consequence of a kind of laziness. As thinkers across the political spectrum (most famously Bourne's former tutor John Dewey) began to push for a kind of wilful, masculine accelerationism, seeing in the war the chance to overturn existing pieties and moral torpor,

Bourne reasoned, by contrast, that war only meant a failure of will and a giving over to defeat. Peace, for Bourne is subtle, complex, and is the task directed to making the future, while war is primitive, easy, and thinks only of the immediate needs of an elite class.

While intellectuals such as Horace Kallen, in his 1915 essay 'Democracy Versus of the Melting Pot: A Study of American Nationality' had argued for a greater rigidity within multiculturalism, suggesting that individual groups should preserve their differences in order to preserve democracy, Bourne went further in his analysis. By bringing discussions of cosmopolitanism and pluralism together with thought on class, Bourne moved understandings of pluralism beyond the nation and into the field of international relations. He noted that

> The official, reputable expression of the intellectual class has been that of the English colonial ... The colonialism of other American stocks was denied a hearing from the start. America might have been made a meeting-ground for the different national attitudes. An intellectual class, cultural colonists of the different European nations, might have threshed out the issues here as they could not be threshed out in Europe. Instead of this, the English colonials in university and press took command at the start, and we became an intellectual Hungary where thought was subject to an effective process of Magyarization' (Bourne, 'The War and the Intellectuals', 6)

Bourne reasoned that the failure of cosmopolitan pluralism in American culture (what he had hopefully called in his 1916 work 'Trans-National America') gave birth to the intellectual laziness that brought the USA into thoughtless action on behalf of British and French interests that in peacetime they had only partially shared. Contrary to Kallen, whose separatist sense of culture saw peace in a certain retreat from interaction between discrete, holistic 'cultures', Bourne advocated for an energetic cosmopolitanism and interactivity that used ongoing, reasoned debate about cultural values as a means to avoid the military conflicts he saw as a result of monolithic thinking and Anglo-Saxon supremacism. This failure of pluralism was a failure, for Bourne, not of 'diversity' alone. It was part and parcel of a wider crisis of the political Left in the period.

While some organisations supported the war on the grounds of its potential for national renewal, or as a site poised to generate the conditions for world revolution or internationalism, others (such as the International Workers of the World and Socialist Party of America) caused the landscape to be riven and along with an escalating surveillance state and vigilante violence ultimately saw the leftist protest energies of the early century overridden, as Mark Whalan has noted.[6] Bourne saw in support for the war an inability to hold back the march of American capitalism (which, perhaps blindly, he regarded as synonymous with American 'whiteness'). As such, rather than conceptualising class and cultural differences as the catalyst that brought society into perpetual ferment and conflict, he saw what Franz Boas had called the plural, cosmopolitan, 'exoteric' life of community (its very complexity) as the means by which peace was to be maintained. Horace Kallen had argued for diversity, but not considered how class relations operated within diverse groups to decide which features of group life constituted the 'core' values of a given culture. He considered culture and class – as have so many Americanists over the years – as separate entities. Attuned to the importance of cultural diversity, Kallen nonetheless thought little on the relationship between culture and class. Bourne, however, considered diversity and political radicalism to be mutually reinforcing projects whose value to the American experiment lay in their combined capacity to provide checks and balances against both the coagulation of pluralism into 'race' thinking (or 'hard' cultural determinism) and corporate capitalist control. Bourne's leftism mobilised 'dissensus' to produce peace, and relied upon an ongoing, perpetual state of microscopic conflict to avoid the macropolitical consolidations of power that would lead to tyranny.

Randolph Bourne and Edith Wharton were on opposite sides of the debate about America's role in the First World War. At least so it would seem. While Bourne advocated for peace at home, Wharton was visiting the frontlines and penning propagandistic journalism in support of a US military intervention to aid Britain and France. Moreover, Wharton conformed perfectly to the class-bound archetype that Bourne identified with interventionist intellectuals in the period. Almost as if he had the Anglo-Dutch mercantilist Wharton in mind specifically, Bourne had written that

> The nerve of the war-feeling centred, of course, in the richer and older classes of the Atlantic seaboard, and was keenest where there were French or English business and particularly social connections. The sentiment then spread over the country as a class-phenomenon, touching everywhere those upper-class elements in each section who identified themselves with this Eastern ruling group ('The War and the Intellectuals', 5)

However surprising it may seem, Bourne's and Wharton's responses to the war did have some parallels. Among their shared concerns was a belief that the American nationalist mind was not up to the task of assimilating information sufficiently to develop a meaningful response to global affairs. As with Undine's mind in *The Custom of the Country*, there was a barrenness of thought, an intelligence deficit, that was identified by both thinkers in this moment. Moreover, as Wharton came to argue in *The Writing of Fiction*, there was moral and aesthetic failing in the concept of totality, which could be found in both Horace Kallen's hard cultural pluralism that kept cultures from meaningful interaction and in a hard, class-bound traditionalist Anglocentrism that was prone to blindness in the face of the multiplicities of the world. To be ethical in their actions, one's vision must be capacious enough to be modest before the sheer potentiality of the future. As I quoted from Rancière at the beginning of this book,

> To become 'modern', that is to get rid of its dependency on the rules of social hierarchy, action simply must be faithful to what can be observed in the everyday life of any ordinary man . . . the truth of the coexistence of the atoms, the multiplicity of micro-events which occur 'at the same time' and penetrate each other without any hierarchy . . .

If the 'modern' is taken to be a political value that sees as legitimate the speech of all in the public sphere, then it follows that its thinkers must be of a radical aesthetic character able to contend with the constantly shifting dynamics of class and culture in everyday life. Advocates of the modern world must be prone neither to the arrogance of supremacism or narcissism, nor to the enervations of a boredom with the world that leads one towards the appeals of tyrannical efficiency.

Second, Bourne and Wharton both identified the interests of big business as being impediments to meaningful and ethical social responses to the world's problems, as well as to the possibility of maintaining cosmopolitan values in the face of a growing nationalistic bellicosity. Both Bourne and Wharton recognised something that has been the main theme of this book – that class concerns exist alongside cultural ones – but not merely in a way that mapped class onto civilisational hierarchies. Even in an age of increasing cultural pluralism, this interaction between exoteric diversity and esoteric economic interests was manifest. What was called for was a kind of interpretive intelligence that could assimilate these diverse interests without kneejerk racial or cultural partisanship. In 'The War and the Intellectuals' Bourne asked, 'Is there no place left, then, for the intellectual who cannot yet crystallize, who does not dread suspense, and is not yet drugged with fatigue?' (13). The irony is that even as they took different sides on debates about the war, Wharton in part answered Bourne's need, and had argued for the same throughout much of her career. In both the pre-war *The Custom of the Country* and the postwar *A Son at the Front* Wharton reasoned that money too often aligned itself with an unthinking nationalism. Where capitalism seemed to give itself over to cosmopolitan thinking it did so only in a circumscribed way that, like Madame de Trezac 'playing' diversity as 'Americanism', advanced the interests of the economic elite. Wharton was a nationalist in some respects for France – at least as it set itself against the imperial project of Hohenzollern Germany – but she advocated for a more thinking form of nationalism that had shades (even if it lacked the outward radicalism) of the redemptive vision of a transnational and deliberative America that Bourne demanded in his essays.

By way of conclusion, I will turn now to a reading of *A Son at the Front*, a novel whose message is that an ethical cosmopolitan culture is one that knows when to gather resources together and when to let go of them. I do so to consider what Wharton saw as the likely outcome of the war in terms of an emergent modernist mind – something that she reasoned would be less truly cosmopolitan than her own micro-generation of artists and more given over to the allure of essentialism in thought and action. In the hero of the novel John Campton's deliberations about the ownership of the portrait of a son who is doomed to death on the frontline, we see Wharton's consideration that cosmopolitanism is often belied by arrogant individualism, but is also beset by the values of the market and by the pull of biology. In contrast to these forces, Wharton advocates for a kind of socially useful position for culture, which she saw in a type of war work such as she undertook for refugees and families affected by brutal, mechanised war. This is the kind of cultural work Undine Spragg, despite her other virtues as a force against entrenched positions, would never undertake. It is a kind of constructive variant of critique, while Undine (and also at points Campton's actions) partake of a kind of critique without an equivalent reconstruction. It is also what William James would call in a powerful essay of 1906 'The Moral Equivalent of War' – an altered use role for the state that foregrounds diverse modes of ethical action over the moral abyss of absolutism and unfettered individualism.

A Son at the Front tells the story of John Campton, an ageing, very successful American painter of the cosmopolitan generation of 1880s and 1890s Paris, whose son George is conscripted into the French military at the outbreak of the First World War. On the eve of his son's departure for the front, Campton draws a sketch of his son asleep that becomes, after many years of separation from him because of boarding school, university and transnational mobility, one of his few existing, material memories: 'They had been parted often, and for long periods: first by George's schooling in England, next by his French military service, begun at eighteen to facilitate his entry into Harvard' (20). A poignant work of formal and spiritual genius, as offers to buy the piece for higher and higher amounts flood in, Campton wrestles with the purpose and value of art in the marketplace and its relationship to personal memory, the right of individuals to hold on to what might benefit the culture writ large, and to mourn the dying masses of modern warfare through the residual forms of art created prior to cataclysmic social change. Consequently, in debating relative forms of value and the power and purpose of letting go of things we hold dear, A Son at the Front returns in a tragic mode to several of the themes of Wharton's more comedic earlier work, The Custom of the Country. As Alice Kelly has argued, 'Wharton's war writing has frequently been discussed – and largely dismissed – as propaganda ... and even Wharton's most steadfast advocates have been quick to dismiss her wartime writing' (*Fighting France*, 14). Yet, it is in the writing in the run-up to the war, and its immediate aftermath, that Wharton's work does in some respects come closest to the formal imperatives she would set out in *The Writing of Fiction*, and must be judged a success according to the terms she laid out there. Matching its ethical imperatives with its urge to maintain and engage formal beauty in the face of destructive forces that threatened to derail art, Wharton's novel *A Son at the Front* in particular has much to say about the intersections of class, culture and war work. Along with *The Fruit of the Tree* (1907), *A Son at the Front* is Wharton's most active engagement with social reform questions. It is an overtly political book that while deviating from some of the norms of the modernist literary culture of the younger generation in being not exactly opposed to the war, is surprisingly forward-thinking in its argument for the role of the state as a regulating force against the private interests that make conflict more likely and as a system for generating the conditions for making art.

When viewed alongside her own hyperactivity in forms of charitable and humanitarian war work, it is possible to see *A Son at the Front* as an attempt to remedy the kinds of problems in the field of capitalist, cosmopolitan culture raised in *The Custom of the Country* through a renewed vision of state or multinational regulatory oversight; a version of the organising intelligence she found wanting in the Gilded Age world of Undine Spragg. The novel predicts a kind of civic internationalism in the realm of the arts, in which America might play an active role, and which looks forward to later twentieth-century state and transnational sponsorship programmes for cultural enrichment, sustainability and growth; a proto-socialist redistribution of wealth that resists the impulses of the conservative forms of philanthropy in which Wharton herself was raised. If the war for Wharton represented a deadening of the intellect, as it did for Bourne, then the renewal lay in the unleashing of a new managerial consciousness operated and controlled by a civil service, of sorts.

In the novel, Wharton advocates (through the figure of Mlle Davril) for a collective pooling of resources that amounts to a form of state sponsorship for the arts in the face of destructive conflict, a position that readers of Wharton who focus on her social position and prejudices might easily overlook. Indeed, there is a sense that in the world of *A Son at the Front*, state reformers operate as a kind of maternal force of care that counteracts the masculine pull of the era towards individualism and force, and whose avatar is Campton, who is unable to let go of or see the social value of his work. She writes:

> [Mlle. Davril] went on to explain that in the families of almost all the young artists at the front there was at least one member at home who practised one of the arts, or who was capable of doing some kind of useful work. The value of Campton's gift, Mlle Davril argued, would be tripled if it were so employed as to give the artists and their families occupation: producing at least the illusion that those who could were earning a living, or helping their less fortunate comrades. 'It's not only a question of saving their dignity: I don't believe much in that . . . The real question, for all of us artists is that of keeping our hands in, and our interest in our work alive; sometimes, too, of giving a new talent its first chance. At any rate, it would mean work and not stagnation; which is all that most charity produces . . .'
>
> Campton listened with growing attention. Nothing hitherto had been less in the line of his interests than the large schemes of general amelioration which were coming to be classed under the transatlantic term of 'Social Welfare'. If questioned on the subject a few months earlier he would have concealed his fundamental indifference under the profession of extreme individualism, and the assertion of every man's right to suffer and starve in his own way. (93)

Davril's plan models an equality between giver and receiver by abolishing the concepts of duty and charity that she argues produce stagnation, and supports the development of artistic creation by advocating for the free use of time for all. While Campton initially represents a kind of aristocratic version of freedom, whose cosmopolitan inattention to the necessities of everyday is held up as a higher value but is really only a mark of privilege, Davril attempts to transfer Campton's freedom from the constraints of socio-economic temporality onto the underclasses, who are consequently made valuable to culture as a result of their diversity and also their new freedom to use their time as they wish. In terms derived from Plato, the underclasses are made able to speak in the public sphere – and shape the destiny of nations – by virtue of their freedom from the private space-time of occupation alone. Davril does not see art as merely productive for the market or the individual at an economic level, and she also recognises that it is powerful precisely because it resists the pull to efficiency that drives the mechanised production that birthed the fascistic, war-consciousness of many of the male population of her generation. The object of this 'Social Welfare' is directed consciously towards the preservation of Beauty, rendered as a socially egalitarian concept. As Mrs Talkett remarks in her speech to Campton late in the novel, which I quoted at the beginning of this section and starts "We must save Beauty for the world; before it is too late we must save it out of this awful wreck and ruin . . .," beauty is understood to be a preservation of difference (a multiplicity in what forms of art from ribbons, to curtains, to flowers and so forth might be defined as beautiful), but it is not wholly synonymous with the interest of the elite class alone, for, as John Campton notes, the kinds of elite minds that made the war happen (or supported it unthinkingly) were mechanical, identical, drab and efficient – trained to quick critique and not to reflective self-culture or spiritual development. In words that echo wholly the sentiment of Randolph Bourne concerning the wealthy, intellectual laziness that leads to bellicose passion, Wharton writes that

> All these young intelligences were so many subtly-adjusted instruments for the testing of machinery of which they formed a part; and not one accepted the results passively. Yet in one respect they were all agreed . . . the German menace must be met . . . on that point speculation was vain and discussion useless. (104)

George's oscillation between weak, uncommitted thinker and committed solider is precisely the dynamic that Bourne attributes to an American mind that searches all too quickly for answers and so falls rapidly to violence. Like his namesake in Stephen Crane's *George's Mother*, George Campton seeks an identity or a fixed position in thought as an answer to the precarity of the modern world.

He wants to know what to do – what form to take for all time – rather than accepting the knowledge that he will never know. This comes from an arrogant solipsism combined with a romantic pull towards the certitude of essences that Wharton and Bourne saw as an especially American moral failing at this moment in history. It is solipsistic, or narcissistic, because it refuses to give up the search for a coherent individual identity and the allure of the decisive action or event for the slower, ongoing work of peace that relies on the continuous, and often contradictory input of the many. This attitude reflects Wharton's comments on modernism as a literary style. For, as Mark Whalan has remarked, Wharton believed that the '[m]odernist's passionate attachment to the idea of originality had led them to abandon the formal lessons that provided . . . perceptive distance . . .' (96). In his belief in 'fighting *for* democracy' as a singular pattern of action or identity, George (like Bourne's American intellectuals) shows his hatred *of* democracy as a contingent, collective practice in the realm of ethics and aesthetics.

In this way, he resembles his father who is unable to comprehend the complex and essential interrelations of nations and powers that make up the phenomenon of 'Europe' and settles on valorising France – a country whose history of revolution points to no meaningful coherence of thought, in fact – as an example of the unity he seeks in his life, and, by extension, for America. Like Wharton, Campton recognises that the history of France provides little evidence of coherence at a political level (the history of repeated revolutions in the nineteenth century shows this more clearly than any other national example, perhaps), but it has an aesthetic politics whose coherence offers solace. Wharton writes that

> The idea of Europe had always been terrifying to them, and indeed to his whole family, since the extraordinary misadventure whereby, as a result of a protracted diligence journey over bad roads, of a violent thunderstorm, and a delayed steamer, Campton had been born in Paris instead of Utica. (26)

For Campton, 'Europe' is defined by a sense of contingency that he interprets as a kind of failure of will. Ironically, then, even as he and George both oppose what they see as German (Prussian) militarism and the proto-fascistic absolutism of the Kaiser, they fall into the trap of opposing authoritarianism with the allure of essences. Cosmopolitan in lifestyle, they are nonetheless both nationalists in habit of thought. Wharton relates this political imaginary to an aesthetic one when she remarks that Campton regularly seeks reassurance in physical, material things, or their representation. She writes that

> Campton had to have reassurance at any price; and he got it, as usual, irrationally but irresistibly, through his eyes. The mere fact that the midsummer sun lay so tenderly on Paris, that the bronze dolphins of the fountains in the square were spraying the Nereids' Louis Phillipe chignons as playfully as ever . . . – all this gave him a sense of security that no criss-crossing of Reuters and Havases could shake. (33)

The European news agencies of Reuters and Agence Havas with their 'criss-crossing' of borders, pluralities and global reach represent an uncertainty that even as he proclaims cosmopolitanism in spirit, Campton is actually only frightened by. But, moreover, this fear is actually a subtly inflected question of class, since the things that Campton values as markers of 'certainty' are actually markers of the suppression of the revolution by Louis Phillipe, whose regime was famous for representing the interests of bankers and industrialists over the working people of France. The thought of a potential Europe of transnational exchange, interconnection and peace mobilises the nationalism and class snobbery that lays latent in Campton's mind. Wharton's tone here is satiric, and reflects, once again, her intellectual parallels with Randolph Bourne and other leftists who questioned the role played by class in conceptions of artistic value, and, in turn, how nationalism was born within the matrix of class and culture. Campton's favoured 'Frenchness' is not a 'European' one (in the sense of being pluralistic and racially-culturally diverse), neither does it see France as a sister nation of America born in revolution, but is one that praises the restoration of monarchy and the export of its culture internationally through the machinations of the elite, banker-industrialist class among whom the American mercantilists of Campton's set are the descendants. He looks at France and sees only himself and

America as he would want it to be. He finds an American 'identity' to bulwark change in a form of cultural difference that is, more truly, a form of elite class solidarity.

This is not to say that Wharton leaves Campton without self-reflexivity about the hows and whys of what he seeks to protect and maintain in the face of war. While never having an epiphany as such – even his ultimate support for Davril's reformist plan is more a way of appeasing his mind than a conviction in socialism of any rigour – he does have instances that come close to a Damascene conversion. When watching his son sleep, Campton realises that his vision of his son's life is partial, and, since the boy lives in his mind as a work of art, that his conception of the hierarchies of art and culture might be similarly limited. 'All night he had lain staring into the darkness', writes Wharton, 'thinking, thinking: thinking of George's future, George's friends, George and women, of that unknown side of his boy's life which, in this great upheaval of things, has suddenly lifted its face to the surface. If war came, if George were not discharged, if George were sent to the front, if George were killed, how strange to think that things the father did not know of might turn out to have been the central things of his son's life!' (45). For a brief moment, the 'ifs' of Campton's thought force him into a speculative futurity that counteracts his otherwise unimpeachable urge to historicise his experience with his son and hold on to a past in which he is a child rather than the future in which he will live as a man. His sense that he does not understand fully the hierarchy of events and individuals in George's life, and more troublingly that Campton himself might not constitute the most important of these, operates as a proleptic disturbance of aesthetic hierarchies, a foreshadowing of the eventual reshaping of the relationship between mimesis and history that the war created. By considering what is missing from the scene that he will never know or understand, and not what is present within it (or what he wishes to be present), Campton's moment of reflection takes on the quality of a truly modern experience shot through with democratic potentiality as cultural hierarchies are abandoned and experience is relativised.

Even as later writers began to think about the position of the USA in the world and disagreed with the dominant Puritanism of their domestic scene, leading to the Lost Generation focus on the experience of exile, on the whole, American writing after the war did not confront the problem of nationalism that spurred on the war with a renewal of a true cosmopolitan spirit of diversity, plurality and opposition to the fixities of essence. Instead, the allure of the concept of the Great American Novel, as well as the New Deal's self-examination of 'Americanness' as a project of social renewal, led to a far stronger emphasis on 'US culture' as its own singular subject of attention. This came hand in hand with a renewal of the question of race through the embedding of eugenics in national policy debates and an aesthetic focus on 'primitivism'. The Boasian dream of imagining the everyday life of groups as a means for a more generous vision of intercultural communication did not, ultimately, survive the war or the twentieth century as a whole. Yet for a brief moment of time, aesthetics appeared as a redemptive, rather than repressive, discourse that reinforced cultural hierarchies and coherencies. This was an earlier phase of modernism that still represents an alternative path through twentieth-century art and culture. One less drawn to 'strong' theorisations of in- and out-group identities. This book has been an attempt to tell this story of art; a pre-modernist theorisation of the modern that renovated realist literary practice to imagine sites and ideas of genuine possibility and social hope without abandoning, indeed even generating, an early version of intersectional critique.

Notes

1. 'Lecture 5', *A Pluralistic Universe*, <https://www.gutenberg.org/cache/epub/11984/pg11984.html> (accessed 15 July 2022).
2. See McGurl, *The Novel Art*.
3. 'A Journal of Civilization' was *The Century*'s subtitle.
4. Ngai, 'Stuplimity'.
5. See Fagg, *On the Cusp*.
6. See Whalan, *World War One*.

Coda: James Huneker, A Decadent Among Modernists

James Huneker is now a somewhat neglected figure in the pantheon of American literary and critical achievement. In his time though (from the 1890s through to his death in 1921) he was perhaps the USA's most revered and respected cultural critic, occupying a position that would eventually, perhaps, be taken by the presently-more-famous H. L. Mencken. A passionate and relentless advocate for cosmopolitanism in art, literature and politics, and opposed to the rising nationalistic fervours of the 1910s that I spoke about in the previous chapter, he was also an unapologetic champion of bohemian morals and a critic of the Puritanical sexual pieties of the Anglo-American bourgeoisie. His life-long bohemianism, campaign for the improvement of aesthetic and cultural values in American literature and art, and wide, international reading might make Huneker an obvious candidate for a position within the fold of the emerging 'high modernism'; or, at the very least, as one of its clear progenitors. Yet, Huneker is more a figure of the transitional (but no less distinct) moment I have outlined in this book. Indeed, he shared with Edith Wharton (who adored his writings on music and theatre especially) and others a suspicion about the meaning and direction of so-called 'modernism' and its various sub-cults in the arts. Moreover, Huneker was quite assuredly the inheritor of the variant of cultural critique associated with José Martí, whom he followed into the major role of society and culture critic at *The New York Sun*.

In his 1919 novel *Painted Veils* (a borderline pornographic romp through the theatre and opera world of Gilded Age

New York), Huneker pokes fun at the then current vogue for forms of 'primitivism', anthropological deep reading, and esoteric orientalism as so much pseudo-intellectual chaff covering more base needs and desires. The novel, which follows the sexual and social exploits of a popular opera singer, Esther Brandés, and her melancholic man-about-town suitor Ulick Invern through a plot involving religious revivals that transform into orgies, orgies that transform into near-religious revivals, and a whole parade of chorus girls in various bohemian locales, opens by calling out the misogyny and voyeurism of literary and artistic history. Huneker quotes from fellow American musician and music critic W. F. Abthorp's transcription of the *Epic of Gilgamesh* in song, turning the account of the passage of Istar (the Sumerian Goddess of fertility, war and sexual love, often seen as the model of the Abrahamic 'Whore of Babylon') through the seven gates of the land of the dead into the structure of his own more profane and less profound novel of a modern woman's sexual exploits. He quotes Abthorp:

> Toward the immutable land Istar, daughter of Sin, bent her steps, toward the abode of the dead, toward the seven-gated abode where He entered, toward the abode whence there is no return.
> At the first gate, the warder stripped her; he took the high tiara from her head.
> At the second gate, the warder stripped her; he took the pendants from her ears.
> At the third gate, the warder stripped her; he took off the precious stones that adorn her neck.
> At the fourth gate, the warder stripped her; he took off the jewels that adorn her breast.
> At the fifth gate, the warder stripped her; he took off the girdle that encompasses her waist.
> At the sixth gate, the warder stripped her; he took the rings from her feet, the rings from her hands.
> At the seventh gate, the warder stripped her; he took off the last veil that covers her body.
> Istar, daughter of Sin, went into the immutable land, she took and received the Waters of Life. She gave the Sublime Waters, and thus, in the

presence of all, delivered the Son of Life, her young lover. (Abthorp in Huneker, *Painted Veils*, i–ii)

Huneker then proceeds to use the structure of the song and the removal of the garments at each liminal zone as the mock-allegorical structure for his own novel, breaking it down into seven 'Gates' in each of which Esther reveals more of her desires and needs to the world as a path to her eventual triumph and overthrow of a morally Puritanical American society in the name of modern diversity and potentiality. Read straight, this opening section of the novel provides a kind of esoteric, ritual code for understanding what is to follow. Yet, Huneker does not let us lose sight of the irony and humour in his understanding that popular 'deep reading', such as came to be *en vogue* following the publication of works such as the Scottish anthropologist James Frazer's diffusionist magnum opus *The Golden Bough* (1890), E. B. Tylor's *Primitive Culture* (1871) and, importantly, Richard Wagner's Ring Cycle, revealed less, perhaps, about humanity's universal patterns of cultural development than they did about nineteenth-century sexual repression and power. After all, *Painted Veils* may be rich in allusions and references to philosophy and art (from Søren Kierkegaard, to Arabian literature, to *Parsifal* as sung at Bayreuth), but it is not really that difficult to understand. The symbolism is not actually that deep (it's mainly about sex) and all the masks of meaning placed by the characters in front of their desires are precisely what the author calls them out for being; so many 'painted veils': gaudy, depthless and not hard to discern as inauthentic. For all its wit and excess, *Painted Veils* is, at core, a satire of emergent forms of American modernism that use allusion to project newness or originality, but are often, in fact, in surprising collusion with the repressive, esoteric and residual impulses of a prior nineteenth-century elitism and its racial–cultural regimes of power.

Painted Veils was not the only time Huneker opposed elitist principals that suggested that understanding the universality of mankind required knowledge of an esoteric ritual or social code that unlocked the relationships between historical peoples. Indeed, he was an advocate for 'high culture', but, as with the figures I have discussed in this book, this did not mean a simply elitist vision of the uses to which culture might be put. Instead, Huneker asked of his readers the exercise of effort, but not with the sense that certain people were inherently incapable of education or development. More often they were just held back.

In an essay on Marinetti and the Italian Futurist Painters, collected as 'The Melancholy of Masterpieces Part 2: The Italian Futurist Painters' in his 1917 collection on the pretensions of the artistic ego, *Ivory, Apes and Peacocks*, Huneker remarks on the trend in current visual art to be 'literary', which is to say, to justify itself not through what appears but by means of a manifesto or a description that often lies beyond one's encounter with it in the pages of a little magazine. He writes, 'The trouble with the Futurist is that he catches the full force of the primal impression, then later loads it with his own subjective fancies. The outcome is bound to be a riddle.' (272) In his broadside against the esoteric and fascistic impulses of Futurism (and the essay is certainly nothing if not a debunking of the political imaginary of this sub-cult of Italian modernism), Huneker notes that in capturing the essence of 'modern' life as they saw it, Marinetti and his ilk were apt to be hostile to the proposition that knowledge might and should be shared, and blind to the fact that in their embrace of 'originality' and passion they were merely placing a veneer on something decidedly older. He notes,

> I purposely mention Marinetti and his manifesto for the reason that this movement in painting and sculpture is decidedly 'literary,' the very accusation of which makes the insurgents mightily rage. For example, I came across in *De Kunst*, a Dutch art publication in Amsterdam, a specimen of Marinetti's sublimated prose, the one page of which is supposed to contain more suggestive images and ideas than a library written in the old-fashioned manner. (263)

Needless to say, Huneker was not much of a fan of Marinetti's prose-poem, and still less his manifestos, in part because they used the claim on originality to perform a bait-and-switch, which was not a work of genius so much as a grab for power and control over the resources of art and culture that lay always already within the reach of all. Better than esoteric modernism for Huneker was the surprisingly hopeful stance of earlier realisms. He writes:

> In what then consists the originality of the Futurists? Possibly their blatant claim to originality. The Primitives, Italian and Flemish, saw the universe with amazing clearness; their pictorial metaphysics was clarity itself; their mysticism was never muddy; all nature was settled, serene, and brilliantly silhouetted. But mark you! they, too, enjoyed depicting a half-dozen happenings on the same canvas. (274)

It is a critical commonplace to note that Aestheticism (nay, Decadence!) such as Huneker's represented a defeated attitude to the world (*fin-de-siècle, fin de globe*) that required the injection of new life through the energies of the European modernist avant-garde. Yet, here, Huneker's decadent claims that nothing on earth is truly original do not sound as though the projects of civilisation and democracy have been wholly defeated. Rather, they sound a note that within the cult of originality (as Wharton would warn) lay a proto-Fascistic impulse to totality that contained (as did Futurism itself) the seed of a genocidal social vision. A world where nothing is wholly original is also a world built on an interpenetration of cultures, changes of use-value, and exchange, where things shift meaning and change continuously and do not require huge ruptures in time to move forwards. He writes dismissively in 'The Melancholy of Masterpieces' that

> The Futurists wish to glorify war—the only health-giver of the world—militarism, patriotism, the destructive arm of the anarchist, the beautiful ideas that kill, the contempt for woman. They wish to destroy the museums, the libraries (unlucky Mr. Carnegie!), to fight moralism, feminism, and all opportunistic and utilitarian measures. (268)

In his critiques of emergent forms of cultish modernism and of anthropological meaning-making in his novels and criticism, Huneker staged a defence of what I have called 'exoteric modernism' – an embrace of the future that relies on excess to generate potentialities in time that are the aesthetic form of a democratic politics. Indeed, Huneker would go further than this in decrying the nationalism of ideas such as the 'great American novel', which he remarked in the collection *Unicorns* (1917) was 'an "absolute", and nature abhors an absolute, despite the belief of some metaphysicians to the contrary' (82), before noting that any claim to greatness or universality was, in reality, 'personal and provincial' (82). If there is to be a 'great American novel [it] will be in the plural; thousands perhaps. America is a chord of many nations, and to find the key-note we must play much and varied music . . . while a novelist may be cosmopolitan at his own risk, a critic should be ever so' (83).

I end with Huneker because as we, once again, debate the relationship between class, culture and nation in the arts, and the fate of 'critique' in the age of 'postcritical' methodologies, is it worth noting, with Huneker and contra Felski, perhaps, that a pessimism or decadence in the realm of culture (an understanding at least that things are seldom original and often poached from the common pool of exoteric experience to shore up an esoteric elite, in Boas's language) does not always mean the defeat of the democratic attitude in the American tradition? It may, indeed, mean its revival. As I have argued across this book, an aesthetic attitude to the world is not apolitical and does not represent a retreat into entrenched and pre-established positions of status. To be decadent and to focus on feelings that may not always be positive, as did the anarchists of Chicago, Stephen Crane or others discussed in this book, is not always to be defeated. Neither does presenting the world as it is mean giving up on its future, or failing in some fundamental way to be critical of its possible directions. In thinking through the 'exoteric' (even the 'realist') in art, we do not think past critique, or foreclose the future, but, rather, find a world that is wonderfully unmade, undecided and ever reborn.

BIBLIOGRAPHY

'A Hellish Deed'. *Chicago Journal*, May 5, 1886.
Abeln, Paul. *William Dean Howells and the Ends of Realism*. London and New York: Routledge, 2016.
Abrams, Lynn. *Oral History Theory*. London and New York: Routledge, 2010.
Agee, James. *Let Us Now Praise Famous Men: Three Tenant Families*. Boston and New York: Houghton Mifflin, 2001.
Ahmed, Sara. *The Promise of Happiness*. Durham, NC and London: Duke UP, 2010.
Anderson, Benedict. *Imagined Communities: Reflections on the Origins and Spread of Nationalism*. London: Verso, 2006.
Arnold, Matthew. *Culture and Anarchy*. Oxford and London: Oxford UP.
Aronoff, Eric. *Composing Cultures: Modernism, American Literary Culture, and the Problem of Culture*. Charlottesville, VA: U of Virginia P, 2013.
Badiou, Alain. *Being and Event*. Trans. Oliver Feltham, London: Continuum, 2005.
Baker, Lee D. *Anthropology and the Racial Politics of Culture*. Durham, NC and London: Duke UP, 2010.
Baldwin, James Mark. *Darwin and the Humanities*. Ithaca, NY: Cornell UP, 1909.
Barnes. Elizabeth. *Love's Whipping Boy: Violence and Sentimentality in the American Imagination*. Chapel Hill, NC: U of North Carolina P, 2011.
Barrish, Phillip. *American Literary Realism, Critical Theory, and Intellectual Taste, 1880–1995*. Cambridge: Cambridge UP, 2001.
Bartel, Kim. 'Kant's Narrative of Hope in the Gilded Age'. *American Literary History*, Vol. 19, No. 3, Fall 2007.
Bartelson, Jens. 'Making Exceptions'. *Political Theory*, Vol. 25, No. 3, June 1997.
Bell, Michael Davitt. *The Problem of American Realism: Studies in the Cultural History of a Literary Idea*. Chicago: U of Chicago P, 1993.
Belnap, Jeffrey and Raúl Fernández (ed.). *José Martí's 'Our America': From National to Hemispheric Cultural Studies*. Durham, NC and London: Duke UP, 1998.
Bentley, Nancy. *Frantic Panoramas: American Literature and Mass Culture, 1870–1920*. Philadelphia: U of Pennsylvania P, 2009.
Berman, Marshall. *All That's Solid Melts to Air: The Experience of Modernity*. London: Verso, 1983.

Best, Stephen and Sharon Marcus. 'Surface Reading: An Introduction'. *Representations*, Vol. 108, No. 1, Fall 2009.
Bloom, James. *Left Letters: The Culture Wars of Mike Gold and Joseph Freeman*. New York: Columbia UP, 1992.
Boas, Franz. 'The Ethnological Significance of Esoteric Doctrines', *Science*, Vol. 16, No. 413, November 1902.
—. *The Mind of Primitive Man*. New York: Macmillan, 1911.
—. 'Scientists as Spies'. *The Nation*, December 1919.
Bourdieu, Pierre. *Distinction: A Social Critique of the Judgement of Taste*. Trans. Richard Nice, Cambridge, MA: Harvard UP, 1984.
Bourne, Randolph. *War and the Intellectuals: Collected Essays, 1915–1919*. Ed. Carl Resek, Indianapolis, IN: Hackett Publishing Co., 1999.
Brace, Charles Loring. *The Dangerous Classes of New York and Twenty Years Work Among Them*. New York: Wynkoop and Hallenbeck, 1872.
Bray, Patrick M. (ed.). *Understanding Rancière, Understanding Modernism*. London: Bloomsbury Academic, 2017.
Briggs, Charles L. 'Genealogies of Race and Culture and the Failure of Vernacular Cosmopolitanisms: Rereading Franz Boas and W. E. B. Du Bois'. *Public Culture*, Vol. 17, No. 1, 2005.
Butler, Judith. 'Precarious Life, Vulnerability, and the Ethics of Cohabitation'. *The Journal of Speculative Philosophy*, Vol. 26, No. 4, 2012.
Campbell, W. Joseph. '1897: American Journalism's Exceptional Year'. *Journalism History*, Vol. 29, No. 4, Winter 2004.
Capper, Charles and Conrad Edick Wright (ed.). *Transient and Permanent: The Transcendentalist Movement in its Contexts*. Boston, MA: Massachusetts Historical Society, 1999.
Cecire, Natalie. *Experimental: American Literature and the Aesthetics of Knowledge*. Baltimore, MD: Johns Hopkins UP, 2019.
Chapin, Frederick H. *The Land of the Cliff-Dwellers*. Boston, MA: Appalachian Mountain Club, 1892.
Clarke, Michael Tavel. 'Lessons from the Past: The Cliff Dwellers and New Historicism'. *Western American Literature*, Vol. 42, No. 4, Winter 2008.
Clifford, James and George E. Marcus. *Writing Culture*. Los Angeles and London: U of California P, 1986.
Coghlan, J. Michelle. *Sensational Internationalism: The Paris Commune and the Remapping of American Memory in the Long Nineteenth Century*. Edinburgh: Edinburgh UP, 2016.
Cohn, Jesse. *Anarchism and the Crisis of Representation: Hermeneutics, Aesthetics, Politics*. Selinsgrove, PA: Susequehanna UP, 2006.
Couser, G. Thomas. *Vulnerable Subjects: Ethics and Life Writing*. Ithaca, NY and London: Cornell UP, 2004.
Crane, Stephen. *Prose and Poetry*. New York: Library of America, 1984.
Cushing, Frank Hamilton. 'My Adventures Among the Zuni'. *Century Illustrated Monthly Magazine*, 1882–83.
Dana, Charles A. *The Art of Newspaper Making: Three Lectures*. London: T. Fisher Unwin, 1895.

Delano, Sterling F. *The Harbinger and New England Transcendentalism: A Portrait of Associationism in America*. London and Canbury, NJ: Associated University Presses, 1983.

Deleuze, Gilles and Felix Guattari. *Kafka: Toward a Minor Literature*. Minneapolis: U of Minnesota P, 1986.

Dimock, Wai-Chee. *Through Other Continents: American Literature Across Deep Time*. Princeton, NJ: Princeton UP, 2006.

Dooley, Patrick. *The Pluralistic Philosophy of Stephen Crane*. Urbana and Chicago: U of Illinois P, 1993.

Eakin, Paul John (ed.). *The Ethics of Life Writing*. Ithaca, NY and London: Cornell UP, 2004.

Elliott, Michael A. *The Culture Concept: Writing and Difference in the Age of Realism*. Minneapolis: U of Minnesota P, 2002.

English, Daylanne K. *Each Hour Redeem: Time and Justice in African American Literature*. Minneapolis and London: U of Minnesota P, 2013.

Erlich, Gloria. *The Sexual Education of Edith Wharton*. Berkeley: U of California P, 1992.

Evans, Brad. *Before Cultures: The Ethnographic Imagination in American Literature, 1865–1920*. Chicago: U of Chicago P, 2005.

—. 'Rethinking the Disciplinary Confluence of Anthropology and Literary Studies'. *Criticism*, Vol. 49, No. 4, Fall 2007.

—. 'Where Was Boas in the Renaissance in Harlem?: Diffusion, Race, and the Culture Paradigm in the History of Anthropology', in *Central Sites, Peripheral Visions: Cultural and Institutional Crossing in the History of Anthropology*, ed. by Richard Handler, 69–98 (Madison, WI: University of Wisconsin Press, 2006).

The Evening World, 24 May 1895.

Fabian, Johannes. *Time and the Other: How Anthropology Makes its Object*. New York: Columbia UP, 1983.

Fagg, John. *On the Cusp: Stephen Crane, George Bellows, and Modernism*. Tuscaloosa: U of Alabama P, 2009.

Feintuch, Burt (ed.). *The Conservation of Culture: Folklorists and the Public Sector*. Lexington: UP of Kentucky, 1988.

Felski, Rita. *Limits of Critique*. Chicago: U of Chicago P, 2015.

Ferguson, Kathy E. 'Gender and Genre in Emma Goldman'. *Signs*, Vol. 36, No. 3, Spring 2011.

Ferrer, Ada. *Insurgent Cuba: Race, Nation, and Revolution, 1868–1898*. Chapel Hill, NC and London: U of North Carolina P, 1999.

Foley, Barbara. *Radical Representations: Politics and Form in U.S. Proletarian Fiction, 1929–1941*. Chapel Hill, NC: Duke UP, 1993.

Foner, Eric (ed.). *The Autobiographies of the Haymarket Martyrs*. New York: Humanities Press, Inc., 1969.

Francis, Richard. *Transcendental Utopias: Individual and Community at Brook Farm, Fruitlands, and Walden*. Ithaca, NY: Cornell UP, 1997.

Frankel, Oz. 'Whatever Happened to "Red Emma"?: Emma Goldman, from Alien Rebel to American Icon'. *Journal of American History*, Vol. 83, No. 3, December 1996.

Gandal, Keith. *The Virtues of the Vicious: Joseph Riis, Stephen Crane and the Spectacle of the Slum*. New York and London: Oxford UP, 1997.
Geismar, Maxwell. *Rebels and Ancestors: The American Novel, 1890–1915*. Boston, MA: Houghton Mifflin, 1953.
Giles, Paul. *The Global Remapping of American Literature*. Princeton, NJ: Princeton University Press, 2011.
—. 'The Parallel Worlds of José Martí'. *Radical History Review*, No. 89, Spring 2004.
Gold, Michael. 'Toward Proletarian Art'. *Mike Gold: A Literary Anthology*, edited by Michael Folsom, New York: International Publishers, 1972.
Goldman, Emma. *Anarchism and Other Essays*. 3rd revised edition, New York: Mother Earth Publishing Association, 1917.
—. *Living My Life: Abridged*. London: Penguin, 2006.
González, Manuel Pedro. *José Martí: Epic Chronicler of the United States in the Eighties*. Havana: Center for Studies on Martí, 1961.
Greenblatt, Stephen and Catherine Gallagher. *Practicing New Historicism*. Chicago: U of Chicago P, 2000.
Hamilton, Kristie G. *America's Sketchbook: The Cultural Life of a Nineteenth-Century Literary Genre*. Athens: Ohio UP, 1998.
Handler, Richard. *Central Sites, Peripheral Visions: Cultural and Institutional Crossing in the History of Anthropology*. Madison: U of Wisconsin P, 2006.
—. 'Raymond Williams, George Stocking, and *Fin-de-siècle* U.S. Anthropology'. *Cultural Anthropology*, Vol. 13, No. 4, 1998.
Hebard, Andrew. *The Poetics of Sovereignty in American Literature, 1885–1910*. Cambridge: Cambridge UP, 2012.
Hegeman, Susan. *Patterns for America: Modernism and the Concept of Culture*. Princeton, NJ: Princeton UP, 1999.
Hellyer, Grace and Julian Murphet (ed.). *Rancière and Literature*. Edinburgh: Edinburgh UP, 2016.
Hinsley, Curtis M. Jr. and David R. Wilcox (ed.). *The 1893 World's Fair and the Coalescence of American Anthropology*. Lincoln: U of Nebraska Press, 2016.
Holt, Hamilton. *The Life Stories of Undistinguished Americans as Told By Themselves: Expanded Edition*. Edited by Werner Sollors. London and New York: Routledge, 2000.
Homberger, Eric. 'Proletarian Literature and the John Reed Clubs, 1929–1935'. *Journal of American Studies*, Vol. 12, No. 2, August 1979.
Howells, W. D. *A Hazard of New Fortunes*. London: The Modern Library Classics, 2002.
—. *Criticism and Fiction*. Project Gutenberg E-Book, 2004. <https://www.gutenberg.org/ebooks/3377> (accessed 15 July 2022).
—. 'Editor's Study', *The Atlantic*, May 1887.
Hughes, Amy E. *Spectacles of Reform: Theater and Activism in Nineteenth-Century America*. Ann Arbor: U of Michigan P, 2012.
Huneker, James. *Ivory, Apes, and Peacocks*. Charles Scribner's Sons, 1915.
—. *Painted Veils*. New York: Boni and Liveright, 1920.
—. *Unicorns*. New York: Charles Scribner's Sons, 1917.
James, William. *A Pluralistic Universe: Hibbert Lectures at Manchester College on the Present Situation in Philosophy*. London: Longman, Green and Co., 1909.

—. *The Principles of Psychology*. New York: Holt and Co., 1890.
Jones, Douglas E. *The Captive Stage: Performance and the Proslavery Imagination of the Antebellum North*. Ann Arbor: U of Michigan P, 2014.
Jones, Gavin. *American Hungers: The Problem of Poverty in U.S. Literature, 1840–1945*. Princeton, NJ: Princeton UP, 2007.
Kaplan, Amy. *The Social Construction of American Realism*. Chicago and London: U of Chicago P, 1992.
Karras, Bill J. 'José Martí and the Pan American Conference, 1889–1891'. *Revista de Historia de América*, No. 77/78, Jan–Dec, 1974.
Kassanoff, Jennie A. *Edith Wharton and the Politics of Race*. Cambridge UP, 1994.
Konstantinou, Lee. 'The Hangman of Critique'. <https://lareviewofbooks.org/article/the-hangman-of-critique> (accessed 17 July 2019).
Kornbluh, Anna. *The Order of Forms: Realism, Formalism, and Social Space*. Chicago: U of Chicago P, 2019.
Lomas, Laura. *Translating Empire: José Martí, Migrant Latino Subjects and American Modernities*. Durham, NC: Duke UP, 2008.
Lawson, Andrew. 'Class Mimicry in Stephen Crane's City'. *American Literary History*, Vol. 16, No. 4, Winter 2004.
Levinas, Emmanuel. *(Entre Nous) Between Us: Essays on Thinking-of-the-Other*. Trans. M. B. Smith and B. Harshav, New York: Columbia, 1998.
Levine, Caroline. *Forms: Whole, Rhythm, Hierarchy, Network*. Princeton, NJ: Princeton UP, 2015.
Levine, Lawrence W. *Highbrow/Lowbrow: The Emergence of Cultural Hierarchy in America*. Cambridge, MA and London: Harvard UP, 1990.
Loraux, Nicole. *The Invention of Athens: Funeral Oration in the Classical City*. New York: The MIT Press, 2006.
Louis A. Perez Jr. *The War of 1898: The United States and Cuba in History and Historiography*. Chapel Hill, NC and London: U of North Carolina P, 1998.
Lowry, E. 'The Flower of Cuba: Rhetoric, Representation, and Circulation at the Outbreak of the Spanish-American War'. *Rhetoric Review*, Vol. 32. No. 2, April 2013.
McGurl, Mark. *The Novel Art: Elevations of American Fiction after Henry James*. Princeton, NJ and Oxford: Princeton UP, 2001.
Manganero, Marc. *Culture, 1922: The Emergence of a Concept*. Princeton, NJ: Princeton UP, 2002.
Martí, José. *Selected Writings*. Edited by Esther Allen, London: Penguin, 2002.
Mead, Margaret. *And Keep Your Powder Dry: An Anthropologist Looks at America*. New York: Berghahn Books, 2000.
Messer-Kruse, Timothy. *The Trial of the Haymarket Anarchists: Terrorism and Justice in the Gilded Age*. New York: Palgrave Macmillan, 2011.
Michaels, Walter Benn. *Our America: Nativism, Modernism, and Pluralism*. Durham, NC: Duke UP, 1995.
—. *The Trouble With Diversity*. New York: Henry Holt and Co., 2006.
Miller, James S. 'Inventing the "Found" Object: Artifactuality, Folk History, and the Rise of Capitalist Ethnography in 1930s America'. *Journal of American Folklore*, Vol. 117, No. 466, 2004.

Mirola, William A. *Redeeming Time: Protestantism and Chicago's Eight-Hour Movement, 1866–1912*. Chicago: U of Illinois P, 2015.

Monteiro, George. *Stephen Crane: The Contemporary Reviews*. Cambridge: Cambridge UP, 2009.

Morgan, Lewis H. *Ancient Society; or, Researches in the Lines of Human Progress from Savagery to Barbarism to Civilization*. New York: Holt and Company, 1907.

Morrison, Hugh. *Louis Sullivan – Prophet of Modern Architecture*. New York: W.W. Norton & Co., Inc., 1963.

Moten, Fred. *Black and Blur*. Durham, NC and London: Duke UP, 2017.

Murphy, Brenda. 'A Woman With Weapons: The Victor in Stephen Crane's *George's Mother*. *Modern Language Studies*, Vol. 11, No. 2, 1981.

Ngai, Sianne. 'Stuplimity: Shock and Boredom in Twentieth-Century Aesthetics'. *Postmodern Culture*, Vol. 10, No. 2, January 2000.

—. *Theory of the Gimmick: Aesthetic Judgment and Capitalist Form*. Cambridge, MA: Belknap Press, 2020.

Noonan, Mark. *Reading the Century Illustrated: American Literature and Culture, 1870–1893*. Kent, OH: Kent State UP, 2010.

Ohler, Paul. 'Forms of Ambivalence to "Tabloid Culture" in Edith Wharton's *The Custom of the Country*.' *English Studies in Canada*, Vol. 36. No. 2–3, June/September 2010.

Olin-Ammentorp, Julie. *Edith Wharton, Willa Cather, and the Place of Culture*. Lincoln: U of Nebraska P, 2019.

Parrington, Vernon. *Main Currents in American Thought: Volume Three: The Beginnings of Critical Realism in America, 1860–1920*. New York: Harcourt, Brace and World, 1958.

Parsons, Elsie Clews (ed.). *American Indian Life*. New York: Viking Press, 1925.

Peirce, Charles Sanders. 'The Fixation of Belief'. 1878. <https://archive.org/details/1877-peirce-fixation-of-belief> (accessed 17 July 2013).

—. 'How to Make Our Ideas Clear'. <http://www.peirce.org/writings/p119.html> (accessed 17 July 2013).

Pittenger, Mark. 'A World of Difference: Constructing the Underclass in Progressive America'. *American Quarterly*, Vol. 49, No. 3, 1997.

Pratt, Lloyd. *Archives of American Time*. Philadelphia: U of Pennsylvania P, 2010.

Puar, Jasbir K. *Terrorist Assemblages*. Durham, NC and London: Duke UP, 2017.

Rancière, Jacques, *Aesthetics and Its Discontents*. Trans. Steven Corcoran, Cambridge: Polity Press, 2009.

—. *Disagreement: Politics and Philosophy*. Trans. Julie Rose, Minneapolis: U of Minnesota P, 1999.

—. *Mute Speech*. Trans. Gabriel Rockhill, New York: Columbia UP, 2011.

—. *The Philosopher and His Poor*. Trans. John Drury, Corinne Oster and Andrew Parker, Durham, NC: Duke UP, 2004.

—. *The Politics of Aesthetics*. Edited by Gabriel Rockhill, London: Bloomsbury Publishing, 2013.

Riis, Jacob A. *How the Other Half Lives: Studies Among the Tenements of New York*. Cambridge, MA and London: Belknap Press, 2010.

Robbins, Bruce. 'Many Years Later: Prolepsis in Deep Time'. *The Henry James Review*, Vol. 33, No. 3, Fall 2012.

Rodseth, Lars. 'Back to Boas, Forth to Latour: An Anthropological Model for the Ontological Turn'. *Current Anthropology*, Vol. 56, No. 6, December 2015.

Roggenkamp, Karen. *Narrating the News: New Journalism and Literary Genre in Late Nineteenth-Century American Newspapers and Fiction*. London: Kent State UP, 2005.

Rotker, Susana. *The American Chronicles of José Martí: Journalism and Modernity in Spanish America*. Trans. Jennifer French and Katherine Semler, Hanover and London: UP of New England, 2000.

Saint-Amour, Paul (ed.). Special Issue: 'Weak Theory, Weak Modernism'. *Modernism/Modernity*, Vol. 25, No. 4. September 2018.

Sapir, Edward. 'Culture, Genuine and Spurious'. *The American Journal of Sociology*, January 1924.

Savransky, Martin. *Around the Day in Eighty Worlds: Politics of the Pluriverse*. Durham, NC: Duke University Press, 2021.

Schaack, Michael. *Anarchy and Anarchists. A History of the Red Terror, and the Social Revolution in America and Europe. Communism, Socialism, and Nihilism in Doctrine and Deed. The Chicago Haymarket Conspiracy, and the Detection and Trial of the Conspirators*. Chicago: F. J. Schulte and Co., 1889.

Schoonover, Thomas D. *Uncle Sam's War and the Origins of Globalization*. Lexington: U of Kentucky P, 2003.

Schwartz, Jesse W. '"Dynamite Talk": William Dean Howells, Racial Socialism, and a Legal Theory of Literary Complicity'. *Nineteenth-Century Literature*, Vol. 73, No. 4, 2019.

Seger, Maria. 'Deferred Lynching and the Moral High Ground in Charles W. Chesnutt's *The Marrow of Tradition*. *Nineteenth-Century Literature*, Vol. 73, No. 1, 2018.

Spencer, David R. *The Yellow Journalism: The Press and America's Emergence as a World Power*. Evanston, IL: Northwestern UP, 2007.

Spies, August. *August Spies' Autobiography: His Speech in Court, and General Notes*. Edited by Nina Van Zandt. Chicago, IL: Nina Van Zandt, 1887.

Stansell, Christine. *American Moderns: Bohemian New York and the Creation of the New Century*. Princeton, NJ: Princeton UP, 2000.

Staub, Michael E. *Voices of Persuasion: Politics of Representation in 1930s America*. New York: Cambridge UP, 1994.

Steele, Janet E. *The Sun Shines for All: Journalism and Ideology in the Life of Charles A. Dana*. Syracuse, NY: Syracuse UP, 1993.

Stein, Gertrude. *Three Lives*. London: Penguin, 1990.

Stevens, Erica. 'Absolutely Novel: The Event and Charles Chesnutt's Paul Marchand, F.M.C'. *Studies in the Novel*, Vol. 50, No. 4, Winter 2018.

Stieglitz, Alfred. 'A Plea for Art Photography in America' (1892). <https://photocriticism.com/members/archivetexts/photocriticism/stieglitz/pf/stieglitzpleapf.html> (accessed 20 March 2022).

Stocking, George W. Jr. (ed.). *A Franz Boas Reader: The Shaping of American Amthropology, 1883–1911*. Chicago: U of Chicago P, 1989.

—. *Race, Culture and Evolution: Essays in the History of Anthropology*. Chicago and London: U of Chicago P, 1982.

—. *Volkgeist as Method and Ethic: Essays on Boasian Ethnography and the German Anthropological Tradition*. Madison, WI: The U of Wisconsin P, 1996.

Strangleman, Tim. 'Class Memory: Autobiography and the Art of Forgetting'. In John Russo and Sherry Lee Linkon (ed.), *New Working-Class Studies*, London and Ithaca, NY: Cornell UP, 2005.

Streeby, Shelley. *Radical Sensations: World-Movements, Violence, and Visual Culture*. Durham, NC and London: Duke UP, 2013.

Taylor, Andrew. 'Reading Resistances in Ralph Waldo Emerson and José Martí'. *Journal of American Studies*, Vol. 55, 2021.

Tone, John Lawrence. *War and Genocide in Cuba, 1885–1898*. Chapel Hill, NC and London: U of North Carolina P, 2006.

Trautmann, Thomas. *Lewis Henry Morgan and the Invention of Kinship*. Lincoln: U of Nebraska P, 2008.

Turner, Victor. *The Anthropology of Performance*. New York: PAJ Publications, 1988.

Ward, Hiley H. *Mainstreams of American Media History*. Boston, MA: Allyn and Bacon, 1997.

Western American Literature, Vol. 42, No. 4, Winter 2008.

Whalan, Mark. *World War One, American Literature, and the Federal State*. Cambridge: Cambridge UP, 2018.

Wharton, Edith. Three Novels of New York: *The House of Mirth*, *The Custom of the Country*, *The Age of Innocence*. New York: Penguin Classics, 2012.

—. *Fighting France: From Dunkerque to Belfort*. Edited by Alice Kelly. Edinburgh: Edinburgh UP, 2015.

—. *French Ways and Their Meanings*. New York: D. Appleton and Co., 1919.

—. *A Son at the Front*. Ithaca, NY: Cornell University Press, 1995.

—. *The Writing of Fiction*. London: Hawthorne Press, 2021.

Williams, Raymond. *Culture and Society 1780–1950*. New York: Columbia UP, 1963.

Wilson, James Harrison. *The Life of Charles A. Dana*. New York and London: Harper and Brothers Publishers, 1907.

Yao, Xine. *Disaffected: The Cultural Politics of Unfeeling in Nineteenth Century America*. Durham, NC: Duke UP, 2021.

Zacaïr, Phillipe. 'Haiti on his Mind: Antonio Maceo and Caribbeanness'. *Caribbean Studies*, Vol. 33 No. 1, 2005.

Zibrak, Arielle. 'The Woman Who Hated Sex: Undine Spragg and the Trouble with "Bother"'. *Edith Wharton Review*, Vol. 32, 2016.

INDEX

Note: page numbers in *italic* refer to figures.

Abbott, Charles, 213
Abeln, Paul, 93, 94
Abrams, Lynn, 75–6
Abthorp, W. F., 235–6
activism, 80
Addams, Jane, 117
'Address Delivered to Judge Gary' (Spies), 82–3, 87
Aesthetic Arts Movement, 157
aestheticism, 14–15, 41, 87, 151–4, 201, 233
   Crane, 153–4, 169
   modernist aesthetics, 49–50
   politics and, 2, 6, 131–6
   Rancière, 14, 15, 22, 33, 41
   realist aesthetic of the everyday, 10–12
   Spies, 88–9
Afterglow, The (England), 213
Agee, James, 179, 180–1
Ahmed, Sara, 61
Alice in Wonderland novels (Carroll), 91
Allen, Esther, 120, 141n27
Althusser, Louis, 156
American Geological Survey, 161
American Guides Series, 179
American Indian Life (Parsons), 45

American Museum of Natural History, New York, 204–5
anarchism, 54, 58, 59, 62, 77–81, 83, 141n27
   anarchist life writing, 76
   and autobiography, 78–81
   Cohn on, 85
'Anarchism: What it Really Stands For' (Goldman), 101
Anarchy and Anarchists (Schaak), 60, *60*
Anasazi (Cliff Dwellers), Navajo, 211–18, 220
Ancient Society (Morgan), 37–8, 85
Anderson, Benedict, 69, 92
Anglo-Saxonism, 21
anthropology, 17, 30–1, 35–6, 38–41, 43–8, 51, 57, 62–3, 201, 205
   anthropological fieldwork, 203
   cultural determinism, 162, 181
   cultural exchange, 161–2
   and esotericism, 45
   four-field approach, 217
   independent invention, 206–7
   professionalisation of, 213
   reckless empiricism, 29
   Wharton and, 211
Anthropology (Kroeber), 179
Anti-Imperial League, 117

archaeology, 211
Argosy, The (London magazine), 142, 143, 144
Arnold, Matthew, 36–7, 50, 159–60, 161
   pursuit of cultural achievement, 167–8
Aronoff, Eric, 22, 45
Art of Newspaper Making, The (Dana), 108–9
'Art of Newspaper Making, The' (Dana), 118, 123
arts
   art as expression, 145
   state sponsorship for, 227–9
   Whartonian theory of, 183–4, 185, 189, 210
Arts and Crafts movement, 72, 87
Associationism, 140n6
Astor, John Jacob, 106
atmosphere, 151–3
'Autobiographical Sketch' (Spies), 75, 76–7, 79, 83–6, 87, 88, 95–6
autobiography
   and anarchism, 78–81
   Goldman, 79–81
   Spies, 76–7, 79, 83–6, 87–9, 88, 95–6

Badiou, Alain, 56, 57
Baker, Lee, 21
Baldwin, James Mark, 215
ballads: working class and, 6
Barnes, Elizabeth, 100, 102
Barrish, Phillip, 23, 156
Bartel, Kim, 93
Bartelson, Jens, 57
'Bartleby the Scrivener' (Melville), 4
Beginnings of Critical Realism in America, 1860–1920, The (Parrington), 108
Bell, Michael Davitt, 29–30
Bellows, George, 218–20, *219*
Belnap, Jeffrey, 120, 131
Benedict, Ruth, 192
Benjamin, Walter, 115
Bennett, Arnold, 142

Bennett, Gordon, 107
Bentley, Nancy, 13, 95, 189, 211
Bering Strait expedition, 35, 161–2, 204–5
Berkman, Alexander, 80–1
Berman, Marshall, 5
Best, Stephen, 26
Bhabha, Homi K., 92
Black, William, 78, 82, 102
blackface minstrelsy, 197
Blaine, James, 113, 122
Bloch, Ernst, 195
Bly, Nelly, 114
Boas, Franz, 17, 50, 159, 160–2, 177, 188, 190–1, 192
   on anthropology, 41, 201
   and Chicago World's Fair (1893), 199
   criticisms of, 40
   culture concept, 21, 34–5, 45, 46, 205, 207
   diffusion, 52n12
   disagreement with Mason, 39, 206
   diversity, 30
   on esoteric doctrines, 41
   and exotericism, 34–48
   Jesup North Pacific Expedition, 161–2, 204–5
   on modernism/culture, 186–7
   origins of ethnic group life, 37
   reckless empiricism, 29
Boasianism, 21, 35, 41, 186–7
bohemianism, 234
   Crane and, 142, 157
   Goldman and, 79
   literary bohemianism, 132
Bolívar, Simón, 125–6
boredom, 210
Bourdieu, Pierre, 23, 31, 49, 137
Bourne, Randolph, 183, 221–4, 229
   class and culture, 225
   and cosmopolitan pluralism, 222–3
   and dissensus, 223
   and First World War, 223–4, 225, 230
   on war, 221–2
Brace, Charles Loring, 155

Briggs, Charles, 164
Brook Farm Transcendentalists, 109–10
Buckle, Henry Thomas, 85
Bunzl, Matti, 22
Bureau of American Ethnology, 35, 36, 161, 163
Burlingame, Edward, 191
Butler, Judith, 5

Campbell, W. Joseph, 106
capitalism, 5, 8, 17
  and cosmopolitanism, 225
  and culture, 202–3
  global capitalism, 192
Carroll, Lewis, 91
Cartesianism, 68
Castro, Fidel, 131
Cather, Willa, 213
Cecire, Natalie, 150
Century Illustrated, The, 191, 193–4, 202
Chapin, Frederick H., 211–13, 214–16
Charles Scribner's Sons, 191–2, 193
Chatterjee, Partha, 92
Chicago
  design schools, 87–8
  post-fire rebuilding, 72–3
Chicago School, 72
Chicago World's Fair (1893), 199–200, 213, 216, 217–18
Clarke, Michael Tavel, 213, 214
class, 56
  and culture, 3–4, 16–26, 30, 31–5, 48, 102, 177, 223, 225
  narratives of, 156
class consciousness, 17
class differences, 23
  and realism, 163
Cliff Dwellers (Anasazi), Navajo, 211–18, 220
Cliff Dwellers, The (Bellows), 218–20, 219
Cliff Dwellers, The (Fuller), 213
Cliff Dwellers Daughter, The (Abbott), 213
Clifford, James, 48, 203
Cohn, Jesse, 85

Collier, John, 179
Comte, Auguste, 148
Conrad, Joseph, 142
'Correspondencia particular del *Partido Liberal*' (Martí), 53
cosmopolitan pluralism, 222–3
cosmopolitanism, 46–7, 191–2, 231, 234
  and capitalism, 225
  Crane, 157–8
  transatlantic cosmopolitanism, 50
  Wharton, 225–6
Couser, G. Thomas, 80
Crane, Stephen, 94, 114, 123–4, 142–82, 229
  aestheticism, 153–4, 169
  bohemianism, 142, 157
  class critique, 171
  cosmopolitanism, 157–8
  democratic aestheticism, 169
  dissensus, 144, 145
  internationalism, 171
  see also *George's Mother*; 'Manacled' (Crane)
critical culturalism, 45
Criticism and Fiction (Howells), 53, 66
Critique of Judgment (Kant), 7, 61
crónicas modernista, 118, 132, 137
Cuba, 111
  America and, 105–6, 107, 112–13
  Martí in, 105
  otherness, 125
  and slavery, 123–4, 126
Cuban War of Independence, 49, 104–5, 117
  in American press, 123
cultural appropriation, 31, 196–9
cultural determinism, 162, 180, 181
cultural development
  intelligence and, 211, 215
  Mason, 39
cultural evolutionism, 216
cultural pluralism, 51, 181, 204, 225
cultural relativism, 21, 22–3, 25, 162
culture, 63, 155–6
  and capitalism, 202–3

culture (*cont.*)
   and class, 3–4, 16–26, 30, 31–5, 48, 102, 177, 223, 225
   as ontology, 56–7
Culture and Anarchy (Arnold), 159–60
culture concept, 21–2, 63
   Boas, 21, 34–5, 45, 46, 205, 207
'Culture, Genuine and Spurious' (Sapir), 63
Cushing, Frank Hamilton, 196, 216–17
   and Zuni, 193–4, 203
Custom of the Country, The (Wharton), 51, 188–9, 190, 192–3, 194–9, 200, 201, 207–9, 211, 220, 224, 225, 227
   boredom, 205, 208–9
   culture concept, 205
   divorce, 203
   intelligence, meaning of, 205–6
   and nationalism, 202

Dana, Charles Anderson, 49–50, 106–11, 112–16, 117–18, 119, 122, 123
   and anarchism, 127–8
   on Cuban nationalism, 124–5
   politics of producerism, 127–8
   and race, 126–7
Dangerous Classes of New York, The (Brace), 155
Darwin and the Humanities (Baldwin), 215
Darwinism, 148
Davis, Richard Harding, 114
Degan, Mattias, 53
'Democracy Versus the Melting Pot: A Study of American Nationality' (Kallen), 222
Derrida, Jacques: trace, concept of, 20
Dewey, John, 221
diaspora, 46–7
diffusion, 52n12
Dimock, Wai-Chee, 92
'Dirigible, A' (Stieglitz), 12
Disinherited Speak, The, 179
dissensus, 31, 82, 103n8, 186, 210

Bellows, 220
Bourne and, 223
Chapin, 214–15
Crane, 144, 145
Eight-Hour Movement and, 71, 72
Rancière, 39, 73, 136
Wharton, 184–5, 186, 198
dissolutionism, 8
divorce, 51, 190, 193, 203, 210
Dooley, Patrick, 154

Eakin, Paul John, 80
'Editor's Study' (Howells), 9
Eight-Hour Movement, 49, 53, 66–7, 68–70, 71–2, 73–5, 86, 100
   '8 Hours for Work, for Rest, for What We Will' engraving, 68–70, 69, 71–2, 73, 80
   and dissensus, 71, 72
Elliott, Michael, 13, 39, 42–3, 156, 159, 190
Emerson, Ralph Waldo, 109, 110, 111, 117, 136, 139, 155
   pursuit of cultural achievement, 167
Engel, George, 54, 55, 83
Engels, Friedrich, 38
England, George Allan, 213
environment, 156
Epic of Gilgamesh, 235
Erlich, Gloria, 192
esoteric doctrines, 36–7, 41, 42
essentialism, 179
   identity essentialism, 162
ethnic particularism, 51
ethnography, 13, 34, 42, 46, 144, 154–5, 192, 203
   ethnographic realism, 19
   photography and, 151
   and representation, 76
'Ethnological Significance of Esoteric Doctrines, The' (Boas), 34, 37
ethnology, 35
eugenics, 233
Evangelina Cisneros affair, 141n17
Evans, Brad, 13, 16, 35, 46–7, 97, 158, 193, 203

on culture, 164
search for authority, 154–5
Evans, Walker, 179
everyday life, 1–2
realist aesthetic of, 10–12
exceptionalism, 180

Fabian, Johannes, 39–40, 200
Fagg, John, 219
Federal Writers' Project, 180
Felski, Rita, 8, 26, 27
Ferrer, Ada, 124, 126, 127
Fewkes, Jesse, 213
Fielden, Samuel, 54, 55
fin-de-siècle art, 16
First Red Scare, 62
First World War, 223–4, 225–7, 230
Fischer, Adolph, 54, 55, 83
'Fixation of Belief, The' (Peirce), 168
'Flaubert's Last Work' (Martí), 128–9
Fletcher, John, 202
folklore, 154–5
Foner, Eric, 78, 95
Foner, Philip, 120, 131
Ford, Ford Madox, 142
Foucault, Michel, 18
Fourier, Charles, 109, 140n6
Fournier, Alex, 218
Frazer, James, 52n12, 236
French Ways and Their Meanings (Wharton), 200
Frick, Henry, 80–1
Fruit of the Tree, The (Wharton), 227
Fuller, Henry B., 213
Fuller, Margaret, 109
Futurism, 237–8

Gallagher, Catherine, 19
Gandal, Keith, 156
Geertz, Clifford, 48
Geismar, Maxwell, 165
George's Mother (Crane), 50, 164–9, 172, 229
reviews, 165
Gilder, Richard Watson, 191
Giles, Paul, 120, 133

global capitalism: and multiculturalism, 192
global politics, 5
Gold, Mike (Irwin Granich), 177–9
Golden Bough, The (Frazer), 236
Goldman, Emma, 79–81, 101
Gómez, Máximo, 105
'Good Anna, The' (Stein), 170
'Good Lena, The' (Stein), 170
Granich, Irwin (Mike Gold), 177–9
Greeley, Horace, 118
Greenblatt, Stephen, 19
Grey, Zane, 213
Grinnell, Julius Sprague, 95
Guarneri, Carl, 110

habit, 168, 169–70
habitus, 22, 23, 31, 44, 131, 150, 163, 170
art as expression of, 145
Hamilton, Kristie, 86
'Hand of Man, The' (Stieglitz), 152, *152*, 153
Handler, Richard, 20
Harbinger, The (Brook Farm in-house publication), 110
Hartman, Saidiya, 62
Haymarket Affair, 48–9, 53–6, 57–8, 63–5, 76–8, 81–2, 96–7, 141n27
Accessory law, 55–6, 58, 64, 96
and *A Hazard of New Fortunes*, 101
as act of terror, 55–6, 57–8
Howells and, 49, 64–5, 93–4, 95
print culture, 63–4
and print media, 77–8
prosecution, 54, 56, 57, 59–60, 62, 63–4, 75, 76, 82, 87, 102
Hazard of New Fortunes, A (Howells), 3–13, 15–16, 17–18, 70–1, 90–4, 97–100, 101–2, 146
class and culture, 3–4
and Haymarket affair, 101
housing and slave trade, 90–1
magazine publishing, 91–2
and racialisation, 90
social hierarchy, 3–9, 10

Hearst, W. R., 50, 105–6, 107, 108, 122, 123, 129, 132, 137
Hegeman, Susan, 13, 21, 37, 38, 39, 42
History of Civilization (Buckle), 85
Holt, Hamilton: lifelets, 172–7
Hour, The (New York weekly), 116–17, 119, 130
   Martí's essays for, 131–9
housing: and slave trade, 90–1
How the Other Half Lives: Studies Among the Tenements of New York (Riis), 155
'How to Make Our Ideas Clear' (Peirce), 168
Howells, William Dean, 3–13, 53, 90–100, 101–2, 146–7, 155
   class and culture, 3–4, 102
   correspondence with James, 93
   definition of literary realism, 93, 94
   and Haymarket Affair, 49, 64–5, 93–4, 95
   Kaplan on, 17–18
   and racialisation, 90
   on realism, 1, 9, 65–6
   realist aesthetic, 10, 11
   on representation, 65
   see also *Hazard of New Fortunes, A* (Howells)
'Howells Fears Realists Must Wait' (Crane), 146–7
human intelligence, 206, 208
Huneker, James, 234–9
   and primitivism, 234–5
Hurston, Zora Neale, 179, 192

identity
   identity essentialism, 162
   identity politics, 22–3
   racial identity, 62
   as tool of state power, 75
immigration, 51
   anti-immigration laws, 58
Impressionism, 138–9
'Impressions of America (By a Very Fresh Spaniard)' (Martí), 116–17, 132–9

intelligence, 120
   and cultural development, 211, 215
   human intelligence, 206, 208
internationalism, 171, 227
Irving, Washington, 86
Ivory, Apes and Peacocks (Huneker), 237

Jackson, William Henry, 213
James, Henry, 18, 86, 142, 184, 190
   Howell's correspondence with, 93
James, William, 3, 41–2, 117, 226
   pragmatism, 168–9
   pursuit of cultural achievement, 167
   stream of consciousness, 183
Jesup North Pacific Expedition, 35, 161–2, 204–5
Jones, Gavin, 16, 24
journalism
   investigative journalism, 114
   new journalism, 114, 115, 121, 122
   yellow journalism, 106, 108, 114, 117, 123, 125, 128, 129, 132, 137

Kallen, Horace, 222, 223, 224
Kant, Immanuel, 7, 61, 88–9
Kapital, Das (Marx), 85
Kaplan, Amy, 3–4, 17–19, 33, 97
   class differences and realism, 163
   on Howells, 17–18
   on realism, 163–4
Kassanoff, Jennie A., 188–9, 193, 196, 211
Kelly, Alice, 226–7
Kipling, Rudyard, 142
Knights of Labor, The (trade union periodical), 76–7, 78
Konstantinou, Lee, 27
Kornbluh, Anna, 6–7, 8, 66, 73–4
Kroeber, Alfred, 40, 45, 179–80

Lamarck, Jean-Baptiste, 148
Lamarckianism, 148–9
Latour, Bruno, 29
Lawson, Andrew, 84
Lay My Burden Down, 179
Lehr-und-Wehr Verein, 56

Let Us Now Praise Famous Men (Agee and Evans), 179, 180–1
Levinas, Emmanuel, 4, 72
Levine, Caroline, 10–11
Levine, Lawrence, 145
Life Stories of Undistinguished Americans as Told By Themselves, The (Holt), 51, 173–7
'Life Story of A Greek Peddler, The' (Holt), 176
life writing
  anarchistic life writing, 76
  lifelets, 172–7
  working-class life writing, 75–6, 80, 81, 86–7, 172–80
Lingg, Louis, 54, 55, 83
literary bohemianism, 132
literary realism, 30–1, 96
  definition of, 92, 94
  Kornbluh on, 6–7
  political formalism of, 6–7
Living My Life (Goldman), 79–81
Lomas, Laura, 111–12, 120, 128, 132
Lum, Dyer, 95–6

McCormick's Reaper Factory, 53
Maceo, Antonio, 105
McGurl, Mark, 144, 185
McKinley, William, 106
magazine publishing, 91–2
Maggie: A Girl of the Streets (Crane), 146, 158
Malinowski, Bronislaw, 17, 203
'Manacled' (Crane), 50, 143–4, 145, 148, 149–51, 154, 157–9, 162, 172
Manganero, Marc, 13
Marcus, George, 203
Marcus, Sharon, 26
Marinetti, Filippo Tommaso, 237
marriage, 193–4
Martí, José, 29, 49–50, 53, 77, 88, 89, 110–17, 128–9
  aesthetic politics, 131–6
  on anarchism/Haymarket anarchists, 141n27
  as colleague, 118–22
  crónicas modernista, 118, 137
  death of, 104–5
  essays for *The Hour*, 131–9
  fine arts articles, 119
  and Haymarket Affair, 94
  Latin American criticism of, 119–20
  on Marx, 120–1, 122
  obituary, 104–5, 106, 110–11, 112, 113–16, 118–19, 122, 129
  politics of, 119–20, 128
  and race, 126–7
Marx, Karl, 5, 85, 120–1, 122
Marxism, 16–17
Mason, Otis T., 39, 206
Mead, Margaret, 25, 192
Mecchia, Giuseppina, 137
'Melancholy of Masterpieces Part 2: The Italian Futurist Painters, The' (Huneker), 237, 238
melodrama, 6, 61–2, 145
Melville, Herman, 4, 26, 34
Mencken, H. L., 234
Mesa Verde National Park, 213
Messer-Kruse, Timothy, 54, 55, 59–60, 76
Michaels, Walter Benn, 17, 162–3
Miller, D. A., 18
Miller, James, 181
Mind of Primitive Man, The (Boas), 43–4, 190–1
Mirola, William A., 74
Moby-Dick (Melville), 26, 34
Modern Instance, A (Howells), 5, 146
modern time, 11–12
modernism: stream of consciousness, 183, 184, 208–9, 210, 219–20
Monteiro, George, 158, 165
'Moral Equivalent of War, The' (James), 226
Morgan, J. P., 106
Morgan, Lewis Henry, 36, 37–8, 85, 148, 216
Morris, William, 87
Moten, Fred, 62
multiculturalism, 17, 24–5, 164, 174–5, 192

Murphy, Brenda, 165
'My Adventures Among the Zuni' (Cushing), 193–4

Nación, La (Argentinian paper), 120–2, 138, 141n27
National Parks, 213
nationalism, 202, 225, 231, 232–3
  Cuban, 124–5, 126
Neebe, Oscar, 54
New Americanism, 18–19, 20
  reading practices, 21–2
New Deal era, 179–80, 233
  culture, 179–81
  Indian New Deal, 179
  literary practices, 76
New Historicism, 18–19, 20, 181
  and critique, 26–7
New York Journal, 105–6, 123
New York Sun, The, 106–8, 127–30, 131
  Cuban nationalism, 124–5, 126
  Martí obituary, 104–5, 106, 110–11, 112, 113–16, 118–19, 122, 129
  as site of alterity, 129–30
New York Tribune, 204–5, *204*
New York World, 105–6, 123–4
Ngai, Sianne, 7, 88–9, 209
Noonan, Mark, 191
North American Review, The, 142
'Nuestra América'/'Our America' (Martí), 120

Ochs, Adolph, 107
Of Grammatology (Derrida), 20
Ohler, Paul, 184, 195
Olin-Ammentorp, Julie, 211
O'Ruddy, The (Crane), 142
otherness, 46, 57, 58, 72, 129–30, 155, 200
  Cubans and, 125
  Spies and, 90

Painted Veils (Huneker), 234–6
Parkinson, Isabelle, 169
Parrington, Vernon, 108, 130
Parsons, Albert, 54, *55*

Parsons, Elsie Clews, 45–6
particularism, 51
Peirce, Charles Sanders, 41, 168–9
Perez, Louis A., Jr., 107
Philosopher and His Poor, The (Rancière), 67
photography, 12–13, 151–3
  atmosphere, 151–3
  and ethnography, 151
  flash photography, 150–1
Pittenger, Mark, 143, 155
Plato, 67, 70
'Plea for Art Photography in America, A' (Stieglitz), 151–2
Pluralistic Universe, A (James), 41–2
political formalism, 6–7, 73–4
politics, 31
  and aesthetics, 2, 6, 131–6
  global politics, 5
  identity politics, 22–3
  of mute speech, 6
  politics of dissent, 49–50
  politics of producerism, 127–8
Pound, Ezra, 32
Powell, John Wesley 37, 192
pragmatism, 168–9
Prairie School, 72
Primitive Culture (Tylor), 236
primitivism, 233, 234–5
print culture, 49–50
  and Haymarket Affair, 63–4, 77–8
  investigative journalism, 114
  Martí's aesthetic politics, 131–6
  new journalism, 114, 115, 121, 122
  tabloid spectacularism, 108
  yellow journalism, 106, 108, 117, 123, 125, 128, 132, 137
  see also *New York Sun, The*
producerism, 127–8
'Profession of Journalism, The' (Dana), 118
Professor's House, The (Cather), 213
Prolet-Kult, 177–8
proletarian culture, 177–8
Proudhon, Pierre-Joseph, 110
Puar, Jasbir K., 64

Pulitzer, Joseph, 50, 105–6, 107, 108, 122, 123, 129, 132, 137
Putnam, Frederic Ward, 199, 204–5

race, 20, 126–7
racial identity, 62
racialisation, 14, 62, 64, 66
   Howells and, 90
   and violence, 82
racism: Cuban, 123–4, 126
Rancière, Jacques, 6, 12–13, 26, 31–2, 36, 44–5, 67, 121, 197, 216, 224
   aestheticism, 14, 15, 22, 33, 41
   on Chapin, 214–15
   on class, 86
   dissensus, 39, 73, 136
   la haine/Chirac, 24
   modern time, 11
   natural order, 90
   on sociology, 153
   warped conjunction, 16
Randall, Elinor, 131
readership: pre-ordained readers, 22–3
realism, 146–7
   aesthetic politics of, 6
   class differences and, 163
   ethnographic realism, 19
   Howells on, 1, 9, 65–6, 92, 94
   Kaplan on, 163–4
   Kornbluh on, 6–7, 66, 73–4
   literary realism, 6–7, 30–1, 92, 94
   realist aesthetic of the everyday, 10–12
   Whartonian realism, 184–5
Red Badge of Courage, The (Crane), 142
relativism, 17, 21, 22–3, 25, 162
representation, 34, 65, 66, 76
representativeness, 6, 19
Richard Bentley & Sons, 143
Riders of the Purple Sage (Grey), 213
Riis, Jacob, 155
ritual, 35, 57, 61, 140n7
Rivers, W. H. R., 37
Robbins, Bruce, 18
Rockhill, Gabriel, 197

Rodseth, Lars, 29, 40, 47, 48
Roggenkamp, Karen, 114, 122
Roosevelt, Theodore, 213
Rotker, Susana, 111, 118, 130, 138

Sahlins, Marshall, 48
Saint-Amour, Paul K., 28, 29
Santayana, George, 191
Sapir, Edward, 63, 192
Savransky, Martin, 175
Schaak, Michael, 60, *60*
Schmitt, Carl, 57
Schwab, Michael, 54, *55*
Schwartz, Jesse W., 62, 95–6
Scribner's Magazine, 190, 191–2, 193, 202
sharecroppers, 179
slave trade: and housing, 90–1
slavery, 134, 179
   Cuba, 123–4, 126
Slosson, Edwin E., 173, 176–7
slum tourism, 8
Small, William, 143
Smith, H. Jay, 217–18
Snead, James, 217–18
social constructivism, 10
social Darwinism, 98, 100
social mobility, 156
social position: and appropriate modes of behaviour, 3–4
social science, 13–14, 23, 35, 98, 148, 155, 190–1
   participant observation, 193–4
   and ritual cultures debate, 35
Sollors, Werner, 174
Son at the Front, A (Wharton), 51, 220, 225–32
Song of the Lark, The (Cather), 213
Spanish-American War (1898), 105, 117; *see also* Cuban War of Independence
speculative fiction, 212–13
Spencer, David R., 106
Spencer, Herbert, 148
Spies, August, 29, 49, 54, *55*, 56, 82–6
   aestheticism, 88–9

Spies, August (*cont.*)
  autobiography, 75, 76–7, 79, 83–6, 87–90, *88*, 95–6
  decadent individualism, 65
  otherness, 90
  on representation/realism, 65, 66
Staub, Michael E., 180
Steele, Janet, 107–8, 127
'Steerage, The' (Stieglitz), 152–3
Stein, Gertrude, 169–71, 172
Stieglitz, Alfred, 12, 13, 151–4, *152*, 172
Stocking, George, 40, 148, 161, 191, 206
'Story of a Play, The' (Howells), 146–7
Stowe, Harriet Beecher, 216
Strangleman, Tim, 75, 76
stream of consciousness, 183, 184, 208–9, 210, 219–20
Streeby, Shelley, 54, 63–4, 77, 125, 134
sublime, 61–2
Sullivan, Louis, 72
suspicion, 8, 26, 27, 38

Taylor, Andrew, 117, 120
temporalities, 211–12
terrorism, 58
Theory of the Leisure Class, The (Veblen), 190
These Are Our Lives, 179
Three Lives (Stein), 169
Tone, John Lawrence, 105, 126
'Towards Proletarian Art' (Gold), 177–8
trace, concept of, 20–1
trades union movement, Chicago, 53–6
transatlantic cosmopolitanism, 50
transnationalism, 49–51
Trautmann, Thomas, 38
'Tribute to Karl Marx, Who Has Died, A' (Martí), 120–2
Turner, Victor, 52n5, 140n7
Twain, Mark, 117
Tylor, E. B., 36, 43, 236

Unicorns (Huneker), 238–9
Unwritten History, 179
USA: manifest destiny, 113

Van Zandt, Nina, 82–3, 86, 87
Veblen, Thorstein, 51, 190
violence
  and racialisation, 82
  and whipping boy, 100–1, 102

Wagner, Richard: Ring Cycle, 236
'War and the Intellectuals, The' (Bourne), 183, 221, 222, 223–4, 225
Wells, H. G., 142, 212
Wetherill family, 213
Whalan, Mark, 223, 230
Wharton, Edith, 29, 183–233
  on aestheticism, 201
  and anthropology, 211
  and archaeology, 211
  class and culture, 225
  and cosmopolitanism, 225–6
  critique of cult of originality, 187–8
  cultural appropriation, 196–9
  dissensus, 184–5, 186, 198
  and divorce, 51, 190, 193, 203, 210
  and First World War, 223–4, 225–7, 230
  on inspiration, 185–6
  intelligence, 210, 211
  and nationalism, 202
  and sexuality, 192, 207–8
  and stream of consciousness, 208–9, 219–20
  theory of art, 183–4, 185, 189, 210
  see also *Custom of the Country, The*; *Son at the Front, A*; *Writing of Fiction, The*
whipping boys/scapegoats: and violence, 100–1, 102
White, Leslie, 40, 192
white supremacy, 21–2
Whitman, Walt, 111
Williams, Raymond, 28

working class
    and ballads, 6
    life writing, 75–6, 80, 81, 86–7, 172–80
    workers, definition of, 67–8
    working-class activism, 80
    working-class life, 89
    working-class literature, 75
Works Progress Administration, 180

Writing of Fiction, The (Wharton), 183–4, 185–6, 198, 208–9, 210, 219–20, 224, 227

Yao, Xine, 124
yellow journalism, 106, 108, 114, 117, 123, 125, 128, 129, 132, 137

zeitgeist: and melodrama, 61
Zibrak, Arielle, 192, 207

EU representative:
Easy Access System Europe
Mustamäe tee 50, 10621 Tallinn, Estonia
Gpsr.requests@easproject.com